NEW-BORN CHILD MURDER

New-born child murder is about women who were accused of murdering their new-born children in the eighteenth century. It explores precisely why certain women were suspected of murdering their children at birth in this period and how they were subsequently treated by their neighbours, families and friends, and by the courts.

This fascinating new book draws heavily on a rich variety of previously unused archival material from the Northern Circuit courts and on a wide range of contemporary printed sources. Individual chapters focus on key issues: attitudes to single women and illegitimacy; the role of medical testimony in local investigations and in court; conflicting public representations of suspects; decision-making in the courts; debates about capital punishment and the administration of justice; and the changes in the law at the turn of the nineteenth century.

This study offers a fresh and challenging approach to the history of women and crime. Clearly written and incorporating an extensive historiographical introduction, *New-born child murder* will appeal to a wide variety of historians and students interested in social, medical, legal and gender history. In the light of recent criminal cases (notably that of Caroline Beale, an English woman arrested in New York on suspicion of murdering her new-born child and of concealing the evidence) this book will also appeal to readers interested in more recent debates about unmarried motherhood, infanticide and the role of medical evidence in the courts.

Mark Jackson is a Research Associate and Lecturer in the Wellcome Unit
for the History of Medicine at the University of Manchester

NEW-BORN CHILD MURDER

Women, illegitimacy and the courts in eighteenth-century England

MARK JACKSON

MANCHESTER UNIVERSITY PRESS

MANCHESTER AND NEW YORK

distributed exclusively in the USA and Canada by St. Martin's Press

Published by Manchester University Press
Oxford Road, Manchester M13 9NR, UK
and Room 400, 175 Fifth Avenue, New York, NY 10010, USA

Distributed exclusively in the USA and Canada
by St. Martin's Press, Inc.,
175 Fifth Avenue, New York, NY 10010, USA

British Library Cataloguing-in-Publication Data
A catalogue record is available from the British Library

Library of Congress Cataloging-in-Publication Data
Jackson, Mark, 1959-
  New-born child murder : women, illegitimacy and the
courts in eighteenth-century England / Mark Jackson
      p.   cm.
  Includes bibliographical references (p.   )
  ISBN 0-7190-4607-6
  1. Filicide—Great Britain—History. 2. Illegitimacy—
Great Britain—History. 3. Unmarried mothers—Great
Britain—History. 4. Medical jurisprudence—Great
Britain—History. I. Title.
KD7967.J33   1996
346.4201'7—dc20
[344.20617]   96-16161
                                                    CIP

ISBN 0-7190-4607 6 *hardback*

First published in 1996

00 99 98 97 96   10 9 8 7 6 5 4 3 2 1

Typeset in Monotype Columbus by Koinonia Limited, Bury
Printed in Great Britain by Bookcraft (Bath) Limited

CONTENTS

Preface   *page* vii

1 **Introduction**   1

Introduction   1
Methods and arguments   2
Sources   16
Conclusion   22

2 **The generation of suspicion: single women, bastardy
   and the law**   29

Introduction   29
The 1624 statute in social context   30
The law and chargeable bastardy in the eighteenth century:
evidence from the Northern Circuit court records   37
Prosecution as a deterrent   45
Prosecution as a process   47
Conclusion   51

3 **Examining suspects: conflicting accounts of pregnancy,
   birth and death**   60

Introduction   60
Detecting signs of pregnancy   61
Detecting signs of labour and child-birth   65
Conflicting interpretations of the signs   74
Conclusion   77

4 **Examining bodies: medical evidence and the
   coroner's inquest**   84

Introduction   84
Legal medicine, coroners' inquests and the investigation
of sudden death   85
Evidence of prematurity and still-birth   90
The lung test   93
Evidence of violence   100
Conclusion   103

5 **Virtuous or vicious: conflicting accounts of accused women** *page* 110

Introduction 110
Suspects as wicked murderers 111
Humanitarian accounts of suspects 113
Opposition to humanitarian accounts 123
Conclusion 127

6 **Evidence in court: the verdicts of inquest, grand and trial juries** 133

Introduction 133
Inquest juries 135
Grand juries 137
Trial jury verdicts 140
Laws of evidence and standards of proof 145
Conclusion 151

7 **Single women, bastardy and the law: the decline and fall of the 1624 statute** 158

Introduction 158
Attempts to repeal the 1624 statute, 1772-6 159
Lord Ellenborough's Act, 1803 168
Conclusion 176

Bibliography 182
Index 199

PREFACE

This book is about the past. It started life ten years ago, as a minor distraction from the rigours of studying clinical medicine in London. Shortly after qualifying, I abandoned the relentless strain of the hospital ward in favour of the imagined sanctuary of academia, and this minor diversion was transformed into a major preoccupation. The initial focus of my historical interest was the manner in which medical evidence came to constitute a central feature of investigations into suspicious infant deaths in the eighteenth century. During the course of my doctoral research, however, my initial narrow examination of medicine and law was necessarily transformed into a much broader exploration of the social, cultural and political factors that led to the identification and prosecution of women for murdering their new-born children in this period. The principal concerns of this book then are precisely why certain women were suspected of murdering their children at birth, and how those women were subsequently treated by their neighbours, families and friends, and by the courts.

This book is also to some extent about the present. In September 1994, Caroline Beale, a young unmarried English woman, was arrested in New York for murdering her new-born child. According to the prosecution, the fact that she had concealed her pregnancy, given birth alone, and subsequently endeavoured to smuggle the child's dead body out of America suggested that she had wilfully killed the child at birth. This assertion was supported by medical evidence apparently demonstrating that the child had probably been born alive. Caroline Beale's defence rested on her insistence that the child was still-born, and on psychiatric evidence that she had been clinically depressed during pregnancy and mentally disturbed at the moment of birth. When the case finally came to court earlier this year, Caroline Beale agreed to plead guilty to manslaughter. In return, she was sentenced to eight months in prison (the period that she had already served on remand), five years' probation, and at least one year of psychiatric treatment. After eighteen months of tense medico-legal negotiations and extensive publicity, Caroline Beale was free to return home to England.

It is clear that many of the issues raised by the prosecution of Caroline Beale are not new. Very similar issues were debated extensively both in and out of the courts in the eighteenth century. Without wishing to make any strong claims about the ability of history or historians to resolve current social and legal problems, I do believe that close examination of past prejudices can shed useful light on present preoccupations. I hope, therefore, that this book not only illuminates a wide range of eighteenth-century debates about unmarried motherhood, illegitimacy, the role of expert medical testimony, and the appropriate means of maintaining law and order, but that it also paves the way for more open exploration of our own attitudes to such issues.

In the course of preparing both my doctoral thesis and the manuscript for this book, I have necessarily benefited from the support, advice, and knowledge of a number of people and institutions. Much of the doctoral research, funded by the British Academy, was originally carried out with the support and encouragement of members of the History and Philosophy of Science Division of the Department of Philosophy at the University of Leeds, namely Geoff Cantor, John Christie, Jon Hodge, and Bob Olby. I am also grateful to a number of individuals who have made detailed comments about certain aspects of my doctoral research, who have supplied me with suitable references, and who have provided me with early opportunities to present and publish preliminary papers on my work. In particular, Cathy Crawford, Michael Clark, Mary Fissell, Mark Jenner, Ludmilla Jordanova, Joan Mottram, Mark Ockelton, John Pickstone, Roy Porter, Bill Speck, Adrian Wilson and readers for Manchester University Press have made constructive comments on various parts or the whole of my work.

I have been fortunate to have been assisted, indeed on occasions nurtured, by some admirable librarians and archivists. In particular, I am indebted to the staff of the Inter-Library Loans and Special Collections sections of the Brotherton Library at the University of Leeds for making the seemingly inaccessible accessible. I would also like to thank staff at the Public Record Office in Chancery Lane for allowing me to monopolise the Northern Circuit court records for many months at a time and, on occasions, for helping me to decipher the rich, but seemingly illegible, language of the depositions. Crown copyright material in the Public Record Office is reproduced by permission of the Controller of Her Majesty's Stationery Office.

More recently, the preparation of the manuscript for this book has been facilitated by the friendly intellectual atmosphere of the Wellcome Unit for the History of Medicine in the University of Manchester. I am particularly grateful to John Pickstone whose offer of full-time employment shortly after I completed my PhD gave me some reason to believe that my attempted transition from doctor to historian might not be entirely fruitless.

I am also grateful to the editorial staff at Manchester University Press and in particular to Jane Thorniley-Walker, Vanessa Graham, and Michelle O'Connell, not only for showing interest in my work but, perhaps more importantly, for understanding the difficulties inherent in producing a coherent and readable manuscript shortly after my wife had given birth to our first child.

It is, appropriately, to my wife and children, that I owe the greatest debt of gratitude. If my conversion from a disillusioned doctor to an aspiring academic, and the successful completion of this book, can be attributed to any single set of circumstances it is to the beguiling blend of excitement and security that infuses my family life. It would be impossible to express the extent to which Siobhán, Ciara and Riordan have transformed my life and my work. I can only begin to thank them for their love and support by dedicating this book to them.

TO SIOBHÁN, CIARA AND RIORDAN

What ever dyes, was not mixt equally;
If our two loves be one, or, thou and I
Love so alike, that none doe slacken, none can die.

John Donne, *The good-morrow*

Introduction

Introduction

This book is about women who were accused of murdering their new-born children in England in the eighteenth century. Its principal concerns are precisely why certain women were suspected of murdering their children at birth in this period and how those women were subsequently treated by their neighbours, families, and friends, and by the courts.

Although it concentrates primarily on the events surrounding the legal processes of accusation and prosecution, this book also deals with a broad array of contemporary social, political, legal and medical issues. While much of the evidence presented in this book is derived from pre-trial and trial court records, I am not interested in simply revealing patterns of prosecution and conviction for new-born child murder in the eighteenth century. I am more concerned with using the extensive court records, together with a variety of other sources, to examine precisely how the actions of certain women were construed by different people in this period and how distinct and often contradictory constructions of those actions were linked to a number of prominent and contentious contemporary debates. In addition to examining the processes by which suspects were identified and brought to trial, this book therefore also explores beliefs about the value, status and appropriate behaviour of single women, attitudes to illegitimacy, and concerns about the maintenance of the poor. It also examines the role of medical testimony and the value of the coroner's inquest in the legal process, investigates legal debates about laws of evidence, standards of proof, and the relative merits of statute and common law, and explores anxieties about the appropriate means of maintaining law and order and administering justice.

This first introductory chapter serves several purposes. By reviewing the benefits and drawbacks of the historiographical methods adopted by the few historians who have already published studies on this subject, the first section of this chapter introduces my own approach to the historical records and their interpretation. The second section sets out the archival sources and evidence on which my arguments are based and explores the advantages and disadvantages of exploiting these particular sources. In the process, this chapter establishes the relevance of this study to historical work in a number of significant areas: the history of women, childhood, and the family; the history of parish life and local administration; the history of medicine; and the history of crime, criminal justice, and legislation.

Methods and arguments

In May 1778, Sarah Sant's neighbours in Weaverham, near Chester, apparently became suspicious that Sarah had secretly given birth to an illegitimate or bastard child.[1] Assisted by a constable and an overseer of the poor, they immediately challenged both Sarah and her mother, Mary, about the suspected birth and began to search the house for evidence of the child. Initially, Sarah denied that she had ever been pregnant. On further pressure from her neighbours and local officials, however, she confessed that she had given birth to a child but insisted that the child had been still-born and that she had not murdered it.

The dead body of Sarah Sant's child was subsequently discovered in a locked box and examined by John Carter and William Thearsby, two surgeons from Northwich. At the coroner's inquest into the cause of the child's death, held on 19 May 1778, these surgeons reported the findings of their initial inspection of the body and, and at the coroner's request, opened the body for further examination. That examination revealed a number of critical signs. First, the child's umbilical cord or navel string had been torn off 'about Four Inches from the Abdomen or Belly'. Second, there was 'a Mark over the upper part of the Wind pipe Similar to a Squeeze or Pinch betwixt the Finger and Thumb'. Third, the lungs appeared to be 'much inflamed and upon the Experiment of putting them into Water they were found to Swim', as the result of which the surgeons concluded that the child had breathed.[2] On the basis of the evidence presented both by the surgeons and by Mary and Sarah Sant's neighbours, the coroner's jury concluded that Sarah Sant, with the assistance of her mother Mary, had murdered her bastard child at birth.

In September 1778, both Sarah and Mary Sant were indicted and tried for the murder of Sarah's illegitimate child at Chester assizes.[3] Sarah Sant was found guilty and sentenced to death. Mary was acquitted. On 22 September, *The Cumberland Pacquet*, a weekly newspaper printed in White-haven and distributed throughout Cumberland, Westmorland, Lancaster and the Isle of Man, contained the following report of the outcome of the trial.

On Friday last, Sarah Sant was executed at Boughton, near Chester, pursuant to her Sentence, and her body given for dissection. – She was attended, at the place of execution, by a Divine; but, in the most pathetic manner, she denied having the least intention of destroying the Child. – And, we hear, that the Mother, on her return home, being received in the Neighbourhood with a coolness she did not expect, hung herself.[4]

The prosecution of Sarah Sant should not be regarded as particularly unusual. Throughout the eighteenth century, many unmarried women who concealed their pregnancies and gave birth in secret, and whose new-born children were later found dead, were suspected by their neighbours of having murdered those children at birth. A large percentage of those women suspected of murder were subsequently prosecuted in the assize courts. Neither should the coolness of Mary Sant's reception in her home town be seen as remarkable. The local hostility that encouraged Mary to hang herself on her return home was a product of the same concerns and suspicions that had initiated prosecution for murder in the first instance.

The unusual feature of Sarah Sant's case is that she was found guilty and hanged. In the eighteenth century, most women indicted for murdering their new-born children were either discharged by a grand jury or acquitted by a trial jury. Of nearly two hundred women indicted in the Northern Circuit courts of Yorkshire, Northumberland, Cumberland and Westmorland between 1720 and 1800, for example, only six women were found guilty and, of those, only two were hanged.[5] Throughout the eighteenth century, strong local suspicions that certain women were murdering their children at birth did not result in convictions in the courts.

Preliminary inspection of assize court records therefore reveals two outstanding features of cases of suspected new-born child murder in this period. First, the overwhelming majority of suspects were, according to the records, unmarried women. Married women and men were apparently infrequently suspected and certainly rarely indicted. The corollary of this is that the majority of the children supposedly murdered by their mothers were referred to in the records as illegitimate or bastard children. The second striking feature of the court records is that, unlike Sarah Sant, the majority of women tried for this crime were not found guilty of murder. Significantly, the high rate of acquittal did not seem to deter people from prosecuting unmarried women for murder. Throughout the eighteenth century, trial courts in parts of England continued to deal with a fairly steady stream of prosecutions. In the north of England, for example, around two or three cases were brought before the grand and trial juries every year until the end of the century.[6]

Contemporary explanations of the persistent prosecution of unmarried women and their customary acquittal focused on two factors. In the first instance, many contemporary writers and witnesses believed that only unmarried women possessed sufficient incentive to kill their children at birth. The single mothers of bastards, they argued, concealed their pregnancies and murdered their children in order to avoid the shame associated with bearing an illegitimate child and to escape the punishments that could be inflicted on them for failing to provide financial support for their children. According to the author of comments published in *The Guardian* in 1713, for example, 'that which generally betrays these profligate Women into it, and overcomes the Tenderness which is natural to them on other Occasions, is the fear of Shame, or their Inability to support those whom they give Life to'.[7] Central to this explanation of the persistent prosecution of unmarried women was a prominent belief that women accused of this crime had in fact killed their children and were therefore guilty of murder.

In accounting for the high acquittal rate of such women, commentators argued that judges and juries in the eighteenth century were treating suspects more leniently than they had previously. This leniency was thought to be particularly evident in the manner in which the courts tended to ignore, or at least to find ways of evading, the provisions of a statute of 1624 that had been passed specifically to facilitate the conviction of unmarried women suspected of committing this crime.[8] Although some writers in this period criticised the way in which increasingly lenient treatment of suspects was allowing murderers to 'escape the Vengeance due to shedders of Innocent Blood',[9] many legal and medical writers in particular considered that the regular acquittal of suspects was an appropriate expression of emergent humanitarian sentiments. From this perspective, informal rejection of the 1624 statute and its formal repeal in 1803 were both manifestations of widespread attempts to reform the criminal justice system along more humanitarian lines in the late eighteenth and early nineteenth centuries.

It is notable that historical studies of this subject have generally adopted contemporary explanations of prosecution and acquittal patterns in this period without question. In recent years, there has been increasing historical interest in what most historians have referred to as 'infanticide'. Historical studies have ranged from broad, but brief, historical overviews of the prevalence and practice of 'infanticide' in a variety of different chronological and cultural settings,[10] to more detailed explorations of 'infanticide' in particular geographical and temporal locations.[11] In addition to these specific works on the subject, historians writing on crime and the courts and on the history of women have included comments on new-born child murder trials in the course of more general discussions about criminal legislation, the administration of justice, the emergence of the insanity defence, and a variety of issues relating to crime and gender.[12] As Mary Nagle Wessling has suggested in her work on infanticide and forensic medicine in Württembergs in the eighteenth century, it is 'no accident that infanticide has emerged as a topic of intense debate in recent historical writing'.[13] As Wessling herself points out, recent attention to the subject can be traced to at least two related developments within social history: to the increasing use of studies of crime and criminality to explore the previously hidden history of ordinary people; and, more specifically, to attempts to rescue women in particular from what has been referred to as 'the periphery of historical enquiry'.[14]

Little of this expanding literature on 'infanticide' has focused in any great depth on England in the eighteenth century. Until recently, R. W. Malcolmson's short essay, 'Infanticide in the eighteenth century', represented the only piece focusing exclusively on this subject in this period. Malcolmson's work, which was published in 1977, was based largely on printed trial reports from sessions at the Old Bailey between 1730 and 1774.[15] More recently, J. A. Sharpe's studies of crime in early modern England and J. M. Beattie's extensive work on crime and the courts between 1660 and 1800 also contain short discussions of 'infanticide' as a type of violent offence. While Sharpe's accounts draw on evidence from the Essex and Cheshire assizes between 1550 and 1750, Beattie's account is derived primarily from the printed trial reports from the Surrey and Sussex assize courts.[16]

The only book previously devoted to the subject in the early modern period is Peter C. Hoffer and N. E. H. Hull's *Murdering Mothers: Infanticide in England and New England 1558-1803*, published in 1981.[17] Like the works of Malcolmson, Sharpe and Beattie, Hoffer and Hull's account of 'infanticide' in the eighteenth century relies almost exclusively on indictments and printed trial reports. Significantly, in covering the alleged murders of infants on two continents over a period of nearly 250 years, Hoffer and Hull have, like most other authors, failed to consider eighteenth-century England in great depth. Although their work is relatively strong on the seventeenth century, especially on the influence of puritanism on both sides of the Atlantic, their discussion of child murder in the eighteenth century is confined to a single, brief chapter.[18]

These previous studies of what historians have generally referred to as 'infanticide' in the eighteenth century have certainly made substantial contributions to the history of crime and criminal legislation. However, these particular studies, and indeed many other historical studies of 'infanticide', are beset with methodological and analytical problems that substantially limit their arguments. These problems concern in particular the terminology used to describe the cases under discussion and the manner in which certain records have been selected and interpreted.

In the first instance, historians writing on this subject have universally used the term 'infanticide' to cover the suspected murders of children at birth. This usage is both anachronistic and confusing. English writers did not apply this term to the murder of children of any age in the eighteenth century. I have found no listing of the word in any law manual or medical text from the period and it does not appear in the surviving court records. Eighteenth-century editions of Samuel Johnson's dictionary referred to 'infanticide' only as the 'slaughter of the infants by Herod'.[19] The term did appear in Benjamin Alexander's 1769 translation of Giovanni Battista Morgagni's *De Sedibus et Causis Morborum*,[20] where it bore the same meaning as the phrases used routinely in English courts to specify the murder of a child at, or just after, birth. However, the word 'infanticide' only came into routine use in the nineteenth century in England, when a number of writers began to focus on the medical and legal issues raised by such cases.[21]

At best, the use of the term 'infanticide' by historians of the eighteenth century is anachronistic. At worst, it can be misleading. While most historians writing in this area have consistently used the term to describe the murders of children at birth,[22] some scholars have covered a much broader range of crimes under the same heading. Hoffer and Hull, for example, discussed the alleged murders of children up to the age of nine years old under the general heading 'infanticide'.[23] Maria Piers, in a broad study entitled *Infanticide: Past and Present*, explored not only the killing of children of different ages but also a variety of forms of child abuse and neglect.[24] As Beattie has suggested in the context of Hoffer and Hull's work, this 'all-inclusive definition removes a good deal of the analytical precision and force of the category "infanticide" … as well as flying in the face of the common meaning of the word'.[25] Such disparate definitions of the term make it difficult to assess different historical accounts.

Although Beattie has correctly identified one of the problems associated with loose definitions, it is not clear what Beattie himself considered to be the 'common meaning' of the word. There cannot have been any common understanding of the term in the eighteenth century since it was simply not used in that period. While the term appeared increasingly in medical and legal texts in the nineteenth century, little attempt was made to clarify its meaning. Infanticide did not constitute a substantive crime in English law until the early twentieth century. The Infanticide Act of 1922 directed that any woman who was found to have caused the death of her 'newly-born' child could, 'under certain conditions', be convicted of infanticide, a form of manslaughter rather than murder. Those circumstances allowing the courts to reach a verdict of infanticide rather than murder were the mother's failure to recover fully from giving birth, by reason of which 'the balance of her mind was then disturbed'.[26] In 1938, the term 'newly-born' was clarified to mean 'a child under the age of twelve months'.[27] It is this legal definition of the word that remains prominent in the late twentieth century. Since the current 'common meaning' of 'infanticide' therefore differs considerably from the meaning attributed to it by most historians, the persistent use of the term to refer either to the murder of children at birth or to the murder and abuse of older children can be misleading.

In order to avoid the implications of current legal usage of the term 'infanticide', I have used the contemporary phrases 'new-born child murder' or 'the murder of new-born children' throughout this book. In addition, I have focused exclusively on those cases to which these phrases were routinely applied in the eighteenth century, namely the suspected murders of children at birth. It is clear that, for a number of reasons, such cases raised a substantially different set of legal, medical and social issues from those raised by the suspicious deaths of older children. First, the suspected murder of a child around the time of birth posed specific problems of proof for the eighteenth-century courts. Those problems, related primarily to the difficulties associated with proving that a dead child had in fact been born alive, became much less conspicuous the longer a child lived after birth. Second, the trials of unmarried women indicted for murdering their children at birth were subject to a specific statutory presumption in the eighteenth century. A statute of 1624 had established that any woman who concealed the death of her illegitimate or bastard child, thereby concealing whether it had been born alive or not, was to be held guilty of its murder.[28] The provisions of this statute, and the assumptions inherent in its construction, defined the circumstances in which suspicions of murder were generated and established the legal conditions in which evidence about the births and deaths of new-born children was collected and assessed. Although the terms and implications of the 1624 statute were challenged in the eighteenth century, it continued to dominate discussions of new-born child murder until its repeal in 1803. Finally, the suspicious deaths of new-born illegitimate children in particular formed a discrete topic for a variety of contemporary commentators. The suspected murders of bastard children at birth attracted the professional and personal interest of lawyers, magistrates, coroners, medical practitioners, philosophers, members of parliament, and clergymen. Disputes about the character, conduct and responsibility of single women accused of murdering their children at birth also captivated the writers of ballads and broadsheets in this period.

A second set of methodological problems inherent in previous historical studies of new-born child murder in the eighteenth century concerns the manner in which historians have selected and interpreted court records. Malcolmson, Sharpe, Beattie, and Hoffer and Hull (and indeed most other historians working in this area) have relied almost exclusively on indictments or printed trial reports for their accounts.[29] Although, in 1977, Malcolmson pointed to the potential value of a large collection of surviving depositions from the Northern Circuit courts, this rich archival source has not been previously used.[30] This reliance on formal indictments and published trial reports, rather than on more detailed records of local investigations into the activities of suspects and their accusers, can be traced to the dominant historiographical approaches adopted by historians researching this area.

In a recent essay on historical approaches to crime and criminal justice in eighteenth-century England, Joanna Innes and John Styles suggested that, over the last twenty years, the study of crime and criminal law has become one of the 'most exciting and influential areas of research in eighteenth-century history'.[31] According to Innes and Styles, recent historical interest in crime is the product of three influential 'tendencies within the "new" social history'.[32] The first and, according to Innes and Styles, the most important, tendency is 'history from below'. Exemplified by the work of E. P. Thompson, this approach 'emphasizes the need to explore and imaginatively to reconstruct the experiences of the dispossessed and inarticulate'.[33]

The second influential tendency within social history draws on 'the methods of positivist social science'.[34] According to Innes and Styles, this approach, best illustrated by Beattie's early work on crime and the courts in the eighteenth century, is characterised by a particular reliance on criminal statistics. They argue:

> The social scientific approach emphasized the discovery and explanation of significant patterns, particularly statistical patterns, in social behaviour. This entailed treating crime as a 'social fact' and using aggregate crime statistics to identify and measure continuities and change. Those who adopted this approach sought explanations for the patterns they found not in the meanings of actions for individual or collective social actors (as in history from below), but instead in correlative (and arguably causal) relationships between a variety of social facts, for example crime and dearth, or crime and political tension, or crime and the Industrial Revolution.[35]

The third tendency within social history to have influenced the historiography of crime comprises what Innes and Styles refer to as the 'reform perspective'. This perspective, exemplified by the work of Radzinowicz on the history of English criminal law, has 'traditionally entailed accepting at least a substantial part of the account of eighteenth-century society and its institutions propounded by late-eighteenth- and early-nineteenth-century reformers'.[36]

While Innes and Styles rightly point out that these 'tendencies do not represent three opposed schools',[37] it is noticeable that historians writing on cases of suspected new-born child murder have routinely adopted the approaches of positivist social science and reformist historiography rather than incorporate the theoretical claims and methodological strategies of historians writing 'history from below'. This historiographical orientation has clearly influenced their selection and interpretation of sources.

The influence of positivist social science is evident in a number of ways. First, most historians have quite explicitly used court records (especially indictments) to count the number of crimes committed and to chart changing levels of crime, or patterns of prosecution, over time. For Sharpe (whose comments on 'infanticide' in the seventeenth and eighteenth centuries are mostly presented in a chapter fittingly entitled 'Measuring Crime, Measuring Punishment'), 'counting offences' remains a useful exercise in spite of the difficulties associated with many of the court records.[38] While Beattie was clearly interested in more than simply establishing prosecution and conviction rates in the course of his monumental survey of crime and the courts in the long eighteenth century, he also used indictments (the 'central core' of his evidence) to generate what he referred to as a 'Homicide Count'.[39] Both Sharpe and Beattie subsequently employed their figures to generate tables and graphs illustrating changing levels of 'infanticide' prosecutions and convictions during the course of the seventeenth and eighteenth centuries.[40]

The statistical approach evident in Sharpe and Beattie's studies is, however, most clearly expressed in the work of Hoffer and Hull, whose explicit aim was to produce 'reliable data bases for statistical comparisons' between different periods and different geographical settings.[41] The quantitative approach adopted by these authors is set out both in a short preparatory chapter on their sources and methods and in a series of appendices containing detailed statistical analyses of their 'data'.[42] In addition, the main text is replete with tables employed not only to depict the changing frequency of 'infanticide' prosecutions and convictions but also to demonstrate the supposedly statistical significance of the figures derived from the records.[43] Significantly, Hoffer and Hull (and indeed other authors) have used not only indictments but also printed trial reports to further their quantitative analysis. Although published trial reports provide an excellent opportunity to examine the nature of proceedings in court and to explore popular representations of those proceedings, they have usually been employed simply to furnish more data for statistical purposes.

There have been substantial disputes about the use of court records to measure and chart long-term and short-term fluctuations in criminal behaviour in this way.[44] However, while there might be some dispute about precisely what indictments can tell us, there is little doubt about what they fail to tell us. Indictments do not provide any detailed information about the nature of the alleged crime or about the circumstances leading up to the event. They do not reveal any information about the manner in which suspicions were aroused or about how a suspect's neighbours and local officials attempted to substantiate those suspicions either before the magistrate or coroner or in the trial courts. They also fail to provide details of those cases that were dismissed by the magistrate or coroner and were therefore not tried at the assize courts. By recording events in a set legal formula and by registering the outcome of the trial with an unqualified verdict of 'guilty' or 'not guilty', indictments also reveal little about the complexity and cultural significance of conflicting accounts of events and competing interpretations of the evidence. The quantitative analysis of indictments therefore tells us little about what certain actions and their consequences might have meant either for individual actors (suspects, witnesses, prosecutors, jurors, and judges) or for a community at large.

The influence of positivist social science, apparent in the routine reliance on indictments and trial reports as a source of quantitative evidence, is also visible in the attempts made by certain historians to correlate changing levels of new-born child murder with certain socio-economic conditions. Thus, Hoffer and Hull have attempted to explain 'changes in multiple-year totals of infanticide as a function of environmental forces – the external causes of the crime'.[45] In a passage that betrays their interest both in quantifying crime and in delineating the causes of criminal behaviour, they suggest:

> Economic needs, sexual norms, medical and demographic events, and levels of stress and violence in the society as a whole all had measurable effects upon the frequency of infanticide prosecutions – enabling us to calculate the composite effects of external conditions upon the amount of infanticide tried in the courts.[46]

Although Hoffer and Hull appear here to have acknowledged an important distinction between factors leading to the commission of crimes and those leading to prosecution, the main focus of their discussion is in fact directed towards explaining what they have referred to as the 'environmental causes of infanticide'[47] rather than exploring the factors determining whether or not a suspect was prosecuted. Their narrow emphasis on offences and offenders, rather than on the processes whereby certain types of behaviour were evaluated by different people in different settings, is evident not only in the book's title, *Murdering Mothers*, but also in the authors' self-conscious endeavour to probe what they refer to as 'the inner motivation of individual offenders'.[48]

This approach, evident not only in Hoffer and Hull's work but also in that of many other historians, is sustained by two related, but deeply problematic, assumptions that lie at the heart of positivist criminology. First, many historians have openly assumed, like some eighteenth-century commentators, that women accused of this crime had in most cases murdered their children. The point has been made most explicitly by Malcolmson:

> Although only a minority of infanticide cases involved an actual criminal conviction, we can safely assume that most instances of suspected infanticide were genuine in the sense that someone was responsible for the baby's death. On a few occasions the wrong person may have been suspected and accused, but when a dead baby was found in a pond, a barn, an outhouse, a box or buried in a garden, there is little reason to doubt that it had probably been murdered, or at the least deliberately not kept alive. If there were a few instances of reputed infanticide in which a baby actually was still-born or accidentally died in the course of delivery, they were almost certainly very much in the minority. Unless, then, the evidence clearly indicates that the mother intended to keep her baby, or that death resulted from misadventure, it seems reasonable to regard the great bulk of suspected infanticides as actual infanticides, and to presume that there was a guilty party somewhere.[49]

This assumption that most suspects were indeed guilty of new-born child murder fails to take account of substantial (although admittedly controversial) contemporary doubts about the guilt or criminal responsibility of these women. These doubts were firmly expressed not only in the works of medical and legal writers in the eighteenth century but also, and perhaps more significantly, in the form of acquittals by the courts. Retrospective assumptions of the suspects' guilt thus fail to acknowledge, or often even to consider, the wide variety of factors on which verdicts were based. In particular, they tend to privilege the accounts of events offered by witnesses and prosecutors over the accounts of events offered by accused women themselves. This asymmetry should be challenged. Although it may well be the case that single women possessed sufficient motive to conceal their pregnancies and murder their children at birth, it may also be the case that a woman's neighbours had sufficiently strong reasons to prosecute her for murder regardless of whether there was any immediate evidence that her child had been murdered. One of the central arguments of this book concerns precisely this point. I shall argue later that the critical element in determining the pattern of prosecutions and convictions for new-born child murder in the eighteenth century was the nature of local and legal responses to certain forms of behaviour rather than the commission of 'crimes'.

The second related assumption underlying the positivist approach to court records is that the 'actual crime rate' greatly exceeded the number of cases reaching court, that is, that beneath the official statistics lurked a 'dark figure' of crime unknown to the authorities and beyond the reach (but not beyond the imagination) of the historian. This assumption is evident in many studies of new-born child murder. For Sharpe, writing on the seventeenth century, the '"dark figure" of undetected infanticides must have been very great'.[50] In his work on crime and punishment in the eighteenth century, Frank McLynn similarly suggested that 'the level of indictments for the offence was very low when compared with the presumed actual rate of infanticide'.[51]

Both historians and criminologists have pointed out that there are considerable conceptual and practical problems with the 'dark figure' of crime.[52] As Christina Larner has suggested, the 'dark figure' of crime 'gives an objective status to certain actions as crimes which they do not actually have. Individual actions can only be defined as crimes by courts of law.'[53] Debates about the magnitude of the "dark figure" of crime or about the levels of 'actual crime' (as distinct from 'recorded crime') can therefore divert attention from the extent to which the meanings of concepts such as crime, guilt, innocence and responsibility were constantly negotiated within particular, but shifting, social contexts. Allegiance to the concept of a 'dark figure' of crime has also tended to focus the historical gaze exclusively on offences and offenders and to obscure the mechanics of the processes whereby suspicion was generated, evidence collected, and guilt or innocence established.

In addition to overlooking the complex mix of factors that informed the decisions and actions of suspects, witnesses, prosecutors, judges and jurors, an historical emphasis on offences and offenders has, perhaps ironically, precluded the development of a richer account of the lives of women in this period. By assuming the guilt of the accused and by uncritically accepting prominent contemporary male accounts of the motives and actions of suspects, historians have failed to acknowledge the extent to which the legal process and medical theory and practice were themselves gendered. In addition, positivist preoccupations with counting cases of new-born child murder and locating the environmental causes of those murders have deflected attention from the extensive involvement of women in generating suspicions, initiating investigations and prosecutions, and in giving evidence in the courts. Thus, previous studies have underestimated both the extent to which women were active participants in the legal process and the manner in which women themselves helped to define and maintain the boundaries of acceptable female behaviour.[54] Significantly, even works focusing exclusively on women and crime have demonstrated these limitations.[55]

If most studies of new-born child murder exhibit the features and limitations of the positivist approach to the history of crime, they also manifest many of the attributes and liabilities of what Innes and Styles have referred to as the 'reform perspective'. According to this approach, 'changes in society, in ideas and in policy thought to have taken place in the late eighteenth and early nineteenth centuries' are considered to be a 'major watershed in English social and political development'.[56] From this perspective, the apparent decline in prosecutions for new-born child murder, the increasing rarity of convictions, and the eventual repeal of the 1624 statute in 1803 were all manifestations of a major shift in attitudes and policy from the harsh, even unjust, approach exemplified by seventeenth- and early eighteenth-century courts and society to the more reasoned and more humane approach adopted by the courts, the public and parliament at the turn of the nineteenth century. For Hoffer and Hull (whose discussion of 'infanticide' in the eighteenth century appears in a chapter fittingly entitled 'Reform, England and New England, 1700-1803'), repeal of the 1624 statute not only legitimated the leniency already shown by judges and jurors but also represented an appropriate convergence between law and humane public opinion.[57] In a similar vein, Sauer has suggested that the 'unfairness' of the 1624 statute was 'replaced by a more equitable law' in 1803.[58]

Significantly, the 'reform perspective' relies heavily not only on the interpretations of contemporary writers, but also on the quantitative evidence furnished by the statistical approach. Thus, Hoffer and Hull's assertion that the attitudes of the courts and the public were softening in this period is dependent on their attempts to demonstrate steadily declining prosecution rates and the low rate of conviction for this crime.[59] In a similar manner, changing levels of indictments led Sharpe to conclude that there was an 'infanticide wave' around the turn of the seventeenth century in England and that the 'rise of infanticide in the second half of the sixteenth century, and its eighteenth-century decline which led to the repeal of the Jacobean statute in 1803, makes it ... one of the distinctive offences of the period'.[60]

There are problems with adopting the methods and interpretations of the 'reform perspective'. First, it is not entirely clear that the quantitative evidence upon which this approach rests can be used to support the assertions made by most historians. Evidence from the Northern Circuit counties, where approximately two women were tried each year for most of the eighteenth century, suggests that the prosecution rate may not have fallen uniformly throughout the country in this period.[61] Even if we accept that the prosecution rate fell in relation to the rising population and rising levels of illegitimacy,[62] it seems inappropriate to interpret this fall simply as evidence of public sympathy for suspects. Reliance on formal indictments and trial reports as a source of quantitative evidence has severely under-estimated the extent and persistence of local hostility towards suspects. As will become apparent in subsequent chapters, depositions of witnesses taken before magistrates and coroners suggest that neighbours, friends and relatives continued to condemn suspects throughout the century. Their disapproval could carry fatal consequences. It should be remem-bered that, in 1778, Sarah Sant was found guilty of murder and hanged, and that her mother, apparently distressed at the nature of her reception at home after her acquittal, was reported to have hanged herself.

A second reason for challenging the 'reform perspective' concerns its assessment of the circumstances surrounding repeal of the 1624 statute. Repeal of this statute cannot adequately be explained either as a product of liberal reforming efforts to introduce more humane and equitable laws or as the direct result of unanimous public sympathy for accused women expressed in the form of declining prosecution rates. The 1803 statute was introduced by a conservative Lord Chief Justice, Lord Ellenborough, who, by his own admission, was primarily concerned with increasing the conviction rate for this offence. As I shall argue later, the terms of the 1803 statute should be interpreted not primarily as a direct consequence of falling prosecutions (even if this trend could be clearly established) or of emerging humanitarian sympathies with the accused, but as the result of a persistent belief that certain women were being acquitted inappropri-ately for this crime.

Of course, not all historians writing on new-born child murder in the eighteenth century have indiscriminately adopted either the positivist approach or the 'reform perspective'. Although much of Beattie's work certainly focused on charting fluctuating indictment levels during the long eighteenth century, his brief discussion also included a perceptive account of the manner in which the offence was variably formulated and punished in that period.[63] However, by relying almost exclusively on indictments as a means of quantifying crime levels and by endorsing contemporary assumptions about 'murdering mothers' and lenient juries, most historians have certainly applied the methods of positivist social science and reformist historiography more thoroughly than they have pursued the kind of analysis proposed by historians advocating 'history from below'. It is perhaps ironic that, although recent historical interest in new-born child murder may have stemmed from the arousal of historical curiosity in the previously hidden experiences of ordinary people, and, in particular, the experiences of women, historians writing specifically on this crime have not acknowledged critical developments in either social history or gender history.[64]

It is clear that my own work on cases of suspected new-born child murder in the eighteenth century has benefited considerably from previous historical works. However, my approach clearly differs substantially from that of earlier works on the subject in a number of ways. First, the main focus of this book is not on the commission of 'crimes' by 'criminals' (nor on measuring those crimes and criminals) but on the processes whereby certain women were suspected of, and prosecuted for, murder. It therefore involves discussions not only of those factors that were thought by contemporaries to lead women to kill their children but also, more pertinently, of those circumstances that aroused suspicions of murder in the neighbourhood and led to prosecution. In outlining the broad social context and the narrow local conditions in which suspicions of murder were generated, I shall argue that the persistent prosecution of single women for the murder of their new-born children stemmed from concerns about the appropriate behaviour of unmarried women, about the concealment of what were regarded as illicit sexual relationships, and, perhaps most importantly, about the financial burdens of bastardy.

Second, I am concerned with the precise manner in which evidence was assembled and evaluated in different settings. In particular, I shall explore how witnesses and suspects formulated conflicting accounts of pregnancy, birth and death, and how they attempted to substantiate those conflicting accounts both locally and in the trial courts. Much of the evidence used to support competing accounts of events was obtained from close physical inspection of bodies, both the bodies of accused women and those of dead children. As a result of this focus on bodies as a source of evidence, medical testimony became central to the courts' efforts to distinguish between live- and still-birth, to determine the cause of death, and to assess the likelihood of murder in individual cases. For a number of reasons, medical witnesses were rarely able to answer such questions with any certainty. Perhaps paradoxically, it was this lack of certainty that proved most useful to the courts. As I shall argue, uncertainties in the medical evidence allowed judges and juries sufficient flexibility to accommodate conflicting accounts of events and to steer a middle course between the rigours of statute law, parochial concerns about the poor rates, and emerging humanitarian concerns.

The contribution of medical practitioners was not confined simply to presenting evidence derived from the examination of bodies. A number of medical practitioners also contributed to contentious debates about the character and conduct of single women accused of murdering their new-born children. In particular, some medical practitioners publicly opposed a persistent belief that suspects were vicious murderers by promoting a novel, and ostensibly humanitarian, account of the intentions and actions of such women. As I shall argue in more detail later, this novel appraisal of the behaviour of suspects held discrete professional and personal benefits for its advocates.

Conflicting accounts of pregnancy, birth and death and competing interpretations of the character and conduct of accused women were thrown into sharper relief by the accusatory flavour of the legal process in England and by the adversarial nature of proceedings in court. Trials of women accused of murdering their new-born children constituted a public and dramatic form of theatre within which conflicting presentations and interpretations of the evidence were fiercely disputed. However, verdicts were not only influenced by issues directly related to the alleged crimes under discussion. As I shall argue, judges and juries were also constrained by contemporary attitudes to various aspects of the law. In particular, the admission and weight of certain evidence was determined by rules governing, or at least used to legitimate, the actions and decisions of the various juries and by changing laws of evidence and standards of proof in this period.

Although the trial court was perhaps the most visible, and in many ways the most decisive, forum for discussion, it was not the only one. Reports of suspected murders appeared in local and national newspapers and attracted the attention of writers and publishers of ballads and broadsheets. The subject also occupied the consideration of members of parliament. In the last few decades of the eighteenth century, attempts to reform the criminal law included efforts to repeal the 1624 statute. Careful analysis of these unsuccessful efforts and of the successful repeal of that statute in 1803 suggests that parliamentary debates about detecting, trying and punishing women accused of this crime were part of broad, and unresolved, debates about the appropriate administration of justice in this period. As will become apparent, close scrutiny of the manner in which these and other critical issues were discussed can reveal the nature and complexity of the relationship between law and public opinion.

Sources

As Kermode and Walker have recently suggested in a collection of articles on women, crime and the courts in early modern England, it is 'becoming increasingly apparent that qualitative material can tell us far more about the activities of ordinary people than can aggregates of litigation alone'.[65] However, although recent articles and conference papers on 'infanticide' have hinted at the benefits to be gained from plundering a variety of archival sources to explore gender issues and developments in legal medicine, work has largely been confined to studies of the German states.[66] There has been little historical interest in utilising eighteenth-century English court records in a similar way. This reluctance to exploit the qualitative strengths of the English archives seems all the more lamentable given the rich array of records available to the historian. In contrast to many previous studies, the arguments presented in this book rely heavily on an intensive study of one particular set of archival sources, namely the Northern Circuit assize court records. It is worth examining in detail the origins and attributes of assize court records in general and the features of the Northern Circuit records in particular.

When a woman was suspected of murdering her new-born child in the eighteenth century, it was customary for her neighbours and local parish officers to interrogate her verbally and, on occasions, to examine her physically. After these initial informal investigations, the woman's accusers informed either a local justice of the peace or a coroner (or sometimes both officials) of their suspicions. The magistrate or coroner was then obliged by statute to question the witnesses (on oath) and suspects (without oath) and to record their statements in writing.[67] These written statements, which were to be certified at the next assize sessions, were referred to as 'depositions'.[68] The formal verdict of the inquest jury, expressed in a standard document written on parchment and known as an 'inquisition', was also returned to the assize courts.

If one or more magistrates considered that there were sufficient grounds for suspicion or if the coroner's inquest returned a verdict of murder, the magistrate or coroner was obliged to commit the suspect to gaol (or, at the least, to bail her) to await trial at the next assize session.[69] Details of prisoners awaiting trial were drawn up by the sheriff and listed in printed 'gaol calendars' shortly before the assize sessions opened. In addition, magistrates and coroners were required to bind all witnesses 'by Recognizance or Obligation' to appear in the assize courts either to give evidence or to prosecute the woman.[70] The details of those bound to appear were recorded and returned to the assize court in the form of written 'recognizances'.

At the first assize session after committal to prison, a formal 'bill of indictment', drawn up by the clerk of the court, would be preferred against a suspect. This process involved an initial assessment of the case by a grand jury of at least twelve, and often more than twenty, men. If the grand jury considered that there was sufficient evidence for further inquiry, the indictment would be marked 'true bill' and the woman would be arraigned and tried. If, on the other hand, members of the grand jury decided that there was insufficient evidence against the suspect, the indictment would be marked *ignoramus* or 'not found' and the woman would be 'discharged by proclamation'. Grand and trial jury verdicts were recorded not only at the foot or on the reverse of the indictments but also in 'gaol books' and 'minute books' from the assize circuits. In some cases, assize clerks also drew up a separate 'bill of costs' detailing the costs incurred in bringing the witnesses and prosecutors to court and in drawing up the various legal documents.

The historical value of these various court records depends upon an understanding of how the documents were produced, what information they routinely contained, and how they were used within the legal process. Gaol calendars, gaol books and minute books contain relatively little information about the circumstances leading to prosecution. According to manuals for assize clerks available in this period, calendars were simply to specify 'by what Justices of Peace, the Prisoner was committed, and for what cause'.[71] In addition to supplying these details, some gaol calendars also show the date of committal to prison, and, occasionally, provide the names of those witnesses upon whose oath the prisoner stood charged. Minute books and gaol books generally contain the names of the grand and trial jurors, the order of proceedings, the nature of the charges and pleas, and the verdicts. Occasionally, judicial comments about a particular case or session were recorded in these books. By and large, however, the main value of these particular records is restricted to tracing the outcome of particular cases.

As formal statements of the charge being brought against the accused, indictments also reveal little of the circumstances that generated suspicions of murder. The indictment was officially to include the name and address of the party indicted, the time and place where the crime was allegedly committed, the name of the victim, and the nature of the instrument (if any) with which the act had been committed. The offence itself was to be described using the appropriate 'Words of Art' (such as 'feloniously' and 'murdered') and the indictment was to conclude that the offence had been committed 'against the peace of the said Lord the King'.[72] In the context of new-born child murder trials, if the mother was to be tried under the statute of 1624, it was also necessary for the indictment to 'contain this special matter, that the prisoner was deliverd of a child, which by the laws of the kingdom was a bastard, and that it was born alive, and shew how she kild it'.[73] Although it was not strictly necessary, some Northern Circuit indictments also concluded that the offence had been committed 'against the Form of the Statute [of 1624] in such Case made and provided'.[74]

According to legal theory, these components of the indictment were to be expressed with as much certainty as possible. Any material errors, omissions or inconsistencies were supposed to render the indictment void.[75] In practice, as J. S. Cockburn has pointed out, 'the law, as reflected in assize trials, settled for less stringent standards of drafting'.[76] As Cockburn has argued, demonstrable inaccuracies in indictments reduce their reliability as historical documents.[77] There are further limits to the historical value of indictments. As Beattie has suggested, indictments defined and categorised offences in such a way that a variety of different acts could be subsumed under a single legal definition.[78] In the process, the finer details of the offence, the possible motives and the degree of violence involved were lost. As I have already suggested earlier in this chapter, indictments surviving from new-born child murder trials give few indications of the circumstances of particular cases, reducing alleged murders to a standard description. In many cases, the indictment simply specified in routine fashion that the accused woman 'then and there with both her hands aforesaid affixed about the Neck of the said Female bastard Child so being alive as aforesaid Feloniously Voluntarily and of her Malice Forethought did Choak and Strangle of which said Choaking and Strangling … the aforesaid Female bastard child instantly died'.[79] Although indictments provide no clear account of the alleged crime, they can be used to retrieve the names of the witnesses who gave evidence in court, the pleas of the accused and the verdicts of the grand and trial juries.

According to Cockburn, records that were drawn up locally by coroners and magistrates are more likely to contain accurate information than indictments.[80] Recognizances and inquisitions provide the names and occupations of many of the witnesses as well as the location of events. Occasionally, they also furnish limited details of circumstances leading to suspicion in individual cases. However, like indictments, both recognizances and inquisitions were formal legal documents drawn up according to a standard design. As a result, they generally contain little detailed information about the apparent nature and interpretation of events.

There is, however, one class of court records drawn up by local officials that constitutes a particularly rich source of information about the circumstances surrounding cases of suspected new-born child murder, namely the written statements, or depositions, of witnesses and suspects. The pre-trial examination of witnesses and suspects, and the written record of their evidences (which were to be signed or marked by informants), served a number of functions within the legal process. First, it enabled a woman's neighbours to present their reasons for suspecting that the woman had murdered her child. Second, it provided suspects with a preliminary opportunity to rebut those suspicions and present their own accounts of events. Although accused women were probably not obliged to answer the questions put to them during this pre-trial examination,[81] any failure to respond to local investigations may have been regarded as a cause of suspicion in itself.[82] In the circumstances, most accused women were prepared to risk self-incrimination and answer the questions put to them.

Taking and recording statements also enabled the magistrate or the coroner and his jury to clarify and assess the conflicting accounts of events presented to them and to reach some preliminary assessment of the case. In certain circumstances, depositions could also be used as evidence in the trial courts.[83] Significantly, the form and content of depositions were clearly influenced by official involvement in their production. Depositions were generally recorded in the third person and in a formal language unlikely to have been spoken spontaneously by either witnesses or suspects. In addition, although some suspects were apparently invited to speak freely in response to the accusations made against them, it is clear that in many cases their depositions simply comprised the answers to unrecorded questions posed by a magistrate, coroner, or clerk, or by neighbours present at the hearing.[84] The extent to which the content of the depositions accurately reflected the evidence of witnesses and suspects may also have been limited by procedural guidelines. It is possible, for example, that some clerks responsible for transcribing statements merely followed statutory directions by including only as much evidence 'as shall be material to prove the Felony',[85] rather than recording the whole of a deponent's testimony.

In spite of prescribed limitations on their production, depositions constitute one of the richest sources of evidence about cases of suspected new-born child murder (and indeed many other crimes) in the eighteenth century. They provide information about initial grounds for suspicion, about motives for prosecution, about the manner in which suspects were interrogated and examined, and about the ways in which certain circumstances and signs were interpreted by different participants. Depositions also offer a means of exploring the relative involvement, expertise and authority of midwives and male medical practitioners and of assessing the changing significance of medical evidence and inquests in this period. In addition, they provide an opportunity to consider the extent to which witnesses, suspects and officials were aware of the provisions of both statute and common law in these cases. By providing a wealth of incidental information about many aspects of eighteenth-century society, depositions also constitute an invaluable qualitative source not only for criminal historians but also for historians interested in social, medical, and gender history.

Many of the arguments presented in this book rely on careful analysis of the records surviving from the Northern Circuit assize courts between approximately 1720 and 1810. The Northern Circuit was the longest and most arduous circuit in the country. Comprising the counties of Yorkshire, Northumberland, Cumberland, and Westmorland, the circuit demanded a round trip from London of approximately 650 miles through some of the most dangerous terrain in the country, notably the Scottish borders.[86] Since the circuit judges also visited the separate jurisdictions of the County Palatinates of Durham and Lancaster, judicial business could last over five weeks during the long summer circuit when assize sessions were held in all six jurisdictions.[87]

Assize sessions for the county of Yorkshire (probably the most populous county in England in this period)[88] were held twice yearly throughout the century. Sessions for the county were held at the Castle in York, part of which served as the county gaol. Sessions for the City of York were held separately at the Guildhall immediately before the county business was opened.[89] As a result of hazardous travelling conditions during the winter, the circuit judges only visited Northumberland, Cumberland and Westmorland during the summer. Assize sessions for Northumberland were held at Newcastle-upon-Tyne (and occasionally at Morpeth), those for the town being convened in the Guildhall and those for the county in the Moot-Hall in the Castle bailey. Sessions for Cumberland and Westmorland (two of the smallest, least populous and most isolated shires in the country) were held at Carlisle and Appleby respectively. The number of cases of suspected new-born child murder that reached these northern assize courts was roughly proportional to the populations of these four counties.[90]

The records surviving from these Northern Circuit sessions are extensive, particularly after 1720. Gaol books and minute books recording the activities of most of the Northern Circuit courts survive from 1713 and 1714 respectively. There are no surviving indictment files from the first two decades of the eighteenth century. But from 1722, files containing not only indictments but also inquisitions, recognizances, gaol calendars and bills of costs are available from almost every year of the century. There are also a number of miscellaneous papers and books surviving from 1730 onwards. It is, however, the quantity and quality of the depositions (which are comprehensively indexed in the Public Record Office catalogues) that makes the Northern Circuit records such a rich archival source. Depositions survive only variably from the cases heard in the Northern Circuit courts in the first two decades of the century. However, from 1720 onwards they are available not only from most of the cases that reached the trial courts but also from inquests that did not result in the trial of a particular woman for the murder of her child.[91]

One further advantage of studying the Northern Circuit is the availability of a number of local newpapers (such as *The York Courant, The Leeds Mercury, The Leedes Intelligencer* and *The Cumberland Pacquet*) which regularly reported suspected murders and events at the assize courts.[92] There are, however, disadvantages to focusing exclusively on the activities of the Northern Circuit courts. Although the archival sources are extensive, there are few printed transcripts of trial proceedings in the northern courts comparable to those available from the Old Bailey Sessions and the Surrey and Sussex assizes.[93] Only the trials of Dorothy Shutt in 1776 and Elizabeth Pickhaver in 1777 were transcribed and published in a collection of transcripts covering trials at the Castle of York between 1775 and 1778.[94] Although depositions (when studied in conjunction with lists of the witnesses that were sworn in court) can be used to infer the nature of the evidence presented and discussed in the assize courts, it is necessary to move beyond the Northern Circuit for a more detailed investigation of the evidence considered by grand and trial juries. I have therefore supplemented my scrutiny of the Northern Circuit records by examining a selection of trial reports from the Old Bailey (referred to as the Old Bailey Sessions Papers) and from proceedings at the Surrey and Sussex assize sessions (referred to as the Surrey and Sussex Assize Proceedings).

It is important to recognise, however, that not even printed trial reports necessarily presented accurate accounts of the evidence or of the factors that influenced juries. Printed reports were abridged to make them suitable for popular consumption and they give few direct indications of the juries' reasons for reaching certain verdicts. The bases for the decisions of the juries in new-born child murder trials and the range of contemporary attitudes to the crime must therefore be inferred from a wider range of sources. In order to explore the full range of contemporary attitudes to the suspected murders of new-born children, I have therefore also made extensive use of a variety of printed sources: texts written specifically for lawyers, magistrates, coroners and medical practitioners; local and national newspaper reports; printed ballads and broadsheets; parliamentary debates and printed bills and statutes; published articles and books; and the letters and diaries of medical practitioners, parsons and magistrates.[95]

Conclusion

This book focuses on recorded cases of women accused of murdering their new-born children in the eighteenth century. It is, however, more than a microhistory of a singular crime. Archival and printed sources relating to cases of suspected new-born child murder provide access to consistently hidden aspects of eighteenth-century life. Court records furnish historians with an opportunity to examine the mechanics of poor law administration and to analyse anxieties about the maintenance of law and order at a local level. They also allow a detailed analysis of public perceptions of pregnancy, birth and death and an exploration of the tensions between midwives and male medical practitioners, and between medical practitioners and the law. In addition, the records provide a means of exploring the complexity of the legal process (from initial accusation through to the verdict of the trial jury and, where appropriate, sentencing) and give access to broader public and parliamentary debates about the appropriate administration of justice. Perhaps more significantly, assize court records and published sources together offer an invaluable opportunity to reconstruct the lives of certain women in this period. Depositions, in particular, render the actions and intentions of women accused of murdering their new-born children and of their neighbours more clearly visible to the historical eye.

Significantly, the extensive survival of the Northern Circuit records also provides an opportunity to examine change across time. While this book draws upon evidence of the processes of accusation and prosecution from particular settings at particular moments in time (that is, from particular cases), it also analyses the manner in which those general processes changed throughout the eighteenth century. This entails more than simply revealing patterns of prosecution and conviction. It also involves a detailed examination of the ways in which statute and common law were variably interpreted, implemented and amended, of the manner in which certain types of evidence were variably interpreted by suspects, witnesses, and the courts, and of the extent to which appraisals of guilt and innocence were constantly renegotiated not only in the courts but also in medical and legal writings and in parliament.

Notes

1 Throughout the eighteenth century, the terms 'bastard' and (less frequently) 'illegitimate' were routinely used to describe children born out of wedlock. I have used these terms interchangeably throughout the book, without intending any offence by either term.

2 The depositions, inquisition and indictment for this case are in the Public Record Office in Chancery Lane, CHES 24/171/6.

3 'Assizes' were the regular court sessions held by Westminster judges in each county in England and Wales for the purpose of administering justice.

4 *The Cumberland Pacquet*, (22 September 1778), p. 2.

5 These figures are derived from the Northern Circuit court records which are discussed in detail below, pp. 16-22.

6 For a discussion of the records from which these figures are derived, see below, pp. 16-22, and fn. 61 below.

7 *The Guardian*, 105, (11 July 1713).

8 The statute, discussed at length in Chapter 2 below, was 'An Act to prevent the Destroying and Murthering of Bastard Children', 21 Jac. I c. 27, 1624.

9 This was the opinion expressed by Daniel Defoe in his *The Generous Protector, or a Friendly Proposal to Prevent Murder and Other Enormous Abuses, By Erecting an Hospital for Foundlings and Bastard-Children*, (London, 1731), p. 9.

10 For broad chronological overviews of what writers have usually referred to as

'infanticide', see: D. Seaborne Davies, 'Child-killing in English law', *Modern Law Review*, 1 (December 1937), 203-23; William A. Langer, 'Infanticide: a historical survey', *History of Childhood Quarterly*, 1 (1974), 353-66; Maria W. Piers, *Infanticide: Past and Present*, (New York, W. W. Norton and Company, 1978); Beverley A. Montag and Thomas W. Montag, 'Infanticide: A historical perspective', *Minnesota Medicine*, (May 1979), 368-72; Keith Wrightson, 'Infanticide in European history', *Criminal Justice History*, 3 (1982), 1-20; Glenn Hausfater and Sarah Blaffer Hrdy, *Infanticide Comparative and Evolutionary Perspectives*, (New York, Aldine Publishing Company, 1984).

11 See, for example: Richard C. Trexler, 'Infanticide in Florence: New sources and first results', *History of Childhood Quarterly*, 1 (1973), 98-116; Barbara A. Kellum, 'Infanticide in England in the later middle ages', *History of Childhood Quarterly*, 1 (1974), 367-88; Keith Wrightson, 'Infanticide in earlier seventeenth-century England', *Local Population Studies*, 15 (1975), 10-22; R. Sauer, 'Infanticide and abortion in nineteenth-century Britain', *Population Studies*, 32 (1978), 81-93; Lionel Rose, *The Massacre of the Innocents: Infanticide in Britain 1800-1939*, (London, Routledge and Kegan Paul, 1986); James Lee, Cameron Campbell and Guofu Tan, 'Infanticide and family planning in late Imperial China: the price and population history of rural Liaoning, 1774-1873', in Thomas G. Rawski and Lillian M. Li (eds.), *Chinese History in Economic Perspective*, (Berkeley, 1992), pp. 145-76; William LaFleur, *Liquid Life: Abortion and Buddhism in Japan*, (Princeton, 1992); Johanna Geyer-Kordesch, 'Infanticide and medico-legal ethics in eighteenth century Prussia', in Andrew Wear, Johanna Geyer-Kordesch and Roger French (eds.), *Doctors and Ethics: The Earlier Historical Setting of Professional Ethics*, (Amsterdam, Rodopi, 1993), pp. 181-202; Mark Jackson, 'New-born child murder: a study of suspicion, evidence, and proof in eighteenth-century England', (PhD thesis, Leeds, 1992); Margaret L. Arnot, 'Infant death, child care and the state: the baby-farming scandal and the first infant life protection legislation of 1872', *Continuity and Change*, 9:2 (1994), 271-311; Mark Jackson, 'Suspicious infant deaths: the statute of 1624 and medical evidence at coroners' inquests', in Michael Clark and Catherine Crawford (eds.), *Legal Medicine in History*, (Cambridge, Cambridge University Press, 1994), pp. 64-86; Mary Nagle Wessling, 'Infanticide trials and forensic medicine: Württembergs 1757-93', in Clark and Crawford (eds.), *Legal Medicine in History*, pp. 117-44; Mark Jackson, 'Developing medical expertise: medical practitioners and the suspected murders of new-born children', in Roy Porter (ed.), *Medicine in the Enlightenment*, (Amsterdam, Rodopi, 1995), pp. 145-65; Mark Jackson, '"Something more than Blood": conflicting accounts of pregnancy loss in eighteenth-century England', in Rosanne Cecil (ed.), *The Anthropology of Pregnancy Loss*, (Berg, 1996).

12 See: Roger Smith, *Trial by Medicine: Insanity and Responsibility in Victorian Trials*, (Edinburgh, Edinburgh University Press, 1981); J. A. Sharpe, *Crime in Seventeenth-century England: a County Study*, (Cambridge, Cambridge University Press, 1983); J. A. Sharpe, *Crime in Early Modern England 1550-1750*, (London, Longman, 1984); Shelley Day, 'Puerperal insanity: The historical sociology of a disease', (PhD thesis, Cambridge, 1985); J. M. Beattie, *Crime and the Courts in England 1660-1800*, (Oxford, Clarendon Press, 1986); Clive Emsley, *Crime and Society in England, 1750-1900*, (London, Longman, 1987); Frank McLynn, *Crime and Punishment in Eighteenth-century England*, (London, Routledge, 1989); R. Short, 'Female criminality 1780-1830', (M. Litt thesis, Oxford, 1989).

13 Wessling, 'Infanticide trials and forensic medicine', p. 117.

14 Jenny Kermode and Garthine Walker (eds.), *Women, Crime and the Courts in Early Modern England*, (London, UCL Press, 1994), p. 1. This interesting collection of essays contains little mention of cases of suspected new-born child murder.

15 R. W. Malcolmson, 'Infanticide in the eighteenth century', in J. S. Cockburn (ed.), *Crime in England, 1550-1800*, (London, Methuen, 1977), pp. 187-209.

16 Sharpe, *Crime in Seventeenth-century England*; Sharpe, *Crime in Early Modern England*; Beattie, *Crime and the Courts*.

17 Peter C. Hoffer and N. E. H. Hull, *Murdering Mothers: Infanticide in England and New England 1558-1803*, (New York, New York University Press, 1981).

18 Hoffer and Hull, *Murdering Mothers*, pp. 65-91.

19 Samuel Johnson, *A Dictionary of the English Language*, (London, 1755). Later editions, published in 1756, 1778, 1785, and 1799, defined 'infanticide' in the same terms.

20 Giovanni Battista Morgagni, *The Seats and Causes of Diseases*, tr. Benjamin Alexander, (3 vols. , London, 1769), vol. I, p. 538.

21 For a bibliography of some of the relevant nineteenth-century literature, see: Sauer, 'Infanticide and abortion'; Rose, *The Massacre of the Innocents*. For more general discussions of the increase in literature on legal medicine in the nineteenth century, see: Thomas Rogers Forbes, *Surgeons at the Bailey: English Forensic Medicine to 1878*, (New Haven, Yale University Press, 1985); Catherine Crawford, 'A scientific profession: medical reform and forensic medicine in British periodicals of the early nineteenth century', in Roger French and Andrew Wear (eds.), *British Medicine in an Age of Reform*, (London, Routledge, 1991), pp. 203-30.

22 For Beattie (*Crime and the Courts*, p. 113), 'infanticide' was 'the killing of a baby at or very soon after birth'.

23 Hoffer and Hull, *Murdering Mothers*, pp. xiii-xiv.

24 Piers, *Infanticide*.

25 Beattie, *Crime and the Courts*, p. 113, fn. 84.

26 'An Act to provide that a woman who wilfully causes the death of her newly-born child may, under certain conditions, be convicted of infanticide', 12 & 13 Geo. 5 c. 18, 1922.

27 'An Act to repeal and re-enact with modifications the provisions of the Infanticide Act, 1922', 1 & 2 Geo. 6 c. 36, 1938.

28 21 Jac. I c. 27, 1624.

29 Malcolmson, 'Infanticide'; Sharpe, *Crime in Early Modern England*; Beattie, *Crime and the Courts*, p. 19; Hoffer and Hull, *Murdering Mothers*, pp. xiii-xix.

30 Malcolmson, 'Infanticide', p. 190.

31 Joanna Innes and John Styles, 'The crime wave: recent writing on crime and criminal justice in eighteenth-century England', in Adrian Wilson (ed.), *Rethinking Social History*, (Manchester, Manchester University Press, 1994), p. 201.

32 Innes and Styles, 'The crime wave', p. 202.

33 Ibid., pp. 202-3.

34 Ibid., p. 203.

35 Ibid., p. 203.

36 Ibid., p. 204. See Leon Radzinowicz, *A History of English Criminal Law and its Administration from 1750*, vol. I, (London, Stevens and Sons Limited, 1948).

37 Innes and Styles, 'The crime wave', pp. 204-5.

38 For his comments on the value of criminal statistics, see Sharpe, *Crime in Early Modern England*, pp. 41-44.

39 Beattie, *Crime and the Courts*, pp. 19-20, 639-43.

40 Sharpe, *Crime in Early Modern England*, pp. 55, 61; Beattie, *Crime and the Courts*, p. 114.

41 Hoffer and Hull, *Murdering Mothers*, p. xvii.

42 Ibid., pp. xii-xix, 165-84.

43 Ibid., pp. 24-5, 29, 55.

44 See, for example, discussions in: Innes and Styles, 'The crime wave', pp. 209-15; Sharpe, *Crime in Early Modern England*, pp. 41-4; J. M. Beattie, 'Towards a study of crime in 18th century England: a note on indictments', in Paul Fritz and David Williams (eds.), *The Triumph of Culture: 18th Century Perspectives*, (Toronto, A. M. Hakkert Ltd. , 1972), pp. 299-314; J. S. Cockburn, 'The nature and incidence of crime in England 1559-1625: a preliminary survey', in Cockburn (ed.), *Crime in England*, pp. 49-71; Douglas Hay, 'War, dearth and theft in the eighteenth century: the record of the English courts,' *Past and Present*, 95 (1982), 117-60; J. A. Sharpe, 'The history of violence in England: some observations', *Past and Present*, 108 (1985), 206-15; Law-

rence Stone, 'A rejoinder', *Past and Present*, 108 (1985), 216-24; J. S. Cockburn, 'Patterns of violence in English society: homicide in Kent 1560-1985', *Past and Present*, 130 (1991), 70-106.

45 Hoffer and Hull, *Murdering Mothers*, p. xi.

46 Ibid., p. xi.

47 This phrase appears in the title of Chapter 5 of Hoffer and Hull, *Murdering Mothers*, p. 113.

48 Hoffer and Hull, *Murdering Mothers*, p. xi.

49 Malcolmson, 'Infanticide', pp. 191-2.

50 Sharpe, *Crime in Seventeenth-century England*, p. 137.

51 McLynn, *Crime and Punishment*, p. 114.

52 For a critical discussion of the problems of 'dark figures' in criminology, see Jason Ditton, *Controlology: Beyond the New Criminology*, (London, Macmillan, 1979), pp. 17-24.

53 Christina Larner, *Enemies of God: The Witch-hunt in Scotland*, (London, Chatto and Windus, 1981), p. 63.

54 A similar point is made with regard to witchcraft prosecutions by Jim Sharpe, 'Women, witchcraft and the legal process', in Kermode and Walker (eds.), *Women, Crime and the Courts*, pp. 106-24.

55 See, for example, Short's explicit reliance on positivist social science in 'Female criminality'.

56 Innes and Styles, 'The crime wave', p. 204.

57 Hoffer and Hull, *Murdering Mothers*, pp. 87-91.

58 Sauer, 'Infanticide and abortion', p. 82.

59 Hoffer and Hull, *Murdering Mothers*, pp. 65-91.

60 Sharpe, *Crime in Early Modern England*, pp. 61, 109.

61 An extensive search of the surviving Northern Circuit records revealed the following number of cases reaching the assize courts each decade: 1720-29 – 15; 1730-39 – 30; 1740-49 – 24; 1750-59 – 25; 1760-69 – 30; 1770-79 – 25; 1780-89 – 19; 1790-99 – 20. There were also twenty-four trials for this crime in the first decade of the nineteenth century.

62 A point made by Beattie, *Crime and the Courts*, p. 122.

63 Beattie, *Crime and the Courts*, pp. 113-24.

64 In addition, they have ignored critical developments in the field of criminology that in the last two or three decades have challenged the assumptions and findings of positivist criminology. For a discussion of so-called 'new criminologies' (such as control theories, labelling, conflict theories, radical criminologies and feminist criminologies), see Katherine S. Williams, *Textbook on Criminology*, (London, Blackstone Press Limited, 1991), pp. 245-308.

65 Kermode and Walker, *Women, Crime and the Courts*, p. 5. The authors cite Natalie Zemon Davis, *Fiction in the Archives: Pardon Tales and their Tellers in Sixteenth-century France*, (Cambridge, Polity Press, 1987) as an example of how certain records can be used in a qualitative, rather than quantitative, manner. Articles in their own collection also demonstrate how effectively court records can be used.

66 Geyer-Kordesch, 'Infanticide and medico-legal ethics in eighteenth century Prussia'; Wessling, 'Infanticide trials and forensic medicine: Württembergs 1757-93'; Alison Rowlands, '"Inhuman and unnatural": Infanticidal women in sixteenth- and seventeenth-century Germany', paper presented to an international conference entitled 'Gender and Crime in Britain and Europe Early Modern and Modern' held at Roehampton Institute, London, 2-4 April 1995.

67 The duties of coroners and magistrates were set out in 'An Act touching Bailment of Persons', 1 & 2 Ph. & M. c. 13, 1554, and 'An Act to take Examination of Prisoners suspected of any Manslaughter or Felony', 1 & 2 Ph. & M. c. 10, 1555.

68 A deposition was 'the Testimony of a Witness, otherwise called a Deponent, put down in Writing by Way of Answer to Interrogatories exhibited for that Purpose' – Giles Jacob, *New Law Dictionary*, (5th ed., 1744), 'Deposition'.

69 Matthew Hale, *History of the Pleas of the Crown*, ed. Sollom Emlyn, (2 vols. , London, 1736), vol. II, pp. 120-1. I have found only one case from the Northern Circuit court records where a woman accused of murdering her new-born child was bailed rather than committed to gaol. In 1733, Ann Medd and her brother George were bound by £100 and £50 respectively to ensure that Ann appeared to answer the charge against her – the recognizances are in ASSI 44/49. In addition, in 1767, John White and his sureties were bound in a total of £2,500 for John to appear to answer charges concerning the death of the illegitimate child of Ann Usher, who had already been acquitted of the murder – the recognizances are in ASSI 44/82.

70 1 & 2 Ph. & M. c. 10, 1555.

71 T. W. , *The Office of the Clerk of Assize: Containing The Form and Method of the Proceedings at the Assizes, and General Gaol-delivery, as also on the Crown and Nisi Prius Side*, (London, 1676) – see the sample Calendar and notes in the preface to the main text.

72 On the drafting of indictments, see: Hale, *Pleas of the Crown*, vol. II, pp. 165-93; Jacob, *New Law Dictionary*, 'Indictment'.

73 Hale, *Pleas of the Crown*, vol. II, p. 288. See also Edward Hyde East, *A Treatise of the Pleas of the Crown*, (2 vols. , London, 1803), vol. I, pp. 348-9.

74 Fletcher Rigge, clerk to the Northern Circuit from 1772, frequently concluded indictments with these words. But see Hale, *Pleas of the Crown*, vol. II, pp. 190, 289.

75 According to Jacob, 'If one material Part of an Indictment is repugnant to or inconsistent with another, the Whole is void' – Jacob, *New Law Dictionary*, 'Indictment'. See the discussion of this point in J. S. Cockburn, 'Trial by the Book? Fact and theory in the criminal process, 1558-1625' in J. H. Baker (ed.), *Legal Records and the Historian*, (London, Royal Historical Society, 1978), pp. 60-79.

76 Cockburn, 'Trial by the Book?', p. 62.

77 J. S. Cockburn, 'Early-modern assize records as historical evidence', *Journal of the Society of Archivists*, 5 (1975), 215-31.

78 Beattie, 'Towards a study of crime', p. 302.

79 From the indictment against Elizabeth Boswell, 1735, ASSI 44/49.

80 Cockburn, 'Early-modern assize records', pp. 224-6.

81 The canon law rule against self-incrimination (*nemo / nullus tenetur seipsum prodere* – no-one is bound to betray themselves) was cited by Michael Dalton in 1619 in support of his assertion that the examination of suspects should be taken without oath and was gradually adopted in the common law courts during the late seventeenth and early eighteenth centuries – Michael Dalton, *The Countrey Justice*, (London, Professional Books Limited, [1619] 1973), p. 273. In the eighteenth century, Gilbert also cited the privilege in support of voluntary examinations – Geoffrey Gilbert, *The Law of Evidence*, (Dublin, 1754), p. 99. For a discussion of the canon law rule and its adoption in the courts, see M. R. T. Macnair, 'The early development of the privilege against self-incrimination', *Oxford Journal of Legal Studies*, 10 (1990), 66-84.

82 Dalton, *The Countrey Justice*, p. 275.

83 For the circumstances in which depositions could be read in evidence, see: Hale, *Pleas of the Crown*, vol. II, p. 284; Jacob, *New Law Dictionary*, 'Deposition'.

84 According to the depositions, Frances Harrison (1795, ASSI 45/38/3/51) was simply asked by the coroner 'if she had a mind to say any thing about the Child that was found in the Canal'. Mary Thorpe (1800, ASSI 45/40/2/240-1) was similarly asked 'what she hath to say in her defence'. By contrast, Ann Benison (1788, ASSI 45/36/2/10-12) was interrogated at length both in front of the coroner's jury and in private.

85 The instructions in the Marian statutes, 1 & 2 Ph. & M. c. 13, 1554, and 1 & 2 Ph. & M. c. 10, 1555.

86 On the length and arduous nature of the Northern Circuit, see: *Browne's General Law List*, (London, 1799), p. 254; J. S. Cockburn, *A History of English Assizes, 1558-1714*, (Cambridge, Cambridge University Press, 1972), pp. 38-46, 51-2.

87 The court records from the assize sessions in Durham and Lancaster were produced separately from those of the other northern counties and are stored separately in the

Public Record Office at DURH 15-19 and PL 26-28. I have not studied the records of these palatinate jurisdictions in any depth.

88 According to the census of 1801, Yorkshire was then the most populous county in the country, with a population of 858,892.

89 Occasionally, the summer circuit also incorporated a session at Kingston-upon-Hull. The locations and times of the sessions are given in the minute and gaol books, ASSI 41 and 42.

90 Accurate estimates of the populations of the Northern Circuit counties is not possible until the first Census Report in 1801. Using that report as a guide, however, the respective population and case proportions (between 1730 and 1799) were as follows: Yorkshire – 73.1/70.7; Northumberland – 13.4/12.6; Cumberland – 10/13.2; Westmorland – 3.5/3.4. Interestingly, however, the proportions of cases recorded from the three Yorkshire Ridings differed from the population proportions. The respective population and case proportions in Yorkshire were: West Riding – 65.7/48.8; North Riding – 18.1/31.7; East Riding – 16.2/17.1. Although further research into the parishes and townships in which cases arose is needed, these figures may reflect differences in the urban/rural composition of the three Ridings. The West Riding contained most of the county's large towns, where the mothers of dead new-born children would be difficult to trace. In small rural communities of the North Riding, however, it may have been difficult for a single woman to conceal her pregnancy and labour, or to hide the body of her dead child, from her neighbours. See also the discussion in Chapter 2.

91 Full details of these records are in the bibliography.

92 *The York Courant* was first published consistently every week from 1725. *The Leeds Mercury* was published inconsistently from the second decade of the eighteenth century, while *The Leedes Intelligencer* was printed every Tuesday from 1754. *The Cumberland Pacquet* appeared weekly from 1774.

93 For an account of the Old Bailey Sessions Papers, see John H. Langbein, 'The criminal trial before the lawyers', *The University of Chicago Law Review*, 45 (1978), 263-316. On the Surrey and Sussex Assize Proceedings, see Beattie, *Crime and the Courts*, pp. 23-5.

94 These two cases are contained in a bound collection of trial proceedings, *The Trials at Large of the Felons in the Castle of York, 1775-8*, a copy of which is housed in York City Reference Library.

95 I have retained original spellings throughout when quoting from contemporary sources. However, all dates prior to 1752 (when the start of the new year was moved from 25 March to 1 January) have been converted to 'new style'; for example, an inquest held on 23 March 1721/2 would be referred to as having been taken on 23 March 1722.

2

The generation of suspicion: single women, bastardy and the law

Introduction

One prominent and persistent feature of new-born child murder trials in the eighteenth century is that the overwhelming majority of defendants were women. More particularly, the majority of women accused of this crime were, according to court records and contemporary reports, unmarried women. In the Northern Circuit courts, for example, over ninety per cent of defendants were women. Of these women suspects, over ninety per cent were referred to as 'single women' or 'spinsters', or, more rarely, as 'widows'. Correspondingly, virtually all of the children allegedly killed at birth were described in the records as bastard children. By contrast, married women and men were infrequently indicted for this crime. Of 207 defendants indicted in the Northern Circuit courts between 1720 and 1799, only eight were married women and only seventeen were (unmarried) men, both usually indicted as accessories to the murder of an illegitimate child by the child's unmarried mother.[1]

Although the terms 'single woman' and 'married woman' were not necessarily mutually exclusive in the eighteenth century, even after the passage of Hardwicke's Marriage Act in 1753,[2] it seems clear that most local and legal attention was directed towards the outcome of the pregnancies of women defined both by local communities and by the courts as unmarried. Contemporary preoccupations with unmarried women and with the fate of their illegitimate children stemmed from a variety of factors, notably from anxieties about the appropriate behaviour of single women and about the role of women in the family, from concerns about the concealment of illicit sex, and, perhaps most importantly, from fears about the financial burden of increasing numbers of illegitimate children. Significantly, the parameters of debates about such issues were defined by the law, both by general legislation relating to the maintenance of bastard children and by a specific statute of 1624 governing the rules of evidence in cases of suspected new-born child murder. Attitudes to the construction of these laws were also central to the decision-making process in the courts and to parliamentary debates on the subject. The aim of this chapter, though, is to explore the legal and cultural context in which suspicions of murder were first generated and prosecutions initiated.

The 1624 statute in social context

Until the late sixteenth century, official displeasure at fornication or extra-marital sex and at the birth of bastard children was expressed through the public penance that could be imposed by church courts. In 1576, however, concern at the increasing number of illegitimate children that were being 'left to be kept at the Charges of the Parish where they be born, to the great Burden of the same Parish' served to bring the matter within the jurisdiction of the secular courts for the first time. Legislation passed in that year granted justices of the peace the authority to commit the mothers and reputed fathers of chargeable bastards to gaol if they refused to maintain their children. Although the statute's wording implied a degree of moral censure at the bearing of bastards (since it was described as 'an Offence against God's Law and Man's Law'), its provisions were restricted to the parents of bastards that were likely to be a financial burden on the parish. The statute's principal aim was apparently to prevent the economic, rather than simply the moral, burden of bastardy.[3]

In 1610, further legislation enabled justices of the peace to commit 'every lewd Woman' bearing a chargeable bastard to a House of Correction for one year. If a woman re-offended, she was to be committed until she could provide sureties for her good behaviour. As in the earlier statute, the financial burden that bastardy placed on a parish was of greater immediate importance to the legislators than the belief that bastardy was to 'the great Dishonour of Almighty God'.[4] Significantly, by providing only for the punishment of women, this statute reinforced existing prejudices against unmarried mothers. Although men were theoretically punishable under the terms of the 1576 Act, the majority of punishment orders were in fact directed solely against the women concerned.[5] This asymmetry in the treatment of men and women, evident both in the law and in parochial practice, can be interpreted as a manifestation of a double standard that was applied to male and female sexual experience, a double standard supposedly based, in this instance, on the greater evils seen to be caused by infidelity in wives than in husbands.[6] It may also have been a consequence of the ease with which the mother, rather than the father, of a chargeable bastard could be identified, located and punished.

The statutes of 1576 and 1610 were born out of an urgent need to deter women from bearing chargeable bastards and to relieve parishes of the expense associated with the maintenance of illegitimate children. The significance of these statutes was increased by the passage, in the intervening years, of the first laws for the relief of the poor.[7] These poor laws, which attempted to resolve problems caused by the increase in population that occurred in the sixteenth century and by an associated rise in the number of wandering poor, established a system of poor relief in which newly created overseers of the poor, under the supervision of justices of the peace, could tax every appropriate person in the parish. The money collected from the poor rates in this way was then used to provide work for the able poor and to maintain the aged and impotent poor. The thriftless and idle poor, dissolute and slothful persons who refused to work, and those who were poor as a result of debauchery rather than casualty or sickness, were all seen as undeserving of poor relief, and were to be sent to the common gaol or House of Correction.[8] Significantly, illegitimate children and their single mothers were viewed as unwelcome and undeserving burdens on this system of parochial poor relief.[9]

The success with which the statutes of 1576 and 1610 relieved parishes of the financial burden of bastards was dependent upon the successful identification and punishment of bastard-bearers by the communities in which they lived. Together with the newly established system of poor relief through taxation, these laws exposed the mothers of bastards in particular to the accusations and hostility of rate-paying neighbours. Keen to avoid the burden of supporting a child, neighbours encouraged pregnant single women either to marry or to filiate their children on men who could maintain them. If such strategies failed and the child was likely to require maintenance from rate-payers in the parish, its mother could become extremely unpopular in the neighbourhood.[10] In an attempt to avoid the unpopularity, shame and punishment of poor, unmarried motherhood, some single women apparently attempted to conceal their pregnancies from the neighbourhood and to give birth in secret. If this subterfuge failed and the body of a child was later found dead, a woman's neighbours and parish officers were quick to suspect that the woman had killed her bastard child at birth in order to evade punishment.[11]

Until the third decade of the seventeenth century, it proved singularly difficult to substantiate such suspicions of murder in court. Prior to 1624, all women and men suspected of murdering new-born children were tried according to common law rules of evidence. At common law, the prosecution was required to prove that a dead child had been born alive before attempting to prove murder. Direct evidence of live-birth, in the form of witnesses to the birth, was rare in cases where murder was

suspected and the prosecution inevitably relied heavily upon presumptive
or circumstantial evidence that the child had been born alive and murdered: upon examination of the mother for signs of her having gone to
her full time; upon estimates of the child's maturity and viability; upon
signs of violence on the child's body; and upon accounts of the behaviour
and reputation of the mother. In some instances, such evidence was
sufficient to obtain a conviction for murder,[12] but in many cases convert-
ing the suspicions of neighbours and local officials into convictions
proved difficult.

The problems encountered by the prosecution at common law, together with contemporary hostility towards the bearers of chargeable
bastards, eventually prompted the provision of special evidential rules
facilitating the prosecution of women accused of murdering bastards.
After attempts to legislate on the subject in 1607 and 1610 had failed, 'An
Act to prevent the Destroying and Murthering of Bastard Children' was
passed by the Commons, after amendment in the Lords, on 27 May 1624.
The full text of the 1624 statute was as follows:

> Whereas many lewd Women that have been delivered of Bastard
> Children, to avoid their Shame, and to escape Punishment, do secretly
> bury or conceal the Death of their Children, and after, if the Child be
> found dead, the said Women do alledge, that the said Child was born
> dead; whereas it falleth out sometimes (although hardly it is to be
> proved) that the said Child or Children were murthered by the said
> Women, their lewd Mothers, or by their Assent or Procurement:
> II For the Preventing therefore of this great Mischief, be it enacted by
> the Authority of this present Parliament, That if any Woman after one
> Month next ensuing the End of this Session of Parliament be delivered
> of any Issue of her Body, Male or Female, which being born alive,
> should by the Laws of this Realm be a Bastard, and that she endeavour
> privately, either by drowning or secret burying thereof, or any other
> Way, either by herself or the procuring of others, so to conceal the
> Death thereof, as that it may not come to Light, whether it were born
> alive or not, but be concealed: In every such Case the said Mother so
> offending shall suffer Death as in Case of Murther, except such Mother
> can make proof by one Witness at the least, that the Child (whose
> Death was by her so intended to be concealed) was born dead.[13]

This statute remained in force until 1803. Although its construction
was severely criticised in the eighteenth century,[14] it continued to dominate discussions of cases of suspected new-born child murder both in the
courts and elsewhere until its repeal. Close analysis of the terms and
implications of the 1624 statute, which has often been subjected to
cursory or mistaken interpretations by historians,[15] is therefore central to
any discussion of new-born child murder in the eighteenth century.

Although the 1624 statute marked a significant departure from common law, it did not substitute a 'presumption of guilt, in the room of actual proof against the criminal', as some contemporary commentators and historians have assumed.[16] The statute simply created a legal presumption whereby a woman who had concealed the death of her illegitimate child was presumed to have murdered it. No longer burdened by the problems of proving live-birth, the prosecution nevertheless had to establish that the child's death had been concealed. As Edward Umfreville, coroner for Middlesex, pointed out in 1761, 'if Advantage be to be taken of this Statute *against* the Prisoner, the Concealment must then be proved by Evidence'.[17]

Strictly speaking, the legal presumption of the 1624 statute only operated if the death of a child had been concealed. Although concealment of pregnancy, of birth, and of the dead body of a bastard child might have given a woman's neighbours grounds for suspicion, these circumstances did not bring the case under the statute as some writers have suggested.[18] Zachary Babington, an associate clerk of assize on the Oxford Circuit for twenty years,[19] emphasised this point in his comments on the statute in 1677:

> It is not the burying of the Child, or hiding of it, that makes it Murther upon the Statute (as some have conceived) for if the Child be found dead in Bed by her side, or in her bosome, yet it is Murther; for the word [*conceal*] in the Statute, relates not to the Body of the Infant, but the death of it ...[20]

Babington, and later Giles Jacob (a prodigious compiler of legal books), also insisted that the 1624 statute deprived those convicted of concealing the death of a bastard child from the benefit of clergy, thereby guaranteeing their execution.[21] Babington, for example, discussed both the statute of 1624 and the statute on stabbing of 1604[22] under the same head:

> These two Statutes create no new Offence that was not Felony and Murther before, but only take away Clergy in those two cases, the one of sudden and desperate stabbing (then frequently in use) the other of lewd Whores, who having committed one sin, to avoid their shame, and the charge of a Bastard, would commit a greater, by trusting to their own strength in their Delivery, that they might more privately destroy the Infant, and yet avoid the danger of the Law, because in that case, none for the King could prove the Child born alive, and therefore it was impossible to Indict and Convict her at the Common Law for Murther, although really and in truth it were so.[23]

Although, in practice, proven concealment became punishable as a non-clergyable felony because it was equated with murder, Babington's interpretation is questionable for a number of reasons. First, while sudden stabbing prior to 1604 had been a form of manslaughter amenable to clergy, it had not been a crime to conceal the death of a bastard child prior to 1624. There was therefore no substantive crime from which the benefit of clergy could be removed. Second, the statute, as Babington pointed out, did not create a new offence. The charge remained one of murder, a crime which since 1531 had in any case been non-clergyable.[24] The statute simply directed the evidence in a particular form of murder. Finally, it must be remembered that in 1624 women were not eligible for the benefit of clergy for any crime except simple theft of goods valued at between twelve pence and ten shillings. Only from 1691 could women claim benefit of clergy in all felonies in which it was available to men.[25] So, however the statute was later interpreted, it cannot have been intended to have any effect on benefit of clergy when it was passed.

By virtue of the penultimate clause of the 1624 statute ('whose Death by her was so intended to be concealed'), a mother's intent to conceal the death of her child was material.[26] This clause allowed the courts some discretion to accept or reject certain evidence. If a woman had prepared child's clothes or if she had informed someone that she was pregnant, for example, the courts could assume that she had not intended to conceal the child's death and the defendant could be exempted from the statutory presumption, leaving the case to stand at common law.[27] Conversely, the statute's emphasis on intent could work against the defendant. A suspect's failure to prepare clothes for her child or to arrange for assistance to be available during labour could be seen as evidence of her intent to conceal the child's death. Indeed, for some commentators, a suspect's failure to engage help at the time of delivery (which, together with concealment of pregnancy, was taken as 'sufficient ground' for assuming murder in the Scottish 'Act anent Murthering of Children' in 1690),[28] was regarded as the essence of the offence under the 1624 statute:

> This Statute makes the Supposition good for the King to the Grand Jury, and Jury of Life and Death, and to the Judgment of the Judge in point of Law, that the Child (supposed to be murthered) was born *alive*, and by her murthered, in regard she being a lewd woman, and contrary to the Custome of honest and innocent women (who always desire help in their Labour) chuseth to be delivered alone, this Statute puts the proof upon her (if she will avoid so strong a presumption of Murther) to be sure to have one Witness to prove the Child was born dead.[29]

Proof of concealment, although sufficient to make out a *prima facie* case against the accused, was not quite conclusive, since it could be rebutted by the evidence of one witness that the child had been born dead.[30] If a woman failed to prove that her child had been still-born, however, she was to 'suffer Death as in Case of Murther'.[31]

The construction of the 1624 statute may have been influenced by a number of factors. According to Daines Barrington, a barrister and Recorder of Bristol, the statute owed much to the admiration with which James I regarded Danish law, which at that time included a provision whereby 'the same presumption from concealing the approaching birth, is made the offence itself, and punished capitally'.[32] As Hoffer and Hull have suggested, however, the statute's emphasis on concealment and lewd women embodied principles that had already been established in English case law.[33] The case in question, referred to by legal authorities as an example of one of the diverse manners in which murder could be committed,[34] had been recounted in 1584 by Richard Crompton:

> A harlot is delivered of an infant which she puts alive in an orchard and covers with leaves, and a kite strikes at it with its talons, whereby the infant soon dies, and she is arraigned for Murder, and executed at Chester circa 2. Eliz. as I am credibly informed, because she intends to kill it in this way.[35]

Significantly, the salient features of both the 'kite case' and the 1624 statute (their emphasis on lewd women, concealment and intent to kill) accurately reflected parochial and legislative disapproval of women who produced bastards and the difficulties inherent in prosecuting such women at common law. Although some commentators have suggested that the statute was intended to protect the lives of bastards,[36] the low status of illegitimate children in this period makes it unlikely that this was the legislators' primary concern.[37] On the contrary, the statutory presumption appears to have been aimed primarily at punishing single women who, by concealing their condition, attempted to avoid the shame and punishment that could be inflicted on them under the bastardy laws. The mothers of legitimate children, and the few men accused of the crime, were still to be tried at common law.

Although Hoffer and Hull have suggested that this emphasis on the bearers of bastards and on concealment of sin was a reflection of the moral preoccupations of 'puritan' legislators,[38] Joan Kent has argued that discussions of many of the bills relating to the regulation of 'personal conduct' in the late sixteenth and early seventeenth centuries centered on the social, economic and political, as well as upon the moral, impact of the proposed legislation. She has pointed out that although some puritans were eager to punish all begetters of bastards for having sinned in that particular way, 'the provisions enacted by the Commons continued to distinguish between those parents who agreed to provide for the child and those who left it to be maintained by the parish'.[39] As in the case of legislation concerning the maintenance of bastards and relief of the poor, the 1624 statute should be understood primarily as a response to the economic and social, rather than the moral, problems posed by single women who burdened parishes with bastards.

The 1624 statute was immediately adopted by the courts. Its impact is evident in a number of ways. First, the pattern of indictment changed. According to historians working on the sixteenth and seventeenth centuries, the mothers of both legitimate and illegitimate children were tried for murder in approximately equal numbers before the statute was passed. After 1624, however, the majority of women accused of murder were indicted as unmarried women and the majority of the children allegedly killed were described as bastards in the court records.[40] While this may have reflected the courts' efforts to ensure that as many women as possible were tried under the new statute (for which it was simply necessary for the indictment to specify that the child was a bastard), it may also have been due to the more vigilant detection and presentation of unmarried suspects by their neighbours.

Second, as Hoffer and Hull have suggested, the association between illegitimacy and guilt was strengthened after 1624. Not only were the mothers of bastards more frequently accused of murder than the mothers of legitimate children after that date, but they were also more likely to be found guilty. According to Hoffer and Hull's figures from the Essex assize court records, approximately sixty per cent of all defendants tried between 1625 and 1648 were found guilty.[41] Significantly, however, over seventy per cent of women tried under the terms of the 1624 statute were convicted compared with only thirty per cent of those women to whom the statute did not apply.[42] To some extent, the higher conviction rate for the mothers of bastards was a product of the statute's construction: once the child had been identified as a bastard, proof of murder was facilitated by the statutory presumption. However, it can also be attributed to the persistent local and legislative hostility directed against single women who threatened to burden parishes with chargeable bastards. Significantly, while the 1624 statute clearly reflected contemporary anxieties about the financial burden of bastardy and about the need to deter women from burdening parishes in the future, it also reinforced those anxieties and gave credence to suspicions of murder by selectively facilitating the prosecution of unmarried women.

The law and chargeable bastardy in the eighteenth century: evidence from the Northern Circuit court records

The 1624 statute was the result of prominent social concerns about the effect of rising levels of illegitimacy on the poor rates. Such concerns were also evident in the eighteenth century. Indeed, the problems caused by chargeable bastardy perhaps became more pressing in the eighteenth century than they had been when the 1624 statute was introduced. Bastardy levels rose in England throughout the eighteenth century.[43] Together with a rise in population, and with the lack of employment opportunities particularly for women at the end of the century,[44] the rise in bastardy levels contributed to a rapid and disturbing rise in the poor rates.

The extent of local concern about bastardy and the rates is evidenced by the extreme measures that were sometimes taken to avoid the maintenance of an illegitimate child. In his diary, for example, Thomas Turner, a churchwarden and overseer of the poor in the small Sussex town of East Hoathly, recounted the enormous time, money and effort that he and other parish officers were prepared to expend in order to ensure that George Hyland married Ann Durrant in 1757 in Hyland's place of settlement rather than in East Hoathly.[45] In some instances, pregnant single women would be turned away from towns by parishioners desperate to avoid the burden of a child's settlement. The anxieties and hostility evident in such behaviour were reinforced by legislative measures aimed at decreasing the number of children left to be maintained by the parish. In 1733, 'An Act for the Relief of Parishes' acknowledged that previous legislation was no longer sufficient to indemnify parishes against the charge of bastards and allowed justices of the peace to apprehend any man named as the father of a bastard child and to commit him to prison unless he gave assurances that he would indemnify the parish against the charge of the child. Significantly, the statute's wording betrays the extent to which bastardy had become a secular issue. The bearing of bastard children was no longer described as being against God's law and the women responsible were no longer referred to as 'lewd'. In the eighteenth century, the legislature's sole expressed concern was the financial burden of bastards on the parish.[46]

Parochial concerns about poor rates ensured that the bearers of bastards had greater cause to conceal their pregnancies, and were more often suspected of murdering their children at birth, than the mothers of legitimate children in the eighteenth century. The relevance of contemporary concerns about unmarried women and the problems of chargeable bastardy to suspicions of murder is visible in the Northern Circuit court records in at least three forms: in persistent references to the 1624 statute;

in the link between illegitimacy and the generation of local suspicions; and in the selection of suspects.

References to both statutory and common law rules of evidence relating to new-born child murder trials can be found in a wide variety of contemporary sources. Legal texts written for parish officers, coroners, justices of the peace, lawyers and judges, generally included an account of the 1624 statute.[47] Although these works occasionally misconstrued the statutory presumption,[48] their coverage of the material points was comprehensive and they provided judges and local officials with a detailed knowledge of the law relating to new-born child murder.

There is no direct evidence that these legal texts were consulted.[49] However, records from every stage of the legal process (from initial suspicions through to trial jury verdict) suggest that the terms and assumptions of the 1624 statute dominated proceedings. At the local level, details of the preliminary inquiries conducted in the neighbourhood before official intervention suggest that those involved possessed a working knowledge of the main issues at common law and under the 1624 statute. Witnesses and suspects seem to have been aware of the significance of concealment, of signs of live- and still-birth, of the preparation of child's clothes, and of failing to call for help at the delivery.[50] Such knowledge may have been obtained from local newspaper reports,[51] from previous involvement in similar cases, or from attendance at inquests and trials.

More direct references to the statute can be found in some inquisitions which either explicitly referred to the statute or were drafted using the statute's formal language. The inquisition into the death of Margaret Wanless's child in Northumberland in 1741, for example, concluded that:

> as no Bruises were to be observed thereupon whether the said Child was born Alive or not or killed in her Labour for want of help the said Jurors know not But believe the said Child was so wrapt up by her that she might privately Bury the same to Conceal the Death thereof if the same was Born alive Contrary to the form of the Statute in that Case made and provided.[52]

Some inquest juries were also advised of the terms of the 1624 statute. In 1741, when it appeared that the birth and body of Susannah Stephenson's new-born child had been concealed by Susannah and her mother, the inquest jury declared that:

> Susannah Stephenson ... had by some Means but by what Means does not appear to the Jurors Murder'd the said Male Child or at least the Law (as the Jurors are advised) deems it so it not Appearing to them by any Testimony that any Women or Others were Call'd in to the Birth of the aforesaid Child but on the Contrary it appears to them that its Birth was Intended to be Conceal'd.[53]

The Northern Circuit minute books, gaol calendars and indictment files also demonstrate the statute's presence. Cases in which mothers were committed to gaol because the births and deaths of their still-born children had been concealed, or in which a child was assumed to have been born alive because it had been concealed, are evidence of the pervasive influence of the statutory presumption that concealment constituted evidence of murder.[54] Indeed, these were precisely the kind of cases at which the statute had originally been aimed. More directly, several women were referred to in the records as having murdered their children 'against peace and against Statute', and when Fletcher Rigge took over as clerk for the Northern Circuit assizes in 1772, he began to draw up indictments 'against the form of the Statute in such Case made and Provided', even though most legal authorities were of the opinion that this was unnecessary for trial under the statute.[55]

The 1624 statute was also central to discussions in the trial courts. In 1717, for example, at the trial of Ann Masie at the Old Bailey, the statute itself was read for 'the better Information of the Jury in this Case'.[56] And in 1734, a clerk of the court apparently read the statute in full prior to Mercy Hornby being found guilty of murder at the Old Bailey.[57] There are few detailed records of the trial proceedings in the Northern Circuit courts. However, according to a minute book entry, at the trial of Mary Ingleson and Joseph Hodgson at York in 1743, Justice Abney noted that 'Concealment by the Statute is evidence of murder'.[58]

The Northern Circuit court records testify to the persistent presence of the terms and implications of the 1624 statute throughout the eighteenth century. The records also demonstrate the crucial role of concerns about bastardy, and particularly chargeable bastardy, in generating suspicions and initiating prosecutions. Not only were over ninety per cent of the supposedly murdered children clearly identified as bastards in the records, but it is also likely that several of the remaining children not directly identified as such were illegitimate.[59] In addition, some neighbours and relatives, perhaps prompted by the examining justice or coroner, emphasized the illegitimacy of the dead child in their depositions. At an inquest held in Cumberland in 1738, Eleanor Graham testified that she 'verily beleives that the said Infant was a Bastard by the Laws of the Land she [Jane Johnson] never having a Husband that this Deponent ever heard off But lives as a house servant with David Edgar of Mossband'.[60]

The strength of the association between bastardy and suspicions that a new-born child had been murdered or abandoned is further evidenced by the fact that several inquest juries assumed that a dead body was that of a bastard even though the identity and the marital status of the mother were apparently not known to the jury. For example, the preamble of an inquisition held in March 1753 stated that the body of a child found floating in a beck in Pocklington in Yorkshire was that of 'a Female Bastard Child', in spite of the fact that the mother was never identified.[61] Similarly, an inquest in Westmorland in 1780 was taken 'on View of the Bones of a Child, supposed to be the Bones of a Bastard Child', even though nothing could be discovered about the birth or death of the child, or about its mother.[62]

The strong assumption that a concealed, possibly murdered child, must have been a bastard was based upon a belief that only the mothers of bastards possessed the necessary motive for such concealment and murder, namely the avoidance of the shame and punishment associated with bearing a child chargeable to the parish. Such a belief had gained authoritative support from Sir Matthew Hale's account of a case in 1668 at Aylesbury in which 'a married woman of good reputation' was indicted for murdering her newly born child. The point at issue in this case, which was referred to by eighteenth-century writers, was whether the 'temporary phrenzy' during which she had supposedly committed the act was real and, if so, whether that phrenzy had deprived her of her reason sufficiently to absolve her guilt. Part of the direction to the jury was that 'had there been any occasion to move her to this fact, as to hide her shame, which is ordinarily the case of such as are delivered of bastard children and destroy them; or if there had been jealousy in her husband, that the child had been none of his, or if she had hid the infant, or denied the fact, these had been evidences, that the phrenzy was counterfeit'. By virtue of her good reputation and her evident insanity, 'the jury found her not guilty to the satisfaction of all that heard it'.[63] The assumption that only unmarried mothers of bastard children possessed motives for murder served in this instance to justify the complementary belief that the murder of a new-born child by a married woman, because motiveless, could only be explained in terms of some evident disease.

Depositions from the Northern Circuit courts also suggest that, in some cases, suspicions that a child had been murdered developed directly from concern about a potentially chargeable bastard. Officially, a suspect could not be compelled 'to answer any Questions relating to her Pregnancy' before her delivery because the child would not be chargeable, and the woman would not have committed an offence, until the child had been born alive. As Richard Burn pointed out in his manual for justices of the peace, 'the child cannot be illegitimate before it is born, there being always a possibility that it may be born in lawful wedlock'.[64] However, if a woman was thought to be pregnant with a potential bastard, the neighbours would be sure to 'keep a Stricter Eye upon her'.[65] Subsequent events might then convince them that a child had been born and possibly murdered. In this way, a murder case often originated in suspicions that a woman was bearing a potentially chargeable bastard.

This pattern of events is demonstrated by the following statement made by George Flounders and John Hildray, overseers of the poor, to a justice of the peace concerning Margaret Baker in 1771:

> it appearing to them and it being commonly reported in the neighbourhood that Margaret Baker Singlewoman an Inhabitant of the said Township (who had formerly bore three Several bastard Children there) was big with Child, he this Informant and the said John Hildray on the Eighth Day of May last applyed to her and acquainted her with their suspicion of her being with Child and desired her to go before a Justice of Peace to Filiate the same in order to have the putative Father taken up by a Warrant for the Indempnity of the said Township, and on such application the said Margaret Baker did not Deny that she was with Child but told them that in Case she was with Child such Child should not be chargeable to the said Township and therefore refused to go to make a voluntary filiation thereof as she was by them desired to do. And this Informant further saith that it is generally believed and suspected in the neighbourhood of Sexhow aforesaid that she the said Margaret Baker hath within Eight or Ten Days now last past been privately Delivered of a Bastard Child in her Dwelling house in Sexhow aforesaid She appearing to be not so big or large in her body now ... And this Informant further saith that he hath great reason to suspect and doth suspect that the said Margaret Baker hath really been privately Delivered of a bastard Child within the space of Ten Days now last past And that such Child hath been Murdered by her as no Child hath appeared or been yet Discovered.[66]

The frequent involvement of overseers of the poor in cases of suspected murder itself testifies to the central role of chargeable bastardy since the office of overseer had been created specifically for the purpose of administering the poor rate and providing for the poor of the parish.[67] Overseers and churchwardens (who were *ex officio* overseers) were often requested by the neighbourhood to examine a woman, either during her suspected pregnancy or after suspected delivery, in order to filiate the child and indemnify the parish against its charge or to investigate suspicions of murder. Since they were themselves householders and contributors to the poor rates, it is not surprising that overseers appear to have been diligent in responding to the requests of the parish. On only one occasion did overseers ignore a request to examine a woman, leaving one of the woman's neighbours to investigate the matter, charge her with being pregnant, and arrange for her to be examined by a midwife. Usually such administrative duties were adequately performed by overseers and churchwardens who were frequently bound over to give evidence, to prefer bills of indictment and, if necessary, to prosecute upon them in the assize courts. The only other men to perform this latter function more frequently were constables.[68]

Further evidence of the importance of bastardy and bastard-bearing to the detection and accusation of suspects is provided by those cases in which a woman was assumed to be pregnant or to be the mother of a dead child on account of her having previously burdened the parish with a bastard. When the body of a child was found in a town or village, a woman with a reputation of that sort would be a prime suspect. In August 1719, a young girl found a pig 'Eating a Child which lay Dead in a Dry Ditch'. On hearing of the discovery, Anne Case 'went and speake to One Mary Crawford singlewoman (who had had Three Bastards before and lay under the same Roof with her) and desired her to view the Child, and told her she thought the Child cou'd be none but hers'.[69] As Elizabeth Ryals complained when she was accused of being pregnant again in 1770: 'When one has once done amiss it is common for people to reflect'.[70]

In this context, it is significant that the majority of women tried for murder in the Northern Circuit courts did not come from large towns such as Leeds, Sheffield, or Newcastle, but from small villages and townships. This is not to say that unmarried women became pregnant less frequently, or that dead and abandoned babies were not discovered as often, in large towns. Indeed, the opposite may have been true.[71] However, it is likely that suspects were identified and brought to justice more readily in the country, in small parishes where the proximity of rate-paying neighbours and relatives ensured that the slightest change in appearance or behaviour of an unmarried woman was readily detected, and where the body of a child could be rapidly traced to the woman concerned. Significantly, it was also in such small communities that unmarried women had reputations to lose and were most vulnerable to the shame and humiliation that could be inflicted upon them by their neighbours if their condition was discovered.

Local preoccupations with chargeable bastardy are also evident in the selection of suspects. According to both statute and common law, bastards were children 'born out of lawful Marriage'.[72] The women most susceptible to the charges of their neighbours, those with the greatest motive for concealing their circumstances, and those most likely to be accused of bearing, concealing, and murdering a bastard child were therefore unmarried women, that is single women and widows. Over eighty per cent of the women accused of murdering their new-born children in the Northern Circuit courts were given the addition of 'single woman' or 'spinster' (terms which by this time were used interchangeably to describe unmarried women) by neighbours and local officers, and by the assize courts.[73] Apart from a number of bastard-bearers whose marital status is not defined in the records, the next largest group of women indicted for murder were widows, whose children were also described as bastards.[74] Significantly, two of the women indicted as widows were described as both 'Widow and Single Woman' in the inquest records, presumably in an attempt to emphasize the illegitimacy of their supposedly murdered children and to bring their cases under the statute.[75]

The children of married women were presumed by law to be legitimate. As John Brydall suggested in his work on the law relating to bastardy, 'for whose is the Cow, as it is commonly said, his is the Calf also'.[76] The fact that a legitimate child would be less likely to be chargeable to the parish protected married women from the suspicions and accusations of their neighbours if their children died at birth. In addition, the prosecution of married women for murdering their children was beset by the problems of proving the case at common law. Although the presumption of legitimacy concerning children born in lawful wedlock was not absolute, since there were circumstances that would bastardize the issue of a married woman,[77] and although some married women were indicted for murdering bastards, evidence of marriage (and, in some instances, evidence of conjugal access within the necessary period) was sufficient to exempt the accused from trial under the 1624 statute and resulted in acquittal in several eighteenth-century trials at the Old Bailey.[78]

Married women were rarely accused of, and tried for, murdering their new-born children in the north of England. Of nearly two hundred women indicted between 1720 and 1799, only eight were described as married. Two of these women were charged as accessories to the murder of bastard children born to other single women.[79] A third woman, Jane Hudson, was described in the recognizances taken at the inquest as 'the Wife of Anthony Hudson late of the Burgh aforesaid Woolcomber', and it would appear that the child supposedly murdered was legitimate.[80]

The cases of the remaining 'married' women are complex but informative. Each of the five women was variably described as married or single. In 1757, Sarah Newitt (maiden name Weatherburn), whose husband had 'been out of the Kingdom about Six Years' and who had borne a 'bastard' child to Edward Middlemas, was described in the indictment as 'Sarah Weatherburn otherwise Newitt late of Alnwick ... Singlewoman otherwise Sarah Newitt Widow'.[81] In 1761, Isabel Forster, who had married John Baty around the time at which she had given birth to a child possibly fathered by another man, was indicted as 'Isabel Forster ... Singlewoman otherwise lately called Isabel the wife of John Baty'.[82] In 1762, Hannah Frost also married her husband close to the time at which she had given birth to a child begotten by another man and was indicted twice, the bill against 'Hannah Frost Spinster' being quashed in the courts and replaced by one against 'Hannah the wife of Samuel Frost, Cutler'.[83] In the same year, Hannah Conyers, who according to the recognizances was married to Thomas Doughty, was indicted for the murder of her bastard child as 'Hannah Conyers ... Spinster otherwise called Hannah Doughty ... Spinster'.[84] And in 1796, Christiana Robinson was described as a single woman in the inquisition, as a married woman in the indictment, and in both cases was charged with murdering a bastard.[85]

Carol Wiener and Valerie Edwards have put forward contrasting explanations for the indictment of defendants as both married women and spinsters in the sixteenth and seventeenth centuries. Wiener has suggested that married women were sometimes described as spinsters by justices of the peace in order to prevent the defence of marital coercion and to ensure that such women were suitably punished for their behaviour. Edwards, on the other hand, has argued that the dual addition was insisted upon by the defendant who claimed that she was married as part of her defence.[86] These interpretations should not be regarded as mutually exclusive. Both explanations can certainly be applied in cases of new-born child murder in the eighteenth century. Coroners and justices of the peace, eager to deter women from burdening the parish with bastards, would be keen to refer to a married woman as a single woman, particularly if the child would have been chargeable, in order to facilitate prosecution under the statutory provision of 1624. Conversely, a married woman, although she might have given birth to a child fathered by a man other than her husband, would be insistent that she was married in order to avoid the statute.

It is also possible that there was some genuine confusion about the marital status of women indicted as both single and married. Prior to Hardwicke's Marriage Act, which came into force in 1754, the term marriage was used to include spousals (or betrothals, in which the couple simply agreed, in the presence of witnesses, that they were married), clandestine marriages, and marriages conducted according to canon law by a parson and entered into the parish register. From 1754, only the last form of marriage was considered valid.[87] However, even after the Act, it was customary for couples to engage in sexual intercourse after betrothal but before the church ceremony. In some circumstances, such couples would be considered by their neighbours and relatives to be acceptably married. However, according to the law, the failure of such couples to complete the marriage process with a church wedding once the woman became pregnant could result in the birth of illegitimate (and possibly chargeable) children. Significantly, some members of parliament considered that, by making it more difficult for a woman to enforce a promise of marriage, the Marriage Act would increase both the number of illegitimate births and the number of children murdered at birth.[88]

Interestingly, there appears to have been little discussion, either locally or in the trial courts, as to precisely what constituted 'lawful marriage', either in cases where suspects were indicted as both single and married or in cases where marriage was introduced as a defence against the rigours of the 1624 statute. It may well be that the manner in which a woman's neighbours viewed her situation was a more significant factor in the generation of suspicion than her precise marital status. It is likely that the women described as both married and single in the Northern Circuit records were regarded by their neighbours as 'husbandless' throughout their pregnancies. The neighbourhood would have been aware that their children were potentially chargeable, either because of the husband's absence or because of his refusal to support it. They would perhaps have known, for example, that Hannah Frost's new husband had threatened to leave her 'if the Child did not come in his Time meaning from the time he first had knowledge of her'. It may well have been the knowledge that women such as Hannah Frost were bearing potentially chargeable children, rather than their precise marital status, that created the incentive to prosecute such women for murder.[89]

Prosecution as a deterrent

The Northern Circuit records suggest that prosecutions for new-born child murder were linked to persistent concerns about the burden of illegitimate children on the poor rates. There is clearly a problem with this argument. When a bastard child died at birth, it could not become a burden on the parish. If the financial burden of a bastard was one of the parish's major concerns, why did parishioners prosecute the mothers of dead children, especially when prosecution could be a time-consuming and costly procedure? The fact that few witnesses failed to appear at these trials to give evidence, even before the courts were authorised to recompense them for their time and trouble,[90] suggests that a woman's neighbours had strong motives for prosecution.

It seems unlikely that prosecution reflected a genuine desire to protect illegitimate children. Bastards were stigmatised in the eighteenth century as they had been in previous centuries.[91] This should not be taken to imply that people condoned the murders of illegitimate children simply because they objected to those children being born. Daniel Defoe, for example, insisted that 'I am as much against Bastards being begot, as I am for their being murder'd; but when a Child is once begot, it cannot be unbegotten; and when once born it must be kept'.[92] However, legislative measures dealing with bastardy failed to express concern for the welfare of bastard children. Emphasis was always placed on the moral and social responsibility of the parents, and on relieving the parish of the cost of maintenance. And although the opening of the Foundling Hospital in 1741 suggests some appreciation of the usefulness rather than the burden of bastards, bills proposed to improve the fate of bastards put out to nurse were rejected by parliament in 1773 and 1802.[93] More significantly, apart from rare efforts to ensure that an abandoned bastard was baptised before it expired, little attention was paid to the fate of supposedly murdered children in the townships and villages in which they were born.[94]

If there is no convincing evidence that prosecutions were spurred on by concern for the victims of these alleged murders, there is also little evidence to suggest that accused women were sufficiently 'marginal' or socially isolated prior to their pregnancies to account for their prosecution. Although some women were referred to in the records as having bad characters, there is no evidence to suggest that women such as Esther Carlisle, who had lodged in the same house for a number of years, or young women who still lived at home, were particularly disliked by their neighbours.[95]

In the circumstances, it seems more likely that the prosecution of women who had concealed their pregnancies, given birth to bastard children in private, and whose children were later found dead, stemmed, at least in part, from a need to deter women from producing bastards and from burdening the parish in the future. The prosecution of one unmarried woman could thus be held up as a warning to other unmarried women in the neighbourhood.

The persistent need for a deterrent, in the face of rising poor rates, may account for the prosecution of women for murder even when the bodies of their supposedly murdered children were not found, or when the coroner's inquest had already returned a verdict of still-birth, in situations, that is, where there was no evidence that a murder had been committed.[96] In addition, it may also explain why, in contrast to witchcraft trials, which declined as acquittals became more common, prosecutions for new-born child murder persisted throughout the eighteenth century when convictions were infrequent.[97] Although some writers have suggested that indictments for this crime fell dramatically during the eighteenth century, in the north of England between twenty to thirty women were prosecuted each decade.[98] Although the prosecution rate may have fallen in relation to the rising population and rising levels of illegitimacy, a steady number of prosecutions served to give single women a clear public warning against attempting to avoid the consequences of burdening the parish with bastard children.

Significantly, it was not even necessary for suspects to be convicted of murder for their prosecution to serve as a deterrent. A woman's pregnancy and her subsequent prosecution for murder could embarrass a woman and her family sufficiently for the woman to leave the parish or be sent away after she was acquitted, thus ridding the parish of one unwanted character and deterring others from offending in the same way.[99]

Prosecution as a process

There are clearly other ways in which the prosecution of unmarried women for new-born child murder can be understood. In particular, women accused of this crime can be seen to have contravened a series of informal regulations governing women's conduct. In this context, their prosecution can be regarded as a consequence of the neighbourhood's increasing frustration and anxiety about their behaviour.

First, throughout the eighteenth century, when women were 'understood either married or to be married',[100] singleness itself was regarded with some hostility. Since an enlarging population was viewed by many commentators as a means of improving the nation's wealth, marriage and the family were regarded as both essential components of social order and prerequisites for national prosperity.[101] Accordingly, women 'who through motherhood were the central figures in the family'[102] were thought to serve society best by marrying and producing children in wedlock. In this context, both single women and widows were regarded with suspicion. In some instances, a single woman servant was clearly identified as a sexual threat to the stability of the family in which she served.[103] Perhaps surprisingly, since they may already have produced children, widows were seen as particularly marginal. According to William Alexander in his lengthy *History of Women*:

> As the state of matrimony is of all others the most honourable, and the most desired by women, so that of widowhood is generally the most deplorable, and consequently the object of their greatest aversion.[104]

Single women and widows, who remained outside the family, threatened both familial and national stability and their behaviour was routinely subjected to greater scrutiny than that of their married counterparts. Such close scrutiny, and the hostility from which it stemmed, may have encouraged a neighbourhood to investigate single women and widows, rather than more respectable married women, when their children died at birth.

The second factor that may have increased local suspicions and encouraged further investigations was the suspects' involvement in sexual relationships outside marriage. In many cases, pre-marital sex itself posed no great threat to a couple's neighbours. Although in some circles pre-marital chastity, particularly in young women, became revered as a virtue in the eighteenth century,[105] and although women might be required to perform public penance if fornication was discovered, many couples engaged in pre-marital sexual relationships with impunity, on the condition that they marry if the woman proved to be pregnant. Only if this condition was broken did their relationship become a threat to the neighbourhood. Pre-marital sex was generally a danger to the parish and a source of shame to a woman only if it was likely to lead to the birth of a bastard that would need to be maintained by the parish.[106]

However, there were clearly some situations in which a young woman's loss of chastity could itself cause problems. As Susan Staves has shown, some eighteenth-century fiction highlights the extent to which the seduction of a young unmarried woman was regarded as depriving fathers of their daughters and bringing shame and grief on their families.[107] Such fictional accounts of a family's grief at a daughter's fall find limited support in the Northern Circuit records. Although there is evidence of parental disapproval of a woman's actions, in most cases familial anxieties appear to be linked to the birth of a bastard child rather than to pre-marital sex itself. In 1767, for example, Hannah Warwick testified to a magistrate in Cumberland that she had kept her pregnancy and the birth of a child secret 'for fear of her Parents who she was afraid wou'd be bitter against her'. The depositions suggest that her fears of family disquiet were justified. Hannah's brother testified that he had warned her 'of the Sin and Danger of so Heinous an offence' as giving birth to a bastard child.[108] However, such family attitudes, and the willingness of a suspect's family to give evidence against her on occasions, may well have reflected the shame and disgrace that a woman's sexual behaviour could bring upon her family irrespective of the birth of a bastard child.

Significantly, as Susan Staves has argued, the law recognised the losses suffered by a family as the result of the seduction of single women: 'During the late seventeenth and early eighteenth centuries the courts began to allow a variety of new civil actions that permitted women or their fathers to recover damages from seducers, including both the notorious action for breach of promise of marriage and several less well known actions permitting fathers to collect for a species of trespass and/or the loss of their daughters' domestic services.'[109] As Staves suggests, the rise of civil litigation of this sort, together with increasing legislative emphasis on the economic rather than the moral consequences of fornication, 'reflects a willingness to understand seduction as secular rather than religious experience'.[110]

Just as the sexual activity of a single woman was seen as disrupting a family, so it was regarded as inappropriate behaviour in servants. While in service, women were expected to remain chaste and to ignore the sexual advances of fellow servants, masters and masters' sons, with whom they lived and worked in close proximity.[111] Attempts to warn female servants of the dangers of succumbing to the pleas of such seducers were not always successful. In the north of England, several servant women later accused of murder had been seduced by a fellow servant or by a member of the family in which they served. In a few cases, seduction apparently followed a promise of marriage. In 1773, for example, Mary Sinclair supposedly allowed 'one William Graham a former fellow Servent of hers at the Scotch Arms at Rickergate (who then and long before had made Love to this Examinant) upon repeated Promises of Marriage to have Carnal Knowledge of her Body'. [112]

Significantly, however, concerns about the sexual activity of servants were linked to concerns about chargeable bastardy. If a woman servant became pregnant and hopes of marriage were disappointed, she was likely to be dismissed from her job. Although servants were in theory protected by law from summary dismissal,[113] there are numerous examples in diaries and in the Quarter Session and assize records of women being dismissed from service on account of their pregnancies. In 1782, for example, Elizabeth Leake, suspecting that Ann Goodair was with child, 'insisted on her leaving her Service directly which Ann did so accordingly that Day'.[114] And James Woodforde dismissed several pregnant servants while rector of Weston Longville in Norfolk.[115] Ironically, dismissal worsened the problems for the parish. If the woman had gained a settlement in the parish as a result of her service, she would herself now require maintenance. The birth of her bastard child would simply create a further burden on the parish.

The opportunities available to servants for sexual liaisons and the potential for single female servants to burden the parish in this way aroused local anxieties and ensured that pregnant servants were treated harshly by their rate-paying neighbours and employers. These circumstances, in turn, ensured that servants, perhaps more than any other group of women, possessed strong motives for concealing their pregnancies and giving birth in secret. Such behaviour inevitably aroused suspicions of murder if a child was found dead. It is significant that of the sixty-four accused women whose occupation is given in the Northern Circuit records between 1720 and 1799, fifty-five were described as some form of servant.

In addition to being single and to indulging in sexual activity thought to be inappropriate to their position as daughters or servants, most women accused of murder had also angered their neighbours by attempting to conceal their pregnancies. While concealment no longer carried strong implications of immorality, as it had for puritan legislators in 1624, it nevertheless increased local suspicions about the behaviour of these women.[116] More particularly, concealment thwarted neighbours' efforts to identify the child's father and to protect themselves against the cost of maintenance. In addition, concealment may also have been construed as a particular insult by neighbouring women who would have expected to have been invited to the birth.[117] By defying local customs and local regulations of this type, single women who concealed their pregnancies presented a distinct ideological and practical threat to the community's welfare.

The prosecution of a woman for the murder of her new-born child cannot therefore be interpreted simply as an attempt to deter women in general from burdening the parish in the future. It can also be seen as the inevitable conclusion to a process of persistent inquiry into the behaviour of certain women. The force of suspicion and the momentum for prosecution for murder were generated not only by evidence that a child had been murdered but also by a neighbourhood's anxieties about the behaviour of single women. Local suspicions of single women and early investigations into a possible pregnancy led a woman's neighbours to keep a close eye on her. If, at some stage, the woman no longer appeared pregnant and no child appeared, the neighbourhood inevitably became suspicious that the child had been born and began to investigate the matter further.

Once suspicions had been aroused and the process of investigation had been initiated in this way, local officers were obliged to make inquiries, and, if the mother was thought to have murdered her child, to commit her to gaol to await trial.[118] It is possible that, in some instances, the case against a woman could be dropped at this stage. In 1774, Richard Wyatt, a justice of the peace in Surrey, discharged a servant who was thought to have destroyed her new-born bastard child.[119] However, the extent to which magistrates exercised discretion in this manner is unknown because generally only the records of cases that reached court survive.

On rare occasions, members of the neighbourhood also expressed a willingness to drop the matter. In August 1742, when Mary Hodgson found the body of a male bastard child born to Mary Ingleson, 'she acquainted her Neighbouring Women and she and they agreed to lett it lye where itt was'.[120] In 1773, Mary Sinclair showed the body of her dead child 'to several of her Mothers Neighbours who upon the Examinant telling them that this Child was born without Life all advised that the Infant should be Buried (after being put into the said Box) in a corner of the Garden - which was done accordingly'.[121] However, the fact that these women, along with many others, were eventually indicted and tried for murder, indicates that most neighbours and local officials preferred to pursue their suspicions to their logical conclusion in the courts.

Conclusion

Throughout the eighteenth century, the unmarried mothers of illegitimate children, and particularly of children that would have been chargeable to the parish, were the women most likely to be suspected of murdering their children at birth. Such suspicions of murder can be seen as the product of anxieties about the behaviour of single women and widows, concerns about the concealment of sexual relationships outside marriage, and, more critically, concerns about the maintenance of illegitimate children on the poor rates. While further research on relations at the parish level might help to clarify the motives and interests of those responsible for identifying and prosecuting suspects, it would appear from the Northern Circuit records that the selective prosecution of single women can be accounted for in two major ways: as a means of providing a general deterrent to single women likely to burden the parish in the future; and as the product of mounting local anxieties about the behaviour of particular women.

Significantly, debates about the poor rates, concerns about illegitimacy, and the prosecution of women for murder were strongly influenced by the law. Legislation concerning relief of the poor and the maintenance of bastard children encouraged single women to conceal their pregnancies and give birth in secret and inspired rate-paying neighbours to keep a close eye on the behaviour of those women. Once suspicions had been aroused, the prosecution of single women was facilitated by the availability of the 1624 statute. Although the terms and implications of this statute were fiercely challenged by some writers in the eighteenth century, it is clear that the statutory assumptions about illegitimacy, concealment and murder continued to dominate discussions of the crime both locally and in the courts.

Notes

1 The Northern Circuit records contain details of 207 defendants indicted for the murders of 190 new-born children between 1720 and 1799. Of those 207, 190 were women and 17 were men. Of the women, 155 were indicted simply as single women or spinsters, ten were indicted as widows, two were described as both widows and single women, and eight were referred to as married. The marital status of the remaining women is not available from the records, but it is significant that most of these were referred to as having murdered, or having been accessories to the murder of, a bastard child. Of the 190 children allegedly killed, 182 were defined in the records as bastards.

2 See the discussion below, pp. 44-5.

3 The statute was 18 Eliz. c. 3, 1576. The secular punishment of bastard-bearers can be traced further back than the sixteenth century. See: Doris Mary Stenton, *The English Woman in History*, (London, Allen and Unwin, 1957), p. 83; Keith Thomas, 'The double standard', *Journal of the History of Ideas*, 20 (1959), 195-216. The late sixteenth century, however, saw the beginning of secular legislation on the subject, although that legislation in many ways simply adopted established parochial practice. It should be noted that public penance for bearing a bastard persisted in the eighteenth century. See *The Diary of a Country Parson: The Reverend James Woodforde 1759-1802*, ed. John Beresford, (5 vols., Oxford University Press, 1924-31), vol. I, p. 69.

4 'An Act for the due Execution of divers Laws and Statutes made against Rogues, Vagabonds and sturdy Beggars, and other lewd and idle Persons', 7 Jac. I c. 4, 1610.

5 G. R. Quaife, *Wanton Wenches and Wayward Wives: Peasants and Illicit Sex in Early Seventeenth Century England*, (London, Croom Helm, 1979), pp. 216-17.

6 Thomas, 'The double standard'. See also Ivy Pinchbeck and Margaret Hewitt, *Children in English Society*, (2 vols., London, Routledge and Kegan Paul, 1969-73), vol. I, pp. 200-22.

7 'An Act for the Reliefe of the Poore', 39 Eliz. c. 3, 1597, and 'An Act for the Relief of the Poor', 43 Eliz. c. 2, 1601.

8 Michael Dalton, *The Countrey Justice*, (London, Professional Books Limited, [1619] 1973), p. 87.

9 A burden made heavier by the apparent rise in the proportion of bastard births in the last half of the sixteenth century. See Peter Laslett and Karla Oosterveen, 'Long-term trends in bastardy in England', *Population Studies*, 27 (1973), 255-86; Peter Laslett, 'Introduction: comparing illegitimacy over time and between cultures', in Peter Laslett, Karla Oosterveen and Richard M. Smith (eds.), *Bastardy and its Comparative History*, (London, Edward Arnold, 1980), pp. 1-65; and Richard Adair, *Courtship, Illegitimacy and Marriage in Early Modern England*, (Manchester, Manchester University Press, 1996).

10 Quaife, *Wanton Wenches*, pp. 89-123. Quaife insists that shame and disgrace did not stem merely from 'illicit sex' or from becoming pregnant, but from failing to marry, thereby leaving a child on the parish – Quaife, *Wanton Wenches*, p. 180.

11 According to Hoffer and Hull, trials for new-born child murder increased after 1576. See Peter C. Hoffer and N. E. H. Hull, *Murdering Mothers: Infanticide in England and New England 1558-1803*, (New York, New York University Press, 1981), pp. 7-8. Increasing numbers of trials may have resulted from an increased number of suspicious deaths, from greater vigilance on the part of parishioners, or from inquest and grand juries sending more women to trial. For further figures from this period, see J. S. Cockburn, 'The nature and incidence of crime in England 1559-1625: a preliminary survey', in J. S. Cockburn (ed.), *Crime in England 1550-1800*, (London, Methuen, 1977), pp. 55, 57-8.

12 In 1580, a woman was convicted and hanged even though, according to the clerk, 'it was not directly proved the child was in life' – quoted by J. S. Cockburn in 'Trial by the Book? Fact and theory in the criminal process, 1558-1625', in J. H. Baker (ed.), *Legal Records and the Historian*, (London, Royal Historical Society, 1978), p. 68. For other examples of convictions prior to 1624, see *Middlesex County Records*, ed. J. C. Jeaffreson, (vols. I-VI, The Middlesex County Records Society, 1886-1892), vol. I, pp. 235, 285.

13 *The Journals of the House of Commons* (*JHC*), 1, pp. 368, 370, 1040, 1042 (1607); *JHC*, 1, p. 421 (1610); *JHC*, 1, pp. 769, 778, 786, 793, 796 (1624). The 1624 statute (21 Jac. 1 c. 27) was continued by 3 Car. I c. 4 and 16 Car. I c. 4 until its repeal in 1803.

14 This issue is discussed further in later chapters.

15 The most extensive discussion of the statute is in Hoffer and Hull, *Murdering Mothers*, pp. 20-31. Other comments on the statute have often failed to explore its complexity or to understand its construction – see below, pp. 33-6.

16 Daines Barrington, *Observations on the Statutes, Chiefly the More Ancient*, (2nd ed., London, 1766), p. 424. Historians have also assumed that the 1624 statute reversed a presumption of innocence - see, for example, Thomas Rogers Forbes, *Surgeons at the Bailey*, (New Haven, Yale University Press, 1985), p. 96. It should be noted that neither the presumption of innocence nor the burden of proving a fact beyond reasonable doubt became established as legal maxims until the late eighteenth century. See J. H. Wigmore, *A Treatise on the Anglo-American System of Evidence in Trials at Common Law*, (3rd ed., Boston, Little, Brown and Company, 1940), vol. 9, para. 2497, 2511, and J. B. Thayer, *A Preliminary Treatise on Evidence at the Common Law*, (Boston, Little, Brown and Company, 1898), pp. 551-76. See also the discussion in Chapter 6 below.

17 Edward Umfreville, *Lex Coronatoria: Or, the Office and Duty of Coroners*, (London, 1761), p. 45.

18 See: Thomas Wood, *An Institute of the Laws of England*, (5th ed., London, 1734), p. 355; R. W. Malcomson, 'Infanticide in the eighteenth century', in Cockburn (ed.), *Crime in England*, p. 197; Forbes, *Surgeons at the Bailey*, p. 97.

19 On Babington, see J. S. Cockburn, *A History of English Assizes, 1558-1714*, (Cambridge, Cambridge University Press, 1972), p. 81.

20 Zachary Babington, *Advice to Grand Jurors in Cases of Blood*, (London, 1677), p. 173.

21 For a brief history of the benefit of clergy, see J. M. Beattie, *Crime and the Courts in England 1660-1800*, (Oxford, Clarendon Press, 1986), pp. 88-9, 141-6.

22 The statute on stabbing was 'An Act to take away the Benefit of Clergy for some kind of Manslaughter', 1 Jac. I c. 8, 1604.

23 Babington, *Advice to Grand Jurors*, pp. 173-4. See also Giles Jacob, *New Law Dictionary*, (5th ed., 1744), 'Clergy'.

24 'An Act concerning convicts in Petit Treason, Murder, &c', 23 H. VIII c. 1, 1531.

25 The relevant statutes were 'An Act concerning Women convicted of small Felonies', 21 Jac. I c. 6, 1623, and 'An Act to take away Clergy from some Offenders, and to bring others to Punishment', 3 Will. & Mar. c. 9, 1691.

26 See also Umfreville, *Lex Coronatoria*, p. 46.

27 This point has sometimes been missed by historians. See, for example, Beattie's comment that evidence that a woman had collected linen or prepared a bed was 'beside the point - the statutory offense was concealing the birth', a comment that betrays not only a disregard for the statutory reference to intent, but also a misinterpretation of the legal presumption – Beattie, *Crime and the Courts*, p. 120.

28 Scottish Acts, 1690, c. 50. In Ireland, an Act identical to that of 1624 was passed in 1707 (6 Ann. c. 4) and repealed in 1803 along with the 1624 statute.

29 Babington, *Advice to Grand Jurors*, pp. 174-5.

30 It did not, for example, constitute 'undeniable evidence that she murdered it', as Lord Chief Justice Kelyng suggested in reporting the trial of Ann Davis in 1664 – Sir John Kelyng, *A Report of divers cases in Pleas of the Crown, adjudged and determined in the reign of ... Charles II*, (London, 1708), pp. 32, 33.

31 The nature of the evidence accepted by courts as proof of live- and still-birth is discussed further in Chapter 4.

32 Barrington, *Observations on the Statutes*, pp. 424-8. Barrington was impressed by the fact that three criminal laws in the reign of James I agreed 'exactly with the Danish laws on the same head'. In fact, the English statute did not agree exactly with Danish law, since in Denmark concealment of the approaching birth, not of the child's death, was taken as evidence of murder. See *The Political Works of James I*, (Harvard University Press, [1616] 1918), pp. 312, 332.

33 Hoffer and Hull, *Murdering Mothers*, pp. 8-20.

34 The 'kite case' was referred to by: Dalton, *The Countrey Justice*, p. 218; Matthew Hale, *Pleas of the Crown: A Methodical Summary*, (1678), p. 53; J. Bond, *A Complete Guide for Justices of Peace*, (1685), p. 115; Jacob, *New Law Dictionary*, 'Murder'; Edward Hyde East, *A Treatise of the Pleas of the Crown*, (2 vols., London, 1803), vol. I, pp. 225-6.

35 Sir Anthony Fitzherbert and Richard Crompton, *L'Office et Aucthoritie de Justices de Peace*, (2nd ed., 1584), p. 19.

36 In 1803, Thomas Percival suggested that the statute's aim had been to protect the lives of bastards – see, Thomas Percival, *Medical Ethics*, (Manchester, 1803), p. 80. The same conclusion is drawn by Catherine Damme, 'Infanticide: The worth of an infant under law', *Medical History*, XXII (1978), 12. See also Pinchbeck and Hewitt, *Children in English Society*, vol. I, p. 209.

37 For the extent to which bastards were limited by common, civil, and ecclesiastical laws, see John Brydall, *Lex Spuriorum: Or, the Law Relating to Bastardy*, (London, 1703).

38 Hoffer and Hull, *Murdering Mothers*, pp. 22-3.

39 Joan R. Kent, 'Attitudes of members of the House of Commons to the regulation of "Personal Conduct" in late Elizabethan and early Stuart England', *Bulletin of the Institute of Historical Research*, XLVI (1973), 44.

40 See, in particular, Hoffer and Hull, *Murdering Mothers*, pp. 23-5. See also: Keith Wrightson, 'Infanticide in earlier seventeenth-century England', *Local Population Studies*, 15 (1975), 10-22; and cases in *Middlesex County Records*, vols. I-VI.

41 Hoffer and Hull, *Murdering Mothers*, pp. 23-5. According to Sharpe, the conviction rate in Essex between 1620 and 1680 fluctuated from a maximum of 55 per cent (1630-4) to a minimum of 10 per cent (1655-9) – see J. A. Sharpe, *Crime in Seventeenth-century England: A County Study*, (Cambridge, Cambridge University Press, 1983), p. 134. According to Beattie, of twenty-three women accused of new-born child murder in Surrey between 1660 and 1700, seven were discharged by the grand jury. Of the sixteen women tried, nine were found not guilty and six were convicted (with one verdict remaining unknown) – see Beattie, *Crime and the Courts*, p. 116. For further information on the seventeenth century, see Wrightson, 'Infanticide'. The seventeenth-century Northern Circuit records are not as extensive or as accessible as the eighteenth-century records. Although I have studied occasional cases when the records permit, I have not made a systematic survey of the Northern Circuit records earlier than 1720.

42 Hoffer and Hull, *Murdering Mothers*, p. 25.

43 Adair, *Courtship, Illegitimacy and Marriage*; Laslett and Oosterveen, 'Long-term trends in bastardy in England'. The rise has been attributed to the failure of community sanctions to ensure that pregnant women married, the development of economic conditions unfavourable for marriage, a greater number of casual pre-marital sexual relationships to which no conditions of marriage were attached, and the dislocation of family life caused by wars and transportation. See also: Pinchbeck and Hewitt, *Children in English Society*, vol. II, p. 585; and Edward Shorter, 'Illegitimacy, sexual revolution, and social change in modern Europe', *Journal of Interdisciplinary History*, 2 (1971), 237-72.

44 On changing employment opportunities for women, see Bridget Hill, *Women, Work, and Sexual Politics in Eighteenth-century England*, (Oxford, Basil Blackwell, 1989), Chapter 4.

45 *The Diary of Thomas Turner 1754-1765*, ed. David Varsey, (Oxford, Oxford University Press, 1984), pp. 85-91.

46 'An Act for the Relief of Parishes and other Places from such Charges as may arise from Bastard Children born within the same', 6 Geo. II c. 31, 1733. In 1662, 'An Act for the better Relief of the Poor of this Kingdom' (13 & 14 Car. II c. 12 s. 19, 1662) had also allowed magistrates to use the goods and lands of parents that had fled in order to maintain a child.

47 Richard Burn, *The Justice of the Peace, and Parish Officer*, (3rd ed., London, 1756), p. 90; Umfreville, *Lex Coronatoria* pp. 44-7; Matthew Hale, *History of the Pleas of the Crown*, ed. Sollom Emlyn, (2 vols., London, 1736), vol. II, pp. 288-9; William Hawkins, *A Treatise of the Pleas of the Crown*, (2 vols., London, 1716-21), vol. II, pp. 438-9.

48 See, for example, Thomas Wood's belief that the 1624 statute referred to concealment of birth – Wood, *An Institute of the Laws of England*, p. 355.

49 However, a broadsheet entitled *Albertus the Second: or, the Curious Justice* suggests that magistrates were known to employ legal and medical advice in cases of suspected murder. The broadsheet recounts the activities of a justice investigating the death of a child found drowned in a river. Although the task of identifying the child's mother apparently defeated him, the justice consulted legal and medical texts in order to clarify the issues involved:

> The rest, as I said, to the JUSTICE repair,
> Who sits all-tremendous within his Arm'd Chair;
> Some Law lay before him, suppose *Nelson's Treatise,*
> And learned *Albertus's* Book, *de Secretis.*

The law treatise referred to is probably William Nelson's *The Law of Evidence,* first published in 1717. 'Albertus's Book' is *De Secretis Mulierum,* a popular work based on Albertus Magnus' *De Generatione Animalium,* written in the thirteenth century.

50 See, for example, the questions asked of Martha Gleadhill by Grace Ditch, a midwife, in 1749, in ASSI 45/24/1/38A; and the deposition of Catherine Coulson taken before a magistrate investigating the death of Rebecca Stephenson's child in 1750, in ASSI 45/24/2/105-8. It should be remembered that depositions giving details of local inquiries were transcribed by coroners and magistrates or by their clerks and their content may have been influenced by those officials.

51 *The Cumberland Pacquet* frequently reported suspicious infant deaths and subsequent trials. Occasionally, reference was made to the law: *The Cumberland Pacquet,* (28 June 1778), p. 3.

52 Margaret Wanless, 1742, ASSI 44/57.

53 Susannah Stephenson, 1741, ASSI 44/56.

54 For details of particular cases of this nature, see below Chapter 4. The statutory presumption was not always accurately construed in court records. According to the gaol calendar (in ASSI 44/90ii), Mary Hills was charged in 1775 with 'concealing the Birth of her female Bastard Infant and feloniously murdering the same'. In 1799, Margaret Fenny, was said to have 'conceal'd the body' of her dead child – see the gaol calendar and recognizances in ASSI 44/114i. On only three occasions is the statute's emphasis on concealment of death accurately recorded: in the inquisition into the death of Margaret Wanless's child in 1741 – ASSI 44/57; in the inquisition and depositions concerning the death of Mary Robinson's child in 1759 – ASSI 45/26/3/89-90B, ASSI 44/74; and in the minute book reference to Mary Stolker – ASSI 41/7. However, the gaol calendar (ASSI 44/93iii) records that Mary Stolker was 'charged with concealing the Birth of her male Bastard Infant and suffering it to perish for want of proper Care'.

55 According to Hawkins, (*Pleas of the Crown,* vol. II, p. 438), 'in order to convict a woman by Force of this Statute, there is no need that the Indictment be drawn specially, or conclude *contra formam Statuti*'. See also Hale, *Pleas of the Crown,* vol. II, p. 289.

56 Ann Masie, Old Bailey Sessions Papers (OBSP), July 1717, p. 4.

57 Mercy Hornby, OBSP, April 1734, pp. 108-9. See also: Ann Price, OBSP, April 1681, p. 2; Martha Nook, OBSP, September 1690, p. 1; Ann Leak, OBSP, January 1723, p. 6; Mary Radford, OBSP, January 1723, p. 6.

58 Justice Abney's comment is recorded in ASSI 41/3.

59 Of 190 children allegedly murdered between 1720 and 1799, 182 were described in the records as bastards. Of the remaining eight children, three were born to single women (Mary Briggs, 1753, Margaret Parkinson, 1762, and Jane Thompson, 1778), one was supposedly murdered by its married mother (Jane Hudson, 1779), and one child was thought to have been murdered by a woman other than the child's mother, whose marital status at the time remains unclear (Hannah Jameson, 1764). In the last three cases neither the marital status of the mother nor the legitimacy of the child were recorded (Jane Fountain, 1725, Mary Williamson, 1729, and Mary Benington, 1733). Ninety-eight of the 190 bodies were identified as male and eighty-one as

female. In the remaining cases, there was either no body to be identified or the sex of the child was not recorded.

60 Jane Johnson, 1738, ASSI 45/21/2/44E-H. Similarly, see the evidence of Henry Wilson concerning Elizabeth Bryson (1775, ASSI 45/32/1/38).

61 The inquisition is in ASSI 44/68. Other examples of the same assumption being made at inquests can be found in bundles of inquisitions in ASSI 44/95, 44/103iii, 44/109i, and 44/113i. In contrast, there are inquisitions scattered throughout the records in which an unidentified child was referred to simply as a new-born male or female child, no assumption being made about its legitimacy. It is possible that these inquest juries were aware of the identity and marital status of the children's mothers but chose not to pursue the cases.

62 The inquisition is in ASSI 44/95.

63 Hale, *Pleas of the Crown*, vol. I, p. 36. The case was quoted in full by Umfreville, *Lex Coronatoria*, pp. 132-3.

64 Burn, *The Justice of the Peace*, p. 82; see also Dalton, *The Countrey Justice*, p. 33. Restrictions on examining a pregnant woman were set by 'An Act for the Relief of Parishes', 6 Geo. II c. 31, 1733.

65 The words of Mary Horn, a witness in the case against Mary Dixon, 1765, ASSI 45/28/1/17.

66 Margaret Baker, 1771, ASSI 45/30/1/22-6.

67 'An Act for the Reliefe of the Poore', 1597.

68 The numerous cases in which overseers were bound over to prosecute include: Mary Walker, 1788, ASSI 45/36/2/185, ASSI 44/103i-iv, ASSI 41/8; Tamar Winlaw, 1789, ASSI 45/36/3/226, ASSI 44/104ii. The case in which overseers refused to become involved was Elizabeth Bryson, 1775, ASSI 45/32/1/38, ASSI 44/90i-ii. For one account of the failings of overseers, and of other aspects of the poor laws, see John Townsend, *A Dissertation on the Poor Laws*, (London, 1786).

69 Mary Crawford, 1720, ASSI 45/18/1/23.

70 Elizabeth Ryals, 1770, ASSI 45/29/3/174-5.

71 According to the author of *The Genuine Sentiments of an English Country Gentleman, upon the Present Plan of the Foundling Hospital*, (1759), pp. 21-2, 'the murdering of infants to conceal amours' was almost unheard of in the author's own parish, and was principally a problem of 'some great towns', an opinion reinforced by a popular belief that cities encouraged all manner of vices through the anonymity they afforded offenders.

72 Brydall, *Lex Spuriorum*, pp. 4, 6.

73 On the earlier uses of 'spinster' and 'single woman', see J. H. Baker, 'Male and married spinsters', *The American Journal of Legal History*, 21 (1977), 255-9.

74 Of 190 women indicted between 1720 and 1799, twelve were identified as widows. Although some such children may have been legitimate, that is fathered by the woman's husband before his death (see Francis Deacon, OBSP, No. VIII, October 1733, pp. 207-8), they would have been seen as potentially chargeable by the parish.

75 See the recognizances concerning Elizabeth Pickhaver, 1777, ASSI 44/92i, and the inquisition into the death of Ann Bradbury's child, 1785, ASSI 44/100ii.

76 Brydall, *Lex Spuriorum*, p. 84.

77 Ibid., pp. 87-9.

78 See Ann Leak, OBSP, January 1723, p. 6; Ann Masie, OBSP, July 1717, p. 4; Hannah Bradford, OBSP No. IV, April 1732, p. 109.

79 Ann Bell alias Wood/Ann Dawson, 1738, ASSI 41/3, ASSI 44/53, ASSI 42/5; and Ann Bailey/John Sharp/Elizabeth Sharp, 1762, ASSI 45/26/6/6-7, ASSI 44/77, ASSI 42/7.

80 Jane Hudson, 1779, ASSI 44/94ii.

81 Sarah Newitt, 1757, ASSI 45/26/1/97-102, ASSI 44/72, ASSI 42/5. A woman's confession that her child was a product of adultery did not necessarily make the child a bastard, although in this instance evidence of the husband's absence was probably sufficient to prove the fact, since it was corroborated by other witnesses.

See Burn's comment (*Justice of the Peace*, p. 80) that 'non-access of the husband ought to be proved otherwise than upon the wife's oath'.

82 Isabel Forster, 1761, ASSI 44/76i.

83 Hannah Frost, 1762, ASSI 45/26/6/22-3, ASSI 44/76i, ASSI 44/77, ASSI 41/4, ASSI 42/7.

84 Hannah Conyers otherwise Doughty, 1762, ASSI 45/26/6/13-17, ASSI 44/77, ASSI 42/8. It is also possible that other women with aliases, such as Ann Bell alias Wood and Mary Swinbank otherwise Sumack, were married. In the absence of corroborating evidence of marriage in the records, however, it is more likely that the aliases in these instances indicate that the woman herself was of uncertain or 'double' parentage, that is illegitimate. See Alan Macfarlane, 'Illegitimacy and illegitimates in English history', in Laslett, Oosterveen, and Smith (eds.), *Bastardy and Its Comparative History*, p. 82.

85 Christiana Robinson, 1796, ASSI 45/39/1/108, ASSI 44/111i, ASSI 41/9.

86 Carol Z. Wiener, 'Is a spinster an unmarried woman?', *The American Journal of Legal History*, 20 (1976), 27-31; Valerie C. Edwards, 'The case of the married spinster: an alternative explanation', *The American Journal of Legal History*, 21 (1977), 260-5.

87 See: Lawrence Stone, *Broken Lives: Separation and Divorce in England 1660-1857*, (Oxford, Oxford University Press, 1993), pp. 16-17; John R. Gillis, *For Better, For Worse: British Marriages, 1600 to the Present*, (Oxford, Oxford University Press, 1985), pp. 140-2.

88 See, in particular, Robert Nugent's comments on the Clandestine Marriage Bill in *The Parliamentary History of England*, (1753-1765), XV, col. 18, 20. See also Lawrence Stone, *The Family, Sex and Marriage in England 1500-1800*, (London, Penguin Books, 1990), pp. 397-8.

89 Hannah Frost, 1762, ASSI 45/26/6/22-3. Significantly, the capacity for concerns about poor rates to influence decisions in the legal process is evident elsewhere. As Peter King has demonstrated in his work on property crimes, judges and juries were inclined to be more lenient towards offenders if hanging, imprisonment or transportation was likely to remove a breadwinner from the family and leave children on the poor rates. See Peter King, 'Decision-makers and decision-making in the English criminal law, 1750-1800', *The Historical Journal*, 27 (1984), 25-58.

90 Statutes enabling the payment of prosecutors and witnesses were 25 Geo. II c. 36, 1752; 27 Geo. II c. 3, 1754; and 18 Geo. III c. 19, 1778. The incentive to appear prior to these statutes was the fact that non-appearance could result in having to pay bonds of up to £100. In 1773, for example, Grace Hall was one of the few witnesses whose recognizance was estreated when she failed to give evidence at the trial of Margaret Hedley.

91 See the comments in *The Gentleman's Magazine*, (September 1735), 528. See also Ruth K. McClure, *Coram's Children: The London Foundling Hospital in the Eighteenth Century*, (New Haven, Yale University Press, 1981), pp. 9-12. Karen Clarke has suggested that in the nineteenth century interest in the fate of bastard infants was limited by the lack of legal protection for these 'children of nobody' - Karen Clarke, 'Infanticide, illegitimacy, and the medical profession in nineteenth century England', *Bulletin of the Society for the Social History of Medicine*, 26 (1980), 11-14.

92 Daniel Defoe, *The Generous Protector, or a Friendly Proposal to Prevent Murder and Other Enormous Abuses, By Erecting an Hospital for Foundlings and Bastard-Children*, (London, 1731), p. 14.

93 See Pinchbeck and Hewitt, *Children in English Society*, vol. I, pp. 200-22. Sir Daniel Downright (pseudonym), in his satire *The Bastard Child, Or a Feast for the Church-wardens*, (London, 1768), suggested that wardens were happy for poor bastard children to meet their demise when put out to nurse.

94 In 1776, Dorothy Shutt's abandoned child was baptised just before it died, one of the witnesses saying to the accused, 'Dolly you have done a bad deed and you may thank God your Child was found that it might be made a Christian of' – Dorothy Shutt 1776, ASSI 45/32/2/158-62.

95 Esther Carlisle, 1777, ASSI 45/33/1/14P-S. However, Hannah Jameson, who was indicted for murdering the new-born child of another woman in 1764, was referred to as 'having a general bad Character' (ASSI 45/27/2/80), and Mary Sant, who was indicted with her daughter Sarah for murdering Sarah's child, was apparently convinced that 'many People woud Fee Dr. Filkin to hang her if possible' (CHES 24/171/6). The poverty of some women may also have prejudiced local feelings. In 1745, Jane Barnes was known 'by report, to be poor and at service' (ASSI 45/23/1/ 3D). However, Elizabeth Wilson, knowing Martha Bramhall 'to be a poor Woman', offered assistance in case she was pregnant (1767, ASSI 45/28/3/25-28A).

96 See Elizabeth Webster (1765, ASSI 45/28/1/134-135A, ASSI 44/80, ASSI 41/5), who was indicted and tried even though the inquest found her child to have been born dead. For further discussion of this, see Chapters 3 and 4.

97 Concerning the decline in witchcraft trials, Christina Larner has suggested: 'The steady stream of acquittals must have been a factor in reducing the number of cases brought to court. No officials were going to take trouble to process cases which were likely to be dismissed or ultimately unsuccessful.' See Christina Larner, *Enemies of God: The Witch-hunt in Scotland*, (London, Chatto and Windus, 1981), p. 77. That acquittals did not prevent prosecutions for new-born child murder suggests strong local motives for persisting with accusations.

98 The number of trials in the Northern Circuit courts in each decade between 1720 and 1809 were: 15; 30; 24; 25; 30; 25; 19; 20; and 24.

99 See the case in *The Diary of Richard Kay, 1716-51*, ed. W. Brockbank and F. Kenworthy (Manchester, Chetham Society, 1968), pp. 121-5.

100 Hill, *Women, Work, and Sexual Politics*, p. 221.

101 Donna T. Andrew, *Philanthropy and Police: London Charity in the Eighteenth Century*, (Princeton, Princeton University Press, 1989), pp. 115-27.

102 L. J. Jordanova, 'Natural facts; a historical perspective on science and sexuality', in Carol P. MacCormack and Marilyn Strathern (eds.), *Nature, Culture and Gender*, (Cambridge, Cambridge University Press, 1980), p. 49.

103 See the comments of Ann Dent about 'a Report of too great an Intimacy between the Witnesses Husband and Jane [Jackson]', in Jane Jackson, 1785, ASSI 45/35/2/90-1.

104 William Alexander, *The History of Women*, (2 vols. in one, London, 1779), vol. II, p. 287.

105 See examples in: Vivien Jones (ed.), *Women in the Eighteenth Century: Constructions of Femininity*, (London, Routledge, 1990); Bridget Hill, *Eighteenth-century Women: An Anthology*, (London, Allen and Unwin, 1987).

106 For further discussion, see P. E. H. Hair, 'Bridal pregnancy in rural England in earlier centuries', *Population Studies*, 20 (November 1966), 233-43; P. E. H. Hair, 'Bridal pregnancy in earlier rural England further examined', *Population Studies*, 24 (March 1970), 59-70.

107 Susan Staves, 'British seduced maidens', *Eighteenth-Century Studies*, 14 (1980/1), 109-134.

108 Hannah Warwick, 1767, ASSI 45/28/3/181-2.

109 Staves, 'British seduced maidens', 110.

110 Ibid., 110.

111 Warnings were given by Richard Mayo, *A Present for Servants*, (London, 1693), pp. 39-40; [Elizabeth Haywood], *A Present for a Servant-Maid: Or, the Sure Means of Gaining Love and Esteem*, (London, 1743), pp. 35, 43-9; and Thomas Broughton, *Serious Advice and Warning to Servants*, (4th ed., London, 1763), pp. 21-3.

112 Mary Sinclair, 1774, ASSI 45/31/2/166-8.

113 'An Act containing divers Orders for Artificers, Labourers, Servants of Husbandry and Apprentices', 5 Eliz. c. 4, 1562; Dalton, *The Countrey Justice*, pp. 68, 74; Burn, *Justice of the Peace*, pp. 623-4; William Blackstone, *Commentaries on the Laws of England*, (4 vols., Oxford, 1765-9), vol. I, p. 413.

114 Ann Goodair, 1782, ASSI 45/34/3/51-2.

115 *The Diary of a Country Parson*, vol. I, pp. 232-3, 236; vol. IV, pp. 148-51. Woodforde dismissed one servant even though the child's father had agreed to marry her, but noted that she was no longer able to cope with her work.

116 For further discussion of attitudes to concealment, see below Chapters 5 and 6.

117 See Adrian Wilson, *The Making of Man-midwifery: Childbirth in England, 1660-1770*, (London, UCL Press, 1995), pp. 25-6.

118 Hale, *Pleas of the Crown*, vol. II, p. 139.

119 *Deposition Book of Richard Wyatt, J. P. 1767-1776*, ed. Elizabeth Silverthorne, (Surrey Record Society, vol. XXX 1978), p. 48. See also the case reported in *The Times*, (1 September 1786), p. 2, in which a coroner discharged a suspect. Inquest verdicts of still-birth may also have represented attempts by coroners to ensure that a case was not pursued.

120 Mary Ingleson/Joseph Hodgson, 1743, ASSI 45/22/3/57-60.

121 Mary Sinclair, 1774, ASSI 45/31/2/166-8. According to R. W. England, in the early nineteenth century some women's relatives and friends helped to dispose of dead bodies and to conceal the circumstances surrounding birth and death – see R. W. England, Jr., 'Investigating homicides in Northern England, 1800-1824', *Criminal Justice History*, VI (1985), 105-23. Evidence of such 'collective concealment', as England calls it, appears only rarely in the eighteenth-century records.

3

Examining suspects: conflicting accounts of pregnancy, birth and death

Introduction

In general, the unmarried mothers of illegitimate children were the women most likely to be suspected of murdering their children at birth. The day-to-day identification, investigation and accusation of specific women, however, depended upon a neighbourhood's ability to recognise signs of pregnancy and signs of labour and recent delivery, and to discover and examine the body of the dead child.[1]

Significantly, much of the initial detective work and much of the subsequent investigation into the circumstances surrounding a child's death was carried out unofficially by members of the local community, in particular by local women. Indeed, suspected pregnancies and births and the bodies of dead children attracted the attention of legal authorities only as a result of the persistent interest and agitation of a woman's neighbours, relatives and employers. Although constables, churchwardens, overseers of the poor, justices of the peace, and coroners provided the official channels through which local suspicions were guided, the driving force behind prosecution derived almost exclusively from a woman becoming 'the talk of the greatest part of the people in the Town', as Margaret Porritt put it in her statement to a magistrate in Whitby in 1759.[2]

The prosecution of a woman for the murder of her new-born child was therefore the culmination of a sequence of events that originated in the suspicions, gossip and rumours of the village or township in which the woman lived. The principal aim of this chapter is to explore precisely how local suspicions of murder were aroused by examining in detail the manner in which signs of pregnancy and child-birth were identified and the ways in which those signs were variably interpreted by suspects and witnesses. In the process, I shall argue that conflicting accounts of events given by suspects and their accusers can be understood not only as specific expressions of the broad social and legal context outlined in the previous chapter but also as articulations of particular perceptions of the body and its functions.

Detecting signs of pregnancy

The identification of pregnancy played a critical role in cases of suspected new-born child murder. At the local level, evidence that an unmarried woman was pregnant aroused anxieties about illicit sex, unmarried motherhood, illegitimacy, and the poor rates, and encouraged a neighbourhood to monitor the behaviour of the woman concerned. In both local and trial courts, evidence of pregnancy served to corroborate the testimony of witnesses and prosecutors that the suspect had indeed been pregnant at the appropriate time and, when necessary, to challenge a suspect's denial of pregnancy.

According to eighteenth-century texts on midwifery and medical jurisprudence, a number of signs indicated that a woman was pregnant: nausea and vomiting, particularly in the morning and lasting until the fourth month of gestation; 'difficulty in making water', haemorrhoids, swollen legs, dyspnoea and back pain, all arising from an increase in uterine size; the lack of menstruation; swelling of the abdomen; increase in breast size and development of the areolae; and movement of the child in the womb.[3] Further evidence could be gained by internal examination or 'touching', which after the fourth month would not only confirm pregnancy but also determine how long the woman had been pregnant.[4]

However, interpreting these signs could present problems. In the first place, many of the signs of pregnancy were identifiable only by the woman herself or were readily concealed from others. As Samuel Farr, a physician in Taunton, pointed out in his work on medical jurisprudence in 1788:

> It is not uncommon for women of abandoned characters, or even married women, to conceal and deny their state of pregnancy; and in such cases, no accurate judgment can be formed till a proper examination be made by a medical person, and those signs of true pregnancy be discovered which are generally acknowledged.[5]

If a woman intent on concealing her pregnancy refused to be examined, it was difficult for her neighbours to be certain that she was pregnant. In such circumstances, a child's movement in the womb and evidence to be gained from 'touching' were of no use. It was for precisely this reason that Bartholomew Parr, a medical practitioner in Exeter, later omitted certain signs from his discussion of the medico-legal aspects of suspected pregnancy.

'We have not mentioned the sensation of motion in the uterus,' he wrote in 1809, 'because we proceed on the supposition of concealment.'[6]

The second problem with the textbook signs was that they were considered to be only uncertain indicators of pregnancy. Even midwives apparently found it difficult to identify pregnancy or to distinguish between pregnancy and other conditions solely on the basis of those signs. For example, menstrual disturbances and 'Ascites or dropsy of the Abdomen' could both be confused with pregnancy, especially in the first months of gestation. Such problems, together with an awareness of the consequences of false accusations, led William Smellie, an eminent Scottish man-midwife, to advise medical practitioners to express their opinions about suspected pregnancies with caution:

> On the whole, the difficulty of distinguishing between obstruction and pregnancy in the first months, is so great, that we ought to be cautious in giving our opinion; and never prescribe such remedies as may endanger the fruit of the womb, but rather endeavour to palliate the complaints, until time shall discover the nature of the case; and always judge on the charitable side, when life or reputation is at stake.[7]

In practice, a woman's neighbours were rarely troubled by the equivocal nature of the signs of pregnancy. Confident that time would eventually confirm their suspicions,[8] most neighbours, friends and relatives were quick to confront a woman if there was the slightest suggestion that she was pregnant.

The physical sign most likely to arouse local suspicions was an increase in a woman's size. In 1766, Susanna Bisby suspected that Martha Bramhall, who had periodically worked for Susanna as a domestic servant, was pregnant on account of her 'being more than usually large about the Waist and Hipps'.[9] In 1770, David Glossop, a chapel warden in Ecclesall in the parish of Sheffield, 'thought that the said Elizabeth Ryals by her more than usual Bulk was again with Child'.[10] It was difficult for many women to conceal such appearances from the people with whom they lived and worked. Many suspects were servants living and sleeping in close proximity to other servants, or were still living at home, perhaps sharing a bed or a room with other members of the family.[11] In these conditions, without the luxury of privacy and under the watchful eye of rate-paying neighbours and employers, concealing an expanding waist-line could cause problems. As Bernard Mandeville, a physician from Holland who lived in London and the author of a number of satirical works, pointed out:

> People of Substance may Sin without being expos'd for their stolen Pleasure; but Servants and the Poorer sort of Women have seldom an Opportunity of concealing a Big Belly, or at least the Consequences of it.[12]

A small number of pregnant women did apparently manage to conceal their condition even in the later stages of pregnancy. In October 1744, Jane Barnes applied to Henry Hall, an apothecary in Wigton, Cumberland, 'complaining of a Violent Cough and pains at her Breast and Stomach'. Hall testified at the inquest that Jane's answers to his questions ('particularly whether or no she had any regular return of her Courses') 'took away all his suspicion of, neither did he ever suspect her being with Child'. Nor did he suspect that she had been delivered of a child when he saw her again three days later. When the cause of her 'illness' was later discovered, Hall testified that he had never seen 'her as he remembers, whilst under his Care, without her Cloak ... that she always conceal'd her Case from him'. Elizabeth Pearson, with whom Jane stayed during her 'illness', also testified that she 'did not suspect the said Jane was with Child'. However, Hall's denial of suspicion and Elizabeth's professed ignorance (like that of other women who were in close contact with a suspect during pregnancy and delivery) may have been a means of protecting themselves from the risk of being tried as accomplices.[13]

Some women accused of murder in the Northern Circuit courts attempted to conceal their pregnancies by wearing the kind of loose clothes that were sometimes in fashion and which, ironically, were often recommended for pregnant women by writers on midwifery.[14] As contemporary broadsheets describing cases of suspected murders demonstrate, this strategy was clearly recognised:

> at last she grew so bigg, that she was afraid that it would be Discover'd tho' she us'd ways and means to hide her Condition, as by wearing large Hoop Petticoats, loose Dresses, and several other ways.[15]

In the north of England, such clothing occasionally succeeded in shedding doubts on the suspicions of neighbours. In 1739, George Robinson, who lived in the same house as Sarah Leigh, 'observ'd the said Sarah to be big about the Belly but whether that Bigness was owing to her large Hoop or to being with Child this Informant cannot take upon him to swear'.[16] In other cases, however, such factors simply delayed the appearance, or diminished the extent, of the signs of pregnancy. In 1766, for example, Elizabeth Usher testified at an inquest that 'the said Ann Usher [her sister] being a Woman of large Size and not wearing Stays the usual Signs were not so fully discovered in her as in other Women'.[17]

Few women eventually tried for murder had successfully concealed their pregnancies.[18] Neighbouring women in particular were quick to notice an increase in a woman's size and attempted to corroborate their suspicions with further evidence. For example, periods of illness (such as back pain) sufficient to prevent a woman from working instantly aroused suspicions. In 1763, Mary Hind deposed that some months previously Mary Swinbank had 'declined working as usual and as this Examinant believes on account of her being with Child or a disorder that occasioned a swelling in her Belly'.[19] In some cases, the absence of menstruation added to the certainty. In 1784, Mary Jackson 'observed her [daughter, Jane] narrowly and suspected her of being with Child as she had not any Courses after that Time, that she grew larger in the body'.[20]

Suspicions that a single woman was pregnant spread rapidly around the village or township in which the woman lived or worked. At this stage, a woman's neighbours took one, or both, of two courses of action. First, they confronted the woman directly, charged her with being pregnant and attempted to substantiate their suspicions with their own investigations. Second, they notified overseers of the poor in an attempt to ensure that the child was filiated and that the parish would not be burdened with its maintenance.

Confronted by the accusations of their neighbours and relatives, most suspects vehemently denied that they were pregnant at this stage. When Sarah Crowther was accused by her mistress of being pregnant, she always denied it 'and swore that she was not with Child and damned every person that said she was with Child'.[21] Some women supplemented their denials with alternative explanations for their condition or with demonstrations deliberately intended to dispel suspicion. Martha Bramhall, for example, tried to convince her employer that she was menstruating, and therefore not pregnant, by showing her her under-linen stained with blood.[22] Other women claimed that they were suffering from obstructed menses or from dropsy, or that, like the rest of their family, they were simply pot-bellied.[23] Such explanations may have been rendered plausible by the fact that these conditions were notoriously difficult to distinguish from pregnancy.

However, in general, suspects had little chance of avoiding confrontation simply by denying that they were pregnant. As Mary Windas apparently complained to her mistress in 1786, in the small villages and townships in which many suspected murders occurred (or at least in which they were readily brought to the attention of the authorities), 'people were very busy and always knew other people's Business better than they did themselves'.[24] In such circumstances, neighbours were rarely satisfied with straightforward denials. Although a suspect's neighbours possessed no legal authority to examine her, either verbally or physically, it is clear that many women later accused of murder had been interrogated and physically searched while they were pregnant. Significantly, few suspects refused to be examined, either because they were powerless to resist the pressure exerted on them by their neighbours or because they were relying on the equivocal signs of pregnancy to free them from suspicion.

The verbal and physical examination of a single woman at this stage was usually carried out by neighbouring women, many of whom regarded themselves as experts by virtue of their own experience as child-bearing women.[25] Occasionally, perhaps as an attempt to increase their authority and to encourage a woman to confess her condition, neighbours called in a midwife to assist in searching the suspect,[26] but generally neither midwives nor male medical practitioners were involved in investigations at this stage. When a physical examination was carried out, it usually confirmed suspicions that a suspect was pregnant.[27] Only rarely did a physical search afford a woman any relief from suspicions. In 1764, for example, a midwife and some other women examined Jane Brown and, according to one of the witnesses, declared 'that to the best of their understanding she was not with Child', after which no further notice was taken of her condition until she gave birth five months later.[28]

When parish officers were informed of a suspected pregnancy, they could add little to the formidable pressure already brought to bear on a woman to confess her condition. According to legislation passed in 1733, even justices of the peace could not compel a woman to answer questions 'concerning her Pregnancy, or supposed Pregnancy' until one month after delivery.[29] This did not prevent overseers from assisting a woman's neighbours in their attempts to encourage the woman to confess her condition 'voluntarily' and filiate the child on a man who could provide maintenance. Although pressure of this nature was sometimes successful,[30] many of the women later accused of murder continued publicly to deny that they were pregnant.

Faced with persistent denials of pregnancy, and sometimes with open hostility, neighbouring women and local officials simply watched and waited. In 1765, for example, a suspicion that Mary Dixon was pregnant led Mary Horn to 'keep a Stricter Eye upon her' until some months later she was rewarded with evidence that Mary Dixon had given birth to a child.[31] Eventually, even women who had succeeded in concealing their pregnancies (or at least in stemming the tide of local suspicions), as well as those already under the jealous eye of the neighbourhood, were likely to be betrayed by the more certain signs of labour and recent delivery, or by the discovery of a body.

Detecting signs of labour and child-birth

To a woman attempting to preserve her reputation or to avoid punishment and dismissal from service, concealing the signs of labour and child-birth presented even greater problems than concealing her pregnancy. Apart from a small number of widows who appear to have owned their own homes,[32] most women gave birth in houses belonging to other people, usually to one or other of their parents, or to their master or mistress. Even widows often had lodgers or servants in the house. Since delivery could occur at any time of the day or night, often with people present in the house or even in the room at the time, all women intent on concealment ran some risk of being discovered in labour.[33] Women who had attempted to conceal their pregnancies, and who had persistently denied their condition, were therefore forced to manipulate circumstances in order to be alone at the time of delivery. By feigning illness and retiring to bed or to the privy, by altering the sleeping arrangements so that she had a room or a bed to herself, or by leaving the house for a short while to give birth in a field or yard, a woman could achieve some measure of privacy.[34] Direct witnesses to child-birth were therefore rare.

In the absence of witnesses, the detection of labour and recent delivery by the household or the neighbourhood in which a woman lived depended upon the identification of the accompaniments of child-birth. Many women were thought to be in labour when they became ill, particularly when they were too unwell to work, or if they passed a sleepless night moaning and groaning. On 25 July 1799, William Wilson found his servant, Margaret Fenny, 'to be extreemly ill and unable to do her usual work'. Both Wilson and his wife suspected that Margaret had borne a child, and they sent for a surgeon who apparently confirmed the fact.[35]

Periods of illness were of course interpreted in the light of existing suspicions that a woman was concealing a pregnancy. In December 1756, Mary Colley of Hunmanby in Yorkshire informed a magistrate that at the end of November her daughter, Margaret, had been 'taken very ill which this Informant from the jealousy that she had of her being with Child thought might be the forerunner of her Labour'.[36] A number of women attempted to maintain the impression that they were not pregnant by passing off both labour pains and their general debility as 'an ague', as 'collick', as 'the gravel', or as 'rheumatick pains'.[37] Female neighbours in particular were rarely convinced by these explanations and their suspicions that a child had been born were further aroused by the discovery of blood.

Blood was regarded as a natural product of child-birth, and its presence on the floor, in the privy, in a bed, or on a woman's clothes was interpreted as evidence of recent delivery. References to the blood and general disorder of delivery were often oblique. Witnesses spoke of finding 'unseemly things' or of 'disorderly work', not only implying that delivery had occurred but also imparting a value judgement about the nature and suspected cause of the disorder.[38] In 1742, Mary Hodgson gave evidence that after Mary Ingleson had been ill, she had helped to wash her bed, in which she apparently saw 'a great deal of Corruption and Nastiness'. Jane West testified that she also had seen 'a deal of Nasty Stuff such as she thought could not come from a woman'. Three days later, a child was found buried in a dunghill, and Mary Ingleson and Joseph Hodgson (the reputed father of the child) were charged with its murder.[39]

It was difficult for women to conceal blood. Bloody clothes and bed clothes were frequently discovered, attempts to wash evidence away after dark were noticed, and dripping blood on to the floor or chair could betray those women who attempted to dispel suspicions by working as usual.[40] In their defence, suspects insisted that evidence of blood could be misleading. Several women claimed that the presence of blood simply represented a return of menstruation, thereby confirming their earlier accounts of menstrual obstruction. On 12 January 1792, Mary Wigfield insisted that her illness was because her 'Monthly Courses were stopped which had caused her to be ill, and her Body to swell very much'. The following day, she told her father 'I am better, for my monthly Courses have broke, and I have parted with a deal of Blood', but shortly afterwards she confessed that she had borne a child.[41] When Elizabeth Gregson saw blood on the floor of her servant's chamber, her servant, pointing to the blood, replied: 'now Mistress you see how you have blamed me wrongfully'.[42] Such attempts to divert suspicion, and those attributing the presence of blood to other causes (such as a nose bleed or vomiting), invariably failed. Persistent in their belief that a child had been born, neighbours had no doubts about the implications of blood. As Ann Maycock put it to Sarah Ward in 1796 when she saw blood on the floor, 'I suspect there is something more than Blood and I shall seek for it'. The subsequent search of the house in which Sarah Ward lived revealed 'a Male child lying in a large Earthen Pot ... and dead'.[43]

In order to avoid being betrayed by the pain and blood of child-birth, some women left their jobs and lodgings for a few days to be delivered elsewhere. Even this subterfuge failed. Their absence was itself regarded as suspicious, and when a woman returned, the neighbourhood were quick to notice that she had lost weight. In 1769, Elizabeth Ryals found work as a cleaner of saws in Sheffield and lodged with Alexander Rutter, one of the saw-makers. Rutter and his wife suspected that Elizabeth was pregnant and on several occasions ordered her to find herself other accommodation. On Monday 25 June 1770, Elizabeth told Rutter that she was ill and would not work. She then disappeared until the Wednesday afternoon, when, according to his testimony at the inquest, Rutter 'instantly perceived that she had parted with her Burthen'.[44]

It was perhaps inevitable that a woman who underwent 'a very visible alteration' in this manner,[45] without producing the expected child, should be suspected of having concealed and murdered it. In 1771, an overseer of the poor in Sexhow, Yorkshire, gave evidence that 'She appearing to be not so big or large in her body now ... he hath great reason to suspect and doth suspect that the said Margaret Baker hath really been privately Delivered of a bastard Child within the space of Ten Days now last past And that such Child hath been Murdered by her as no Child hath appeared or been yet Discovered'.[46] And in 1793, Hannah Crawford was charged by the constable of Branxton 'with the suspicion of having born a Bastard Child on Monday the 18th day of March instant, and of having murder'd the said Child, as no account could be got of it'.[47]

Superimposed upon mounting suspicions of pregnancy, signs of labour and recent delivery (sometimes coinciding with the discovery of a child's body rather than with the absence of a child) aroused suspicions of murder and prompted neighbours to intervene more forcibly in a woman's affairs in order to determine the truth of the matter. They were no longer dealing with a potential offence, with a potentially chargeable bastard, but with the birth and possible murder of an illegimate child. Although the pace of the investigation was still set by neighbouring women, local officials, in particular constables and overseers of the poor, played a more prominent part once delivery and murder were suspected.

Once suspicions that a woman had been delivered of an illegitimate child had spread through the village, township or parish in which she lived, her neighbours were eager to encourage her to explain what she had done with the child and to prove her innocence. Neighbouring women were ruthless in their approach, refusing to be distracted from their task and, if necessary, returning on several occasions to elicit answers to their questions. Some witnesses admitted that they had deliberately attempted to trick a suspect into confessing that she had given birth. According to her testimony at an inquest in 1764, Jane Kirby, suspecting that Jane Brown had given birth, searched every corner of Jane's room:

> and from thence went to the House of Easment and looked into the Vaults with a Candle But could see nothing but came back and told the said Jane Brown she had seen the Child in Order to make her Confess But she answered not and this Informant persuaded the said Jane Brown to go to her own room and go to Bed which she did and when she was in Bed this Informant told her she had Murdered her Child but she answered no she never saw it.[48]

Such ploys were often successful but usually unnecessary. On being questioned by their neighbours, most women later tried for murder admitted that they had been pregnant and given birth. However, eager to dismiss accusations of murder, most suspects insisted that they had been delivered of a still-born child and that they had secretly disposed of the child without acquainting relatives and neighbours precisely because the child had been born dead.[49]

At this stage, only a few women persisted in their denials of pregnancy and recent delivery, sometimes supporting their arguments with claims that they could not have been delivered without assistance. In 1792, for example, John Billam, an overseer of the poor for the parish of Rotherham, testified to the coroner that when he questioned Mary Wigfield about reports that she had given birth to an illegitimate child, she replied: 'Jacky Billam do you think it is possible that I shou'd bear a Child by myself, They say I have but it is a Lye I have not'.[50] Midwifery texts generally failed to support these claims. In the late seventeenth century, for example, Percivall Willughby, a physician and man-midwife in Derby, recorded cases of country women being delivered safely without assistance in support of his argument that intervention by midwives was unnecessary in child-birth.[51]

While a suspect was being interrogated, or if she refused to confess to the delivery, her neighbours made every effort to discover a body or some other sign of child-birth in the house or in the vicinity. In some instances, the search was carried out under a warrant issued by a justice of the peace, and the investigation was headed by a constable or overseer of the poor.[52] As in the case of the verbal examination of suspects, the search of a house or lodgings could be extensive. On 30 September 1764, for example, a number of the men of Rosedale in the parish of Middleton in Yorkshire were directed by a magistrate 'to search for a Child or Children which Ann Peirson was suspected to be delivered of'. On searching the first time they found nothing, but on returning to the house, 'they perceived some fresh Earth before the House, which giving them stronger Suspicion, they went in to examine the House more narrowly'. They subsequently discovered the bodies of two female children, 'appearing to them New Born wrapped up together in a Linnen Cloth and buried under a Stone in the Back Kitchen', and 'an old Axe with its head dirty with the same sort of Earth as where the Children were buryed'.[53]

The search of Ann Peirson's house illustrates the manner in which men became involved at this stage of investigations. While they frequently searched for children's bodies, they rarely questioned suspects. Only occasionally did constables and overseers of the poor and, later in the century, male medical practitioners participate in the interrogation of a woman accused of murder.[54] In most cases, the initial inquiry into a suspected murder was carried out by local women whose authority, with or without a warrant from a magistrate or coroner, was usually sufficient to persuade most suspects to cooperate.[55]

In addition to questioning a suspect and searching her room and belongings, neighbours arranged for a physical examination of the suspect for signs of recent delivery. The pressure exerted on a woman to submit to examination could involve physical as well as verbal intimidation. Although most women apparently 'did not hesitate to be so examined' when they were coerced by inquisitive neighbours,[56] if a woman did refuse to cooperate, she could be forcibly restrained. In 1791, when Mary Robinson 'refused to be examined by Mr Stott the Surgeon the Witness and others held her by force untill Mr Stott examined her'.[57]

Occasionally, in the north of England, suspects were physically examined by a 'Jury of Matrons' carefully selected from the neighbourhood as experts in the matter by virtue of their experience as child-bearers.[58] In 1794, for example, Ann Lyth and Sarah Taylor testified at the inquest that:

> they were warned and requested by Mr Robert Proud of Hovingham aforesaid the Constable as well as eleven other respectable Matrons of different Townships or Villages all having had Children and Child bearing Women to wait upon Frances Harrison … Singlewoman with an Intent and on Purpose to inspect and examine her state and condition whether she had lately been delivered of a Child or not.[59]

In most cases of suspected murder, however, the physical examination of a suspect was performed by midwives, or by male medical practitioners (that is, by surgeons, apothecaries, physicians, and man-midwives), rather than by members of the public. Significantly, during the course of the eighteenth century, the pattern of involvement of these practitioners in the examination of suspects changed. Before the middle of the century, it was customary for both local communities and the courts to call in female midwives in order to confirm that a suspect had recently given birth and to examine the dead child's body. Male medical witnesses rarely appeared in the Northern Circuit courts before 1750 and, when they did give evidence, confined their comments to opinions about the corpse.[60]

Midwives summoned to examine suspects and to testify in court were apparently well-practised in midwifery. In 1771, for example, Elizabeth Catchasides testified that 'she hath practised as a Midwife for the Space of Eighteen Years now last past and hath herself bore several Children'.[61] This level of experience may have been considered a material factor in a midwife's ability to determine whether or not a suspect had given birth. In 1757, for example, Isabel Hudson referred to the fact that she was 'lookt upon as a Judge, haveing many Years practic'd the Art of Midwifery'.[62] Since nearly sixty per cent of the midwives testifying before magistrates and coroners signed their depositions, compared with only one quarter of the suspects and remaining female witnesses, it is also likely that most midwives were better educated than the majority of the other women, and some of the men, involved in these cases.[63] Significantly, however, even those midwives who were unable to sign their names, and who may well have been lower in the social scale than their clients, were nevertheless established in the neighbourhood.[64] The official reliance on midwives in this way suggests that contemporary views (and some historical accounts) of midwives as witches and bawds failed to recognise the respectability and status of midwives in some local communities.[65]

Although midwives involved in cases of suspected new-born child murder appear to have been more respectable and more influential than some accounts of midwifery in this period would suggest, and although they spearheaded many local investigations, it is clear that during the course of the eighteenth century their contribution in these cases was limited by the expanding role of male medical practitioners. In the second half of the eighteenth century, neighbours called in far more surgeons and apothecaries than midwives to examine and interrogate suspects and to inspect dead bodies. In addition, in the courts, male practitioners gave opinions about all aspects of these cases, including those that required intimate internal examination of the suspects. Although midwives continued to be involved, particularly in the early local stages of an investigation, they were increasingly subordinate to male medical practitioners. Their contributions were sometimes limited to witnessing the examination performed by a surgeon and on occasions they referred the case to a male practitioner. In 1778, for example, Mary Hopwood, a midwife in the East Riding of Yorkshire, testified that she 'is of Opinion that Hannah Turner had Boarn a Child but was not willing to have the Jury Depend on her Judgment alone, and Desired that an Apothecary should be sent for'.[66]

This transformation in the use of midwives and medical witnesses reflected both broader changes within the practice of midwifery and changing attitudes to the body as a source of evidence. Until the eighteenth century, child-birth was the almost exclusive preserve of women, not only of the mother and a midwife but also of the neighbouring women or 'gossips' who assisted at deliveries.[67] During the eighteenth century, however, in spite of considerable opposition from both male medical practitioners and some midwives, an increasing number of men began to practise midwifery, largely at the expense of the reputation and practice of women. The gradual rejection of the value of female experience and tradition in child-birth which this process entailed is reflected in the growing use of male medical witnesses in suspected cases of new-born child murder.[68]

The declining use of midwives as experts can also be attributed to developments in medical jurisprudence and to changing attitudes to the body as evidence. As I shall argue in the next chapter, when the statutory presumption of 1624 fell into disfavour in the middle of the eighteenth century and a greater number of trials were conducted at common law, the courts placed greater emphasis on medical evidence that the child had been born alive.[69] This evidence required some form of post-mortem dissection. Since women were traditionally excluded from the use of surgical instruments to probe bodies in this way, it was male medical practitioners who were requested to examine the body and give evidence in murder investigations. Consequently, as male practitioners became more prominent in investigations, it became convenient for both a woman's neighbours and the courts to ask medical men, rather than midwives, not only to open corpses but also to search the bodies of suspects for signs of recent delivery.

What particular signs then constituted evidence of recent delivery according to the midwives and medical practitioners who examined suspects and later testified at inquests and in the trial courts? The physical signs most frequently discussed by medical writers and medical witnesses, and which when taken together were considered as proof of delivery, were: relaxation or distension of the vagina; swelling of the genitalia; the flow of the lochia or 'Cleansings'; the open state of the os uteri; a flaccidity or laxity of the abdomen; swollen, hard breasts which produced milk on pressure or suction; and extended areolae.[70] In practice, neither the results of internal examination nor the presence of 'the Discharges usual with lying in women'[71] were viewed by medical witnesses as conclusive because 'Feminine Disorders or Deliverys of Children'[72] could both produce the same appearances. Proof of recent delivery therefore depended almost exclusively upon demonstrating the presence of milk in a suspect's breasts. Thus, in 1788, John Lincoln, a surgeon in Northallerton in Yorkshire, testified that:

> Upon Examination found the Os Tinse or Passage into the Uteris, the Discharge in a State to suspect some substance has passed, No Child appearing was ready to pass the most favourable Construction on the Affair and said she perhaps had had a Miscarridge but gave directions to look to her Breasts for Milk which might Ground Suspicion more strongly.[73]

The presence of milk was usually demonstrated by pressure or suction on the breasts:

> the examinent says he ordered a Woman then present to Draw or suck her Brests and findeing Milk it was put into a Tea Cup and the Milk so taken out of Ann Bennison Breast was sufficient to Certify that she had had a Child.[74]

Milk in a suspect's breasts was regarded by witnesses as the most 'certain Proof' of recent delivery.[75] Although some popular literature reiterated a traditional belief that virgins and the non-pregnant could have a type of milk in their breasts, witnesses were convinced that only recent pregnancy could account for the milk found in the breasts of women examined by them. In 1755, Mary Thompson, midwife, testified before a magistrate that 'she found Milk in her [Ann Stockdale's] Breasts which she never knew any to have that had not been with Child'.[76] Corroborated on occasions by the presence of milk on a woman's clothes 'opposite to the Nipples',[77] milk in the breasts encouraged neighbours to continue their search for a body and to urge the suspect to confess to recent delivery. Indeed, this form of evidence was regarded as so conclusive that many suspects ceased to deny the fact and readily confessed to the birth once milk had been drawn from their breasts. In 1749, Grace Ditch, a midwife from Emley in Yorkshire, testified before a magistrate that she told Martha Gleadhill 'that as She had Milk in her Breast She must have brought forth a Child very lately, upon which the said Martha Gleadhill did Confess that ... She was delivered of a Male Child'.[78]

The damning nature of milk in the breasts led some women to find ways of drying up the flow artificially. In 1768, Elizabeth Woodman was reported to have asked a fellow servant 'if there was not a Method to carry of[f] Milk from one that had bore a Child of the Breast'.[79] At least one surgeon, having failed to find milk in a woman's breasts, did believe that there were methods to achieve this end. In 1752, Francis Taylor, a surgeon from New Malton in Yorkshire, gave evidence before a magistrate that 'it is very possible in his Opinion for the Milk in a Woman's brest to be Dryed away by Art in a Day or two time'.[80] This possibility was questioned by midwifery writers. Although Pierre Dionis and William Smellie both described the use of various applications to drive back milk in women who were 'not willing to give suck' and who wanted to put their children out to nurse, both writers doubted the efficacy of such measures:

> We must not be so credulous as to believe that a Linen-Rag dipt in any Liquor, and applied to the Breasts, will drive back the Milk, and change the ordinary Course of Nature.[81]

In practice, most women later accused of murder had failed to stem the natural flow of milk or to provide convincing alternative explanations for its presence,[82] and the discovery of milk convinced neighbours and local officials that a woman strongly suspected to have been pregnant had finally been delivered of her bastard child.

In addition to confirming that a suspect had given birth around the time when the body of a dead child had been discovered,[83] the demonstration of milk in a woman's breasts determined further issues for the courts. In contrast to some seventeenth-century writers who asserted that women could have milk in their breasts early in pregnancy,[84] in the eighteenth century the presence of milk was taken to indicate that the mother had gone to her full time. It was thus used to rebut a woman's claim that she had been miscarried of a premature, and therefore still-born, child. In 1790, for example, Hannah Pullen testified to a justice of the peace that she had been delivered of a substance 'like a lump of Flesh' only eighteen weeks after she had had 'connections with a person who had carnal knowledge of her Body'. The surgeon who had examined her disagreed:

> he was sent for to examine Hannah Pullen who it was said had Miscarried that on examining her from milk being in her breasts and thus full and distended and from having the Discharges usual with lying in women he has been led by experience to believe that she was at or near her full time nor does her situation agree with the account she gives of the period of pregnancy.[85]

The value of medical opinion concerning recent delivery was recognised throughout the course of investigations into cases of suspected new-born child murder. It was routinely admitted at coroners' inquests and in the trial courts and was employed to facilitate the local interrogation and examination of suspects by relatives and neighbours. In some cases, the simple intervention of a midwife or male medical practitioner clearly encouraged a suspect to confess that she had borne a child. Accordingly, some women accused of murdering their new-born children openly expressed their fear of the testimony of midwives and surgeons. Thus, in 1757, Margaret Young, a midwife in Northumberland, 'was call'd upon to see the said Sarah Newitt, who (upon sight of this Informant) spoke, what! are you (meaning this Informant) come here to swear away my Life – No said this Informant if it had been in my power to have preserv'd your Life and good Name I'd done it'.[86]

Conflicting interpretations of the signs

Local suspicions that a single woman had been pregnant and had subsequently given birth to an illegitimate child encouraged the woman's neighbours to interrogate her, to search her rooms or house for evidence of recent delivery and for signs of the child itself, to examine her physically, and, if no child could be found or if a new-born child was found dead, to accuse her of murder. How did women accused of murder respond to local suspicions and account for the evidence that was being accumulated by their neighbours?

The depositions of suspects before magistrates and coroners suggest that suspects' efforts to dispel suspicions of murder involved several strategies. In the first instance, while most women later tried for murder eventually confessed that they had given birth, they insisted that the child had been still-born. In order to substantiate this claim, a number of women provided their accusers and the courts with a chronological narrative of pregnancy that made explicit the premature and accidental nature of the birth. A suspect's claim that she had been delivered of only a quantity of blood or had been miscarried of a premature still-born child was thus consolidated by reference to the precise times at which sexual intercourse and delivery had occurred. In July 1762, for example, Elizabeth Eltoft supported her claim that she had given birth only six months after conception by insisting that 'on or about the Twenty Fourth day of December last past ... Robert Wilks ... had carnal knowledge of this Examinants body only once and did then beget her with Child'.[87]

As I shall discuss in the next chapter, both lawyers and medical practitioners acknowledged that premature births were likely to be still-births. The inclusion of details supporting claims of prematurity therefore constituted an important element of a suspect's attempts to refute allegations that she had given birth to, and murdered, a live-born full grown child. Suspects' efforts to defend themselves against allegations of maternal neglect or murder at birth were also bolstered by their description of those circumstances that might have caused them to be delivered prematurely. In 1756, for example, Grace Furnace indicated that her child had been born prematurely and dead because she had injured herself lifting 'a Load of Coals'.[88] A recognised association between mechanical injuries of this nature and what were referred to as 'miscarriages' or 'spontaneous abortions', evident in eighteenth-century obstetrical texts,[89] rendered this component of suspects' accounts critical to the process of assessing maternal responsibility.

The terms in which suspects accounted for the births and deaths of their children also make evident a significant slippage between constructions of premature delivery or miscarriage, on the one hand, and menstruation on the other. This slippage functioned at several levels. First, as I have already suggested, some women claimed that the presence of blood on clothes and bed clothes, usually interpreted by their neighbours as indicative of recent delivery, was, on the contrary, a mark of normal menstruation.[90] Blood, suspects were implying, could be misleading as a sign of recent delivery and murder.

This conflation of menstrual blood and the products of premature birth appeared in other guises. Some suspects claimed to have been delivered only of a quantity of blood. In 1730, Prudence Newsome testified that she had been delivered 'of something like bloud of the bigness of her Hand'.[91] And, in 1799, Susanna Staniforth testified that she had been delivered of 'only Blood'.[92] On other occasions, suspects acknowledged that the substance of which they had been delivered possessed more form and substance than blood, but nevertheless denied that that substance constituted a child. Thus, Elizabeth Eltoft admitted that she had been 'delivered of or Miscarried of … a hard substance' but insisted that this substance 'had not the form of a Child'.[93] In this context, it is significant that some women accused of murder, when they did admit to having conceived, referred to it as only 'a false Conception' unworthy of further attention.[94]

In calling to mind the blood loss of menstruation, in referring to the unformed nature of the substance of which they had been delivered, and in emphasising the false nature of conception, suspects were reproducing accounts of female physiology, and in particular of menstruation, conception and pregnancy, evident elsewhere. The slippage between constructions of menstruation and premature birth, for example, is embodied in at least two other locations: in the availability of proprietary medicines ostensibly produced for 'bringing on the menses' but almost certainly serving the alternative function of terminating unwanted pregnancies;[95] and in the belief that menstrual blood yielded 'Nourishment to the Embrio, when suppressed by Conception'.[96]

The conflation of menstrual blood loss and premature birth, reinforced in this way by wider cultural conceptions of female physiology, enabled suspects to produce a coherent account of pregnancy and birth that stressed the accidental and premature nature of labour and delivery and emphasised their own lack of responsibility for the birth and death of their child. In their evidence before magistrates and coroners, suspects could thus reinforce their portrayal of themselves as the innocent dupes of male deceit and seduction by depicting themselves as the hapless victims of a further 'sad misfortune',[97] that of miscarriage. The suspects' use of such phrases to portray themselves as the passive sufferers of tragedy (a portrayal also evident in contemporary ballads and broadsheets)[98] was reinforced by the manner in which terms such as miscarriage and abortion (which were used synonymously to describe the expulsion of the immature products of conception)[99] were incorporated into suspects' accounts of events. Miscarriage was something that happened *to* women rather than something done *by* women.

It is likely that many of the witnesses in these cases, particularly those drawn from the suspects' circle of immediate family and friends or from their fellow-servants, shared many of the suspects' cultural perceptions of menstruation, conception, and pregnancy. However, most witnesses and those responsible for pursuing accusations into the courts adopted interpretations of the evidence that differed significantly from those of the suspects. Thus, witnesses insisted that the presence of blood on a woman's clothes or bed-clothes indicated something more sinister than menstruation or miscarriage.

In addition to rejecting suspects' explanations for the presence of blood, witnesses strongly challenged suspects' accounts of accidental and premature delivery. Such accounts were regarded simply as defensive strategies employed by women to escape both the rigours of local animosity and the severity of the law. Evidence derived from the examination of the women under suspicion or of the products of delivery were generally taken to confirm suspicions that certain women had given birth in secret to live-born children. Moreover, witnesses disputed the picture of a hapless, passive victim implicit in many of the suspects' accounts, particularly if the suspect had given birth to bastard children previously.[100] Fuelled by concerns about bastardy levels and poor rates and about the activities of single women, the testimony of prosecutors and witnesses emphasised the malevolent agency of suspects. According to most witnesses, women who claimed to have given birth to a still-born child or to have been miscarried through no fault of their own, were, on the contrary, clearly to be held culpable for their children's deaths.

Conclusion

When an unmarried woman put on weight, became unable to work, or stopped menstruating, her neighbours rapidly suspected that she was pregnant. If their efforts to force the woman to confess her condition and to filiate the child failed, they simply waited until she was betrayed by the more certain signs of labour and recent delivery. Once the neighbours suspected that an illegitimate child had been born, midwives and male medical practitioners were immediately called in to confirm their suspicions by examining the woman's body.[101] In addition, constables and overseers of the poor, sometimes supported by a warrant from a magistrate or coroner, organised a search of the vicinity in order to discover the child's body.

Faced by the combined authority of neighbouring women, medical practitioners and local officials, most suspects confessed that they had been delivered of a child. However, almost without exception, they denied both that the child had been born alive and that they had murdered it. Such denials failed to dispel local suspicions. Evidence that a woman had concealed her pregnancy and the birth and body of her child, combined with evidence derived from examining the suspect and from inspecting the dead body, aroused suspicions that the child had been murdered and encouraged the woman's neighbours, family and friends to inform a magistrate or coroner of their suspicions.[102] The suspicions of the neighbourhood then provided the grounds for committing the woman to gaol to await trial, sometimes after a short period to allow the suspect to recover from the birth.[103]

The potency of neighbourhood suspicions of murder is evident in the court records. Although some legal writers advised that no person should be convicted of murder in the absence of a corpse,[104] several women were tried for murder without the child's body ever being found.[105] It is possible that some of these women had not been pregnant and that the neighbours' accusations had been misguided. Alternatively, these women may have achieved precisely the level of concealment that had concerned the legislators of 1624 and continued to trouble rate-payers in the eighteenth century. More importantly, however, such cases demonstrate the ability of a woman's neighbours to send her to trial for murder by virtue of suspicions derived solely from the signs of pregnancy and recent delivery.

Notes

1 The formal examination of bodies of dead new-born children was increasingly the province of the coroner and his jury in this period and is discussed in the next chapter.
2 Mary Robinson, 1759, ASSI 45/26/3/89-90B.
3 William Smellie, *A Treatise on the Theory and Practice of Midwifery*, (London, 1752), pp. 141-51; Pierre Dionis, *A General Treatise of Midwifery*, (London, 1719), pp. 125-45, this being one of a number of influential French midwifery texts translated into English in the early eighteenth century; Samuel Farr, *Elements of Medical Jurisprudence*, (London, 1788), pp. 3-9. Uroscopy, recommended by some popular literature on generation, for example, *Aristotle's Compleat Master-Piece*, (11th ed., London, 1725), pp. 34-5, was not mentioned by medical authors.
4 Smellie, *Treatise on Midwifery*, pp. 180-4
5 Farr, *Medical Jurisprudence*, pp. 4-5.
6 Bartholomew Parr, *The London Medical Dictionary*, (3 vols., London, 1809), vol. II, p. 180.
7 Smellie, *Treatise on Midwifery*, pp. 187-8. In the early nineteenth century, Parr, *Medical Dictionary*, vol. II, p. 180, further suggested that untimely and uncharitable judgements concerning pregnancy could lead women to commit suicide.
8 According to Smellie, *Treatise on Midwifery*, p. 188, the problems of detecting pregnancy diminished with time: 'All these diagnosticks are more plain and certain, the nearer the patient approaches to the time of delivery'. For this reason, Christopher Johnson in his translation of Dr. P. A. O. Mahon's *An Essay on the Signs of Murder in New Born Children*, (Lancaster, 1813), pp. 4-5, later shed doubt on the possibility that a woman could 'under any pretext be supposed ignorant of her pregnancy, when the foetus has attained its full time and ordinary size', as some women claimed.
9 Martha Bramhall, 1767, ASSI 45/28/3/25-28A.
10 Elizabeth Ryals, 1770, ASSI 45/29/3/174-5.
11 See, for example: Mary Walker (1726, ASSI 45/18/3/33-5) who shared a bed with her sister; Rebecca Stephenson (1750, ASSI 45/24/2/105-8) who shared a bed with her master's 'Daughter in Law'; or Jane Jackson (1785, ASSI 45/35/2/90-1) who

slept with her mother.

12 Bernard Mandeville, *The Fable of the Bees: or, Private Vices, Publick Benefits*, (2 vols., Oxford, [6th ed., 1732] 1924), vol. I, Remark C.

13 Jane Barnes, 1745, ASSI 45/23/1/3A-E. Similar denials of knowledge about pregnancy or delivery can be found in Mary Wood's testimony that, although she shared a bed with Elizabeth Webster, she did not know that she had been pregnant until she had been delivered - Elizabeth Webster, 1765, ASSI 45/28/1/134-135A. See also the testimony of Mary Walker's sister in Mary Walker, 1726, ASSI 45/18/3/33-5.

14 Dionis, *Treatise of Midwifery*, p. 123: 'A woman with Child must not be kept tight in her Clothes'. See also William Alexander, *The History of Women*, (2 vols., London, 1779), vol. II, pp. 137-8, where he noted that, as a result of the fashion, 'about the years 1759 and 1760 every woman, old and young, had the appearance of being big with child'.

15 'A Full and True Account of a barbarous and bloody Murder Committed by Nelly Salvy, a Cook-Maid, who Liv'd in a Gentlemans House the upper end o Caple-Street, on the body of her own young Child just Born, the 25th of this Instant January 1725', (Dublin, 1725).

16 Sarah Leigh, 1739, ASSI 45/21/3/94-97A.

17 Ann Usher, 1766, ASSI 45/28/2/146-8.

18 The possibility of successful concealment is, however, suggested by inquest verdicts of children killed 'by Person or Persons unknown'.

19 Mary Swinbank alias Sumack, 1763, ASSI 45/27/1/76D-M.

20 Jane Jackson, 1785, ASSI 45/35/2/90-1. Jane was also suspected on account of her familiarity with a man: Ann Dent 'taxed her with being with Child as there was a Report of too great an Intimacy between the Witnesses Husband and Jane'. Suspected sexual activity was rarely mentioned by witnesses as a grounds for suspecting pregnancy. In this instance the accusation, although apparently accurate, may have been expressed for personal reasons.

21 Sarah Crowther, 1786, ASSI 45/35/3/54. Fierce denials were also made by Ann Usher (1766, ASSI 45/28/2/146-8) and Martha Bramhall (1767, ASSI 45/28/3/25-28A).

22 Martha Bramhall, 1767, ASSI 45/28/3/25-28A.

23 See: Ann Stephenson, 1797, ASSI 45/39/2/100; Hannah Leighton, 1793, ASSI 45/38/1/114-17; and Hannah Butler, Old Bailey Sessions Papers (OBSP) No. I, December 1736, p. 26. Ann Stephenson's story that she was suffering from obstructed menses as a result of exposure to cold was compatible with humoral explanations of disease in the seventeenth and eighteenth centuries: see Audrey Eccles, *Obstetrics and Gynaecology in Tudor and Stuart England*, (London, Croom Helm, 1982), p. 75.

24 The words of Mary Windas when she was threatened with dismissal from service because her mistress had heard that she was pregnant – 1786, ASSI 45/35/3/233-4.

25 Most women in the neighbourhood considered themselves competent judges of a suspect's condition. Only the young and unmarried might be regarded as insufficiently experienced to testify. In 1766, Susanna Bisby qualified her comment that Martha Bramhall appeared large by insisting that she was not 'a competent Judge of such Appearances, being not yet seventeen Years of Age' – Martha Bramhall, 1767, ASSI 45/28/3/25-28A.

26 See, for example, Prudence Newsome, 1730, ASSI 45/18/7/47-50.

27 Since the court records are inevitably biased towards those cases in which the pregnancies were discovered, there is no means of telling how many pregnant women succeeded in avoiding local suspicions.

28 Jane Brown, 1765, ASSI 45/28/1/2-6. See also the case of Ann Trotter (1777, ASSI 45/33/1/119) in which a surgeon apparently failed to recognise that Ann was pregnant a week before her delivery.

29 'An Act for the Relief of Parishes and other Places from such Charges as may arise from Bastard Children born within the same', 1733, 6 Geo. II c. 31.

30 Women who later became the subject of settlement and bastardy orders had often filiated the child during pregnancy.

31 Mary Dixon, 1765, ASSI 45/28/1/17.

32 Such as Mary Ward (1738, ASSI 45/21/2/61-2) who lived in Scarborough.

33 Elizabeth Cunny (1725, ASSI 45/18/2/18-20) apparently gave birth in the house of her master 'without acquainting any body with it, tho' some Women were in the room at ye Time of her Delivery'. The fact that people present usually denied any knowledge of the delivery suggests that, as in the case of pregnancy, they were careful to avoid being charged with complicity. The people most likely to be indicted as accomplices, if present at the birth, were the suspect's mother and the child's father: in 1745, Ann and Hester Henderson (ASSI 45/23/1/49B-C, ASSI 44/60, ASSI 41/3) were charged with murdering Hester's bastard child; in 1789, Jane Miller, Jane Hutchinson, her mother, and Richard Caygill, the child's father (see the indictment in ASSI 44/104i), were all indicted for the murder of Jane Miller's child. Friends and neighbours were rarely indicted as accomplices.

Although denying knowledge of labour, the evidence of people present in the house could still be material in the courts. Witnesses could testify that the suspect had not called for help during labour, an omission that would facilitate trial under the 1624 statute, or they could support a suspect's claim that the child had been still-born by testifying that they had not heard a child cry – see Mary Windas, 1786, ASSI 45/35/3/233-4.

34 See, for example, the effort made by Mary Walker (1768, ASSI 45/29/1/169) to ensure that she spent the night of her labour alone 'in a private Room'.

35 Margaret Fenny otherwise Fenwick, 1799, ASSI 45/40/1/55-8.

36 Margaret Colley, 1757, ASSI 45/26/1/22-6.

37 See for example: Ann Parcival (1735, ASSI 45/20/1/95-99A), who 'lay all night in Bed very uneasy pretending she had got an ague'; Mary Ingleson (1743, ASSI 45/22/3/57-60), who 'thought she had the Heart Collick'; and Ann Atley (1746, ASSI 45/23/2/12-13), who 'pretended to be ill of the Gravel'.

38 The words of Elizabeth Cunningham to describe what she had seen in Ann Playforth's room, leading her to suspect recent delivery (1730, ASSI 45/18/7/51-3), and those of Margaret Haw in the case of Jane Brown (1765, ASSI 45/28/1/2-6). The descriptions perhaps reflected a popular view of menstrual blood as venomous, as something of which women needed to purge themselves in order to be healthy - see J. Pechey, *The Compleat Midwife's Practice Enlarged*, (5th ed., 1698), p. 75, quoted in Eccles, *Obstetrics and Gynaecology*, p. 49.

39 Mary Ingleson/Joseph Hodgson, 1743, ASSI 45/22/3/57-60.

40 Eleanor Hayward, midwife, found some bloody clothes 'concealed under a Bed Mattrass' (Jane Miller/Jane Hutchinson/Richard Caygill, 1789, ASSI 45/36/3/120-4); Mary Downey testified that she had seen 'Clothes at several times hanging up in the kitchen commonly made use of by Women in Child bearing, always wash't at night and drying in the Morning' (Elizabeth Woodman, 1768, ASSI 45/29/1/174-8); Christiana Robinson's attempt to work at spinning as normal were foiled by Mary Howey noticing 'a large Quantity of Blood under the Seat that the said Christeana Robinson had been sitting on' (1796, ASSI 45/39/1/108).

41 Mary Wigfield, 1792, ASSI 45/37/3/221-3.

42 Ann Stephenson, 1797, ASSI 45/39/2/100.

43 Sarah Ward, 1797, ASSI 45/39/2/121-2.

44 Elizabeth Ryals, 1770, ASSI 45/29/3/174-5.

45 The phrase is taken from Ann Usher (1766, ASSI 45/28/2/146-8), whose neighbours searched the local coal pits when they suspected that she had been delivered of her child. For similar tell-tale signs of delivery, see the case reported in *The Times*, (12 October 1785), p. 3.

46 Margaret Baker, 1771, ASSI 45/30/1/22-6.

47 Hannah Crawford, 1793, ASSI 45/38/1/48B-D.

48 Jane Brown, 1765, ASSI 45/28/1/2-6.
49 Pheeby Cockshot (1756, ASSI 45/25/4/28-9), for example, told Mary Hoffman, a midwife, that she had left her child in 'the Turfhouse' because it was dead.
50 Mary Wigfield, 1792, ASSI 45/37/3/221-3; see also Hannah Leighton, 1793, ASSI 45/38/1/114-17.
51 Percivall Willughby, *Observations in Midwifery*, ed. H. Blenkinsop, (S. R. Publishers Ltd., Yorkshire, [1863] 1972), pp. 31-5. Similar stories were reported in *The Cumberland Pacquet*, (24 October 1776), p. 3; ibid. (10 June 1777), p. 3; ibid. (28 October 1783).
52 For the use of warrants issued by magistrates or coroners to search or apprehend a suspect, see: Elizabeth Ryals, 1770, ASSI 45/29/3/174-5; Jane Hudson, 1779, in ASSI 44/94ii; Jane Jackson, 1785, ASSI 45/35/2/90-1. The investigation of Mary Pemberton's suspected delivery was headed by an overseer without the need for a warrant – Mary Pemberton, 1765, ASSI 45/28/1/68.
53 Ann Peirson, 1765, ASSI 45/28/1/69-74.
54 For example, George Flower, surgeon in Maltby, Yorkshire, interrogated Ann Stephenson in 1797 about the birth and death of her child (ASSI 45/39/2/100).
55 Only one woman apparently attempted to bribe searchers (with both money and the use of her body) to discontinue their search – Susanna Staniforth, 1799, ASSI 45/40/1/118.
56 The words of Ann Bent, who was 'often times called in to see her Neighbours when they happen to lye in', in describing the reaction of Ann Hollingworth, 1799, ASSI 45/40/1/6-17.
57 Mary Robinson, 1791, ASSI 45/37/2/155. Tamar Winlaw (1789, ASSI 45/36/3/226) and Elizabeth Barnet (1796, ASSI 45/39/1/4-7) also refused to be examined by a midwife or surgeon.
58 On the history of the jury of matrons in both civil and criminal courts, see James C. Oldham, 'On pleading the belly: a history of the Jury of Matrons', *Criminal Justice History*, VI (1985), 1-64.
59 Frances Harrison, 1795, ASSI 45/38/3/51. For other 'Juries of Matrons', see: Elizabeth Pruddam, 1746, ASSI 45/23/2/81-3; Pheeby Cockshot, 1756, ASSI 45/25/4/28-9; Margaret Colley, 1757, ASSI 45/26/1/22-6; Margaret Baker, 1771, ASSI 45/30/1/22-6.
60 I have found only one example of a male practitioner giving evidence in the north of England before 1750. In 1728, William Hornby examined the body of Anne Milburne's child – Anne Milburne, 1728, ASSI 45/18/5/53. According to printed sessions papers, however, surgeons sometimes gave evidence at the Old Bailey and at the Surrey and Essex sessions in the 1730s and 1740s.
61 Margaret Baker, 1771, ASSI 45/30/1/22-6.
62 Sarah Newitt, 1757, ASSI 45/26/1/97-102.
63 Excluding medical witnesses, all of whom signed their depositions, twenty per cent of male witnesses could not sign their names.
64 Although Mary Greenside could not sign her deposition, she had apparently practised midwifery for 'betwixt thirty and forty years' – Ann Bateman, 1761, ASSI 45/26/5/2-3.
65 See, for example, Farr's comments in *Medical Jurisprudence*, pp. 7-8. Farr argued that the determination of pregnancy should not, even on account of decency, be committed to midwives, but should instead 'be entrusted to the more regular practitioner, who being a person of education, would add the influence of his judgment to his examination, and would not be content with a single enquiry, which may be uncertain, but would frequently repeat it, till he had perfectly ascertained the truth'. Similar attitudes to midwives had previously appeared in Willughby's *Observations in Midwifery*, and in contemporary novels. For historical works on the midwife as witch and bawd, see Robert A. Erickson, *Mother Midnight: Birth, Sex, and Fate in Eighteenth-Century Fiction*, (New York, AMS Press, 1986); and T. R. Forbes, *The Midwife and the*

Witch, (New Haven, Yale University Press, 1966), pp. 112-32. For an alternative account, see: David N. Harley, 'Ignorant midwives – a persistent stereotype', *Bulletin of the Society for the Social History of Medicine*, 28 (1981), 6-9; David N. Harley, 'Historians as demonologists: the myth of the midwife-witch', *Social History of Medicine*, 3 (1990), 1-26. Harley has pointed out the limitations of contemporary evidence, noting, for example, that criticisms expressed by man-midwives were influenced by their eagerness to increase their own practices at the expense of those of the midwives.

66 Hannah Turner, 1778, ASSI 45/33/2/137. On the roles of midwives and male practitioners, see David Harley, 'The scope of legal medicine in Lancashire and Cheshire, 1660-1770', in Michael Clark and Catherine Crawford (eds.), *Legal Medicine in History*, (Cambridge, Cambridge University Press, 1994), pp. 45-63.

67 Adrian Wilson, *The Making of Man-midwifery: Childbirth in England, 1660-1770*, (London, UCL Press, 1995), pp. 25-6.

68 The rise of, and controversy surrounding, man-midwifery in the seventeenth and eighteenth centuries is discussed in Wilson, *Man-midwifery*, and in Jean Donnison, *Midwives and Medical Men: A History of Inter-Professional Rivalries and Women's Rights*, (London, Heinemann, 1977), pp. 1-59.

69 See below, Chapter 4. See also the discussion in Mark Jackson, 'Suspicious infant deaths: the statute of 1624 and medical evidence at coroners' inquests', in Clark and Crawford (eds.), *Legal Medicine in History*, pp. 64-86.

70 Farr, *Medical Jurisprudence*, pp. 49-50; Parr, *Medical Dictionary*, vol. II, p. 179.

71 The words of William Tindall, surgeon, in Hannah Pullen, 1790, ASSI 45/37/1/176-8.

72 Francis Taylor, surgeon, could not distinguish between these two possible causes of Ann Young's condition in 1752 – Ann Young/Ambrose Hoyland, ASSI 45/24/4/73-4.

73 Ann Bennison, 1788, ASSI 45/36/2/10-12.

74 Ibid. ; a description of the procedure from the testimony of a constable.

75 The opinion of James Armstrong, surgeon, in the case of Hannah Dodd, 1788, ASSI 45/36/2/38-9.

76 Ann Stockdale, 1755, ASSI 45/25/3/99B-99H. On the possibility of non-pregnant women (and indeed men) having milk in their breasts, see discussions in: *Aristotle's Compleat Master-Piece*, (11th ed., London, 1725), pp. 27-8; William Harvey, *Lectures on the Whole of Anatomy*, tr. C. D. O'Malley, F. N. L. Poynter, K. F. Russell (Berkeley, University of California Press, 1961), pp. 155-6; and Eccles, *Obstetrics and Gynaecology*, p. 53.

77 Frances Harrison, 1795, ASSI 45/38/3/51.

78 Martha Gleadhill, 1749, ASSI 45/24/1/37-38A.

79 Elizabeth Woodman, 1768, ASSI 45/29/1/174-8.

80 Ann Young/Ambrose Hoyland, 1752, ASSI 45/24/4/73-4. Although Taylor failed to find milk, two midwives did find milk in Ann's breasts.

81 Dionis, *Treatise of Midwifery*, p. 287; also Smellie, *Treatise on Midwifery*, pp. 418-19.

82 Margaret Baker, for example, failed to convince inquirers that her milk was due to her three year old child sometimes sucking at her breasts – Margaret Baker, 1771, ASSI 45/30/1/22-6.

83 The importance of establishing a connection between the estimated time of the child's birth and the signs of recent delivery was later emphasised by Johnson, *Signs of Murder in New Born Children*, p. 36. The connection was successfully disputed in the courts by Mary Bristow (OBSP, January 1718, pp. 6-7), and Sarah Clayton (OBSP, February 1760, pp. 88-90).

84 Discussed in Eccles, *Obstetrics and Gynaecology*, p. 53.

85 Hannah Pullen, 1790, ASSI 45/37/1/176-8.

86 Sarah Newitt, 1757, ASSI 45/26/1/97-102.

87 Elizabeth Eltoft, 1762, ASSI 45/26/6/19A. See also Hannah Pullen, 1790, ASSI 45/37/1/176-8.

88 Grace Furnace, 1756, ASSI 45/25/4/58-9.

89 William Smellie, *A Treatise on the Theory and Practice of Midwifery*, (a new and corrected edition, n. d.), pp. 53-4.

90 See, for example, Ann Stephenson, 1797, ASSI 45/39/2/100.

91 Prudence Newsome, 1730, ASSI 45/18/7/47-50.

92 Susanna Staniforth, 1799, ASSI 45/40/1/118.

93 Elizabeth Eltoft, 1762, ASSI 45/26/6/19A. See also Hannah Pullen, 1790, ASSI 45/37/1/176-8.

94 See the evidence in Margaret Baker, 1771, ASSI 45/30/1/22-6; Ann Hollingworth/Robert Bradbury, 1799, ASSI 45/40/1/6-17; Susanna Staniforth, 1799, ASSI 45/40/1/118.

95 Patricia Crawford, 'Attitudes to menstruation in seventeenth-century England', *Past and Present*, 91 (1981), 47-73; Angus McLaren, *Reproductive Rituals: The Perception of Fertility in England from the Sixteenth to the Nineteenth Century*, (London, Methuen, 1984), pp. 89-112.

96 Dr J. Freind, *Emmenologia*, tr. Thomas Dale, (London, 1729), pp. 4-8.

97 The words by which Ann Atley (1746, ASSI 45/23/2/12-13) is reported to have described her pregnancy loss to Mary Hebden.

98 See the discussion below, Chapter 5.

99 For a discussion of the medical and legal uses of these terms in the nineteenth century, see I. J. Keown, '"Miscarriage": a medico-legal analysis', *The Criminal Law Review*, (October 1984), 604-14.

100 As Elizabeth Ryals put it, in response to neighbourhood suspicions that she was pregnant again, 'When one has once done amiss it is common for people to reflect'. Elizabeth had given birth to two illegitimate children who were still alive in 1770 when she was prosecuted for murdering her third bastard child at birth.

101 Obtaining the necessary information for the courts required prompt examination of a suspect since, according to Christopher Johnson in *Signs of Murder in New Born Children*, p. 35, 'in a few days, all the parts resume their natural state'. Prompt examination was, of course, facilitated by the neighbours' willingness to investigate suspects themselves, to inform local authorities, and to request a medical opinion as soon as they suspected that a suspect had given birth to an illegitimate child.

102 In some cases, local suspicions were heightened if a woman fled. Such behaviour was considered to betray 'a consciousness of guilt' – Richard Burn, *The Justice of the Peace, and Parish Officer*, (3rd ed., London, 1756), p. 46. In 1752, an inquest jury had 'great Cause to Suspect' that Mary Briggs was the mother of a child found dead in a pond, but that she had 'fled from Justice'. No further mention of her appears in the records and the inquisition was certified at the Lent assize in 1753 (ASSI 44/68). When Jane Thompson was threatened with examination by a midwife in April 1778, she fled from her place of service, leaving her master 'in a great measure satisfyed that his said Servant had bore a Child or Children'. The inquest jury failed to name Jane Thompson as the mother of a dead child found in the neighbourhood, but three months later she was committed to gaol to await trial (ASSI 45/33/2/131, ASSI 44/93i). See also the case in *The Times*, (12 October 1785), p. 3, in which 'the unfortunate perpetrator of this horrid deed made her escape' before the inquest jury announced its verdict of wilful murder.

103 *The York Courant* (30 September 1760), p. 3, reported that Ann Bateman would be 'committed to the Castle as soon as she is fit to be removed, in order to take her Trial.' See also the case reported in *The Times*, (8 April 1790), p. 3.

104 Matthew Hale, *History of the Pleas of the Crown*, ed. Sollom Emlyn, (2 vols., London, 1736), vol. II, p. 290.

105 See the case of Margaret Baker (1771, ASSI 45/30/1/22-6), who persistently denied that she had been pregnant, and who was prosecuted in spite of the fact that the child to which she was supposed to have given birth was never found.

4

Examining bodies:
medical evidence and
the coroner's inquest

Introduction

The discovery of the dead body of a new-born child aroused suspicions that a single woman in the neighbourhood had committed murder. Bodies were usually discovered in privies or dunghills, in fields or rivers, or hidden indoors under mattresses, in cupboards, or in locked boxes. In many cases in the north of England, the precise location of the body had been elicited during the interrogation of a woman already under suspicion of having concealed her pregnancy and given birth in secret. On occasions, however, the body was discovered accidentally by men on their way to work or by children playing. In these cases, the child's mother had usually already been provisionally identified by her neighbours and she was immediately confronted with the body in order to make her confess. But if the mother's identity was not immediately known, a coroner or justice of the peace could attempt to identify the woman responsible by ordering a general search of 'all Suspected persons' (that is, single women and widows) for signs of recent delivery.[1]

The body of a dead new-born child provided a critical focus for local inquiries and a crucial source of evidence for the courts. Inquisitive neighbours made every effort to see the body for themselves and instantly drew their own conclusions about the cause of the child's death. In accordance with regulations, the body was also viewed by the coroner and his jury at the inquest.[2] In addition, medical practitioners were frequently summoned by neighbours or local officials to examine the body for signs of live- or still-birth and for evidence that the child had been murdered. Medical evidence derived from inspecting the bodies of dead new-born children in this way formed an increasingly prominent part of the evidence presented both locally at inquests and later in the trial courts.

In this chapter, I shall examine in detail the manner in which evidence was collected from the dead body and how that evidence was subsequently interpreted by medical witnesses and by the courts throughout the eighteenth century. In doing so, I shall argue that although medical witnesses may have been unable to answer questions about live- and still-birth and about the cause of death with any certainty, their evidence was nevertheless critical to the courts. Medical testimony enabled judges and juries not only to mediate between the conflicting accounts of events offered by suspects and their accusers but also to incorporate changing attitudes to defendants and to moderate the harshness of statute law (and parochial opinion) with what was regarded as an appropriate measure of mercy. In addition, by examining the status of legal medicine more generally in this period, I shall argue that the need for medical evidence in cases of suspected new-born child murder contributed both to a resurgence of interest in the inquest as a pre-trial inquiry and to the emergence of legal medicine in England.[3]

Legal medicine, coroners' inquests and the investigation of sudden death

The investigation of sudden death in England during the eighteenth century was limited by the low status of the coroner and his inquest, and by the lack of provision for the regular admission of medical evidence in both pre-trial and trial procedures. When the office of coroner was established at the end of the twelfth century, coroners were required to act as keepers of the crown pleas and to collect the revenue due to the crown in connection with those pleas.[4] In the fourteenth and fifteenth centuries, changes in the local and central administration of justice, including the rise of justices of the peace, combined to divest coroners of much of their authority.[5] By the seventeenth and eighteenth centuries, the coroners' decline was marked by their lack of care and diligence in performing their remaining duties. Most inquisitions were noted by the eminent seventeenth-century jurist Sir Matthew Hale to be insufficient, and in 1761 Edward Umfreville, one of the coroners for the county of Middlesex, was prompted by the disrepute into which the office had fallen to publish his private notes in an attempt to encourage 'a general uniform Practice' amongst coroners.[6]

From a medico-legal perspective, one of the most significant features of the decline of the coroner's office is the fact that the coroner's jurisdiction to take inquisitions touching the death of a person *subito mortuis, super visum corporis* had been restricted by a belief that only sudden deaths with manifest evidence of violence warranted inquiry. This view, given authoritative support by Hale,[7] rendered the inclusion of medical knowledge at inquests redundant. When there were obvious marks of violence on a dead body, the cause of death was deemed to be evident even to those not medically trained; and when there were no marks of violence, an inquest was believed to be unnecessary.

The contribution of medical testimony to the investigation of sudden deaths was also limited by the general neglect of legal medicine in England, a neglect which has usually been unfavourably contrasted with the situation in Italy, France, and Germany.[8] The absence, before 1836, of legislative provision for the payment of medical witnesses testifying at inquests discouraged coroners from calling medical evidence.[9] In addition, the lack of a substantial English text or lecture course on medical jurisprudence prior to the nineteenth century limited the forensic knowledge and skill of medical practitioners, restricted the value of their evidence in both coroners' and trial courts, and sometimes discouraged them from appearing as witnesses.[10]

In spite of these limitations, coroners were not always deterred from holding inquests, and medical opinion as to the cause of death was by no means disregarded, during the eighteenth century. This is well illustrated by the large number of investigations held into the deaths of new-born children thought to have been murdered by their mothers. Inquiries into the circumstances of these deaths were performed with a speed and diligence that belies the low status of both coroners and medical evidence in this period. Although there were often no marks of violence on the children's bodies, and although some deaths might therefore have been attributed to natural causes, coroners were routinely notified of, and held inquests into, the deaths of new-born children throughout the eighteenth century. Several inquests in the north of England were held on the same day that the body was discovered and the majority had been convened within two days.[11] Some coroners even managed successfully to summon an inquest jury to view the body and hear the evidence on a Sunday, even though, according to Umfreville, Sunday was "*dies non juridicus,*" whereon no judicial Act ought to be done'.[12]

Medical testimony was a prominent feature of coroners' investigations into new-born child murder and a regular part of trials for this offence. In the seventeenth century, and noticeably more so in the eighteenth, medical testimony as to the cause of death and the possibility of still-birth made significant contributions to discussions of the crime both in and out of court. Indeed, medical writings on problems of proof in these cases, and upon the validity of certain observations made on inspection and dissection of the body of a dead child, are among some of the earliest English works on legal medicine.[13]

Several factors may explain the extent of medical involvement in these cases. Some years ago, J. D. J. Havard suggested that medical interest in new-born child murder may have stemmed from the provisions of the 1624 statute.[14] This proposition certainly seems plausible since the statute provided a focus for many discussions about the crime, discussions that revolved around issues increasingly acknowledged to fall within the cognizance of medical practitioners. However, the statute's impact on the development of legal medicine was not straightforward. Close analysis of the statute and of its application until its repeal in 1803 suggests that it influenced the development of medical evidence in two phases. At first, the statute's emphasis on still-birth encouraged the courts to focus on medical evidence that a child had been still-born. Since such evidence could only be gained by viewing dead bodies, the statute encouraged the post-mortem inspection of dead new-born children, generally by mid-wives or male medical practitioners. Acceptance of this process may have facilitated the development of more extensive examinations of dead bodies for forensic purposes in the eighteenth century.

By the middle of the eighteenth century, however, opposition to the statute's severity and the proliferation of exemptions to it resulted in its virtual abrogation and a return to common law rules of evidence. The decline of the statute, which is discussed in more detail in subsequent chapters, placed renewed emphasis on proof of live-birth and stimulated a prolonged and vigorous discussion of the validity of medical evidence on this point. Although there had been discussions of medical evidence about still-birth, about marks of violence on the child's body, and about tests for live-birth prior to the middle of the eighteenth century, it is noticeable that it was in this period that medical evidence became a prominent issue both in and out of the courts. From this time onwards, the testimony of medical men played an increasingly critical role in investigations into new-born child murder.

The developing interest in medical evidence in the eighteenth century can also be attributed to a growing emphasis on the body as a source of knowledge. In spite of popular antagonism to dissection, the inspection and dissection of bodies became an increasingly important tool in penetrating the secrets of nature, in identifying the seats of diseases, and in understanding the causes of death. The scrutiny and dissection of the corpses of new-born children can be understood as part of this novel interest in probing the depths of the human body.[15] In this context, it is significant that the dissection of dead new-born children was exclusively performed by male medical practitioners, in particular by surgeons. Male surgical dominance can, to some extent, be explained by the traditional exclusion of women from the use of surgical instruments and by physicians' refusal to practise the craft of surgery. It can also be interpreted as a product of a link that developed between the exploration of bodies and gender in this period. As Ludmilla Jordanova has argued, the unveiling and penetration of the human body for scientific purposes in the eighteenth century was to be performed by men. The body itself, when serving as a symbol of nature, as a passive object of rational inquiry, was, by contrast, depicted as female.[16] The development of this gender-oriented rhetoric concerning exploration of the human body reinforced the exclusion of women both from opening corpses and from searching the bodies of suspects for signs of recent delivery.

Significantly, growing interest in medical evidence in cases of suspected new-born child murder was accompanied by renewed interest in the coroner's inquest as a form of pre-trial inquiry. This process is evident in the Northern Circuit records. In the first half of the eighteenth century, it was common for either coroners or magistrates (or sometimes both) to investigate suspected murders and it was not uncommon for magistrates to bring cases to trial despite an inquest verdict of still-birth or natural death.[17] The court records show that from the 1760s this pattern changed. In the last four decades of the century, the majority of suspected new-born child murders were investigated solely by coroners and their juries and it became increasingly unlikely for an inquest verdict of still-birth to be overruled by magistrates.[18] Magistrates' inquiries were generally confined to cases in which no body could be found and where the coroner therefore had no jurisdiction. By the end of the eighteenth century, the inquest had clearly become the major form of pre-trial inquiry into suspicious infant deaths.

The prominence of the inquest in the last half of the century cannot be attributed simply to the improved survival of coroners' records following the passage of 'An Act for giving a proper Reward to Coroners' in 1752.[19] Coroners' depositions and inquisitions, including those from cases not reaching the trial courts, have certainly survived more completely from that date. However, the involvement of magistrates, whose records were unaffected by that statute, declined markedly from the 1760s precisely when the need for medical evidence became prominent. This decline in the involvement of magistrates suggests a shift in attitudes unrelated to record survival.

It is possible that the development of a single pre-trial procedure in these cases was encouraged by the financial implications of the 1752 Act, which allowed coroners to be paid for inquests 'duly taken' and for any travel expenses incurred. Such allowances, if paid, would have increased the cost of investigating sudden deaths by inquest and the performance of two similar inquiries into the same death may have been regarded as an unjustifiable expense. However, this fails to explain why the inquest was preferred to the magistrate's hearing. If finance was to be the deciding factor, it would have been more reasonable to have dispensed with the inquest. Given the larger distances travelled by the small number of coroners in a county, it is likely that the cost of holding an inquest after 1752 was greater than the cost of a magistrate's inquiry.[20]

The records suggest that the resurgence of interest in the inquest as a major form of pre-trial inquiry was closely linked to a growing awareness of the importance of medical evidence in these cases. Inquests could only be held *super visum corporis*, that is upon view of a body. The significance of the view, which was to be on 'the whole Body, not a Part of it', was that it provided the court with evidence. According to Umfreville, an 'Inquisition taken by the Coroner without a *personal View* of the Body is absolutely void; for much of the Evidence ariseth upon the View, and the View ascertains the Death'.[21] When medical evidence derived from the examination of the bodies of dead new-born children became prominent in a new way in the middle of the eighteenth century, the coroner's remit to investigate suspicious deaths only 'upon view of a body' made the inquest the obvious forum for the initial presentation of this evidence. Significantly, by specifically requesting that certain tests be performed and by examining medical witnesses about their findings, the coroner and his jury also encouraged debate about the validity of medical evidence and assisted in the dissemination of medical knowledge.

Although many writers, medical witnesses, judges, lawyers, coroners, and juries acknowledged the importance of medical testimony in cases of suspected new-born child murder, the nature and quality of investigations performed by medical practitioners in the north of England varied considerably. Disparities between practitioners can be attributed both to variations in forensic experience and to the lack of instruction on post-mortem techniques available to medical practitioners called as witnesses. While most coroners in the north of England had investigated a considerable number of suspicious infant deaths,[22] few medical practitioners seem to have had extensive experience of these cases. Of the eighty-two surgeons, apothecaries, and physicians named in the court records between 1720 and 1799, only eight practitioners had certainly examined the bodies of new-born children and presented the evidence at an inquest more than once.[23] Even in those cases, however, greater experience did not guarantee a more detailed post-mortem examination.

Variations in post-mortem technique, from superficial inspection of the body to extensive dissection of its internal cavities, can also be attributed to the fact that, in spite of an increased awareness of the medico-legal issues in these cases, there were no comprehensive guides to the post-mortem investigations that should be performed. However, it is conspicuous that even after Samuel Farr's modified translation of Johann Faselius' *Elementa Medicinae Forensis* was published in 1788, few medical practitioners adopted the systematic and comprehensive approach proposed by Farr.[24] In practice, medical evidence presented at inquests and discussed in the trial courts in the eighteenth century generally focused on three key issues: evidence of prematurity and still-birth; the results of the lung test for live-birth; and evidence of violence.

Evidence of prematurity and still-birth

The simplest way for a single woman to avoid the suspicions and accusations of her neighbours and, if necessary, to prove to a court that her child had been still-born, was to have an assistant at the delivery. Although, according to the seventeenth-century physician Percivall Willughby, a midwife was not absolutely necessary at delivery, her presence nevertheless served 'to avoid all future suspicions, and to free some of the looser sort from the danger of the statute-law, in case that the child should bee found dead'.[25] However, a woman who had carefully concealed her pregnancy in order to preserve her reputation was unlikely to ask for assistance at the birth, and most women tried for this crime had given birth alone.

In the absence of direct witnesses to the birth, the question as to whether a child had been born alive or dead was determined on the basis of circumstantial evidence. In some cases, suspects either claimed that the child had died *in utero* through some injury or accident that had befallen them or they insisted that they had been delivered prematurely of a still-born child as a result of such an injury. Although inquest juries sometimes included such factors in their findings, and although the courts certainly admitted and considered this type of evidence, medical witnesses rarely commented on such matters.[26] In 1788, Farr also listed twenty-three signs of still-birth that could be discovered by examining suspected mothers and the bodies of dead children.[27] However, apart from occasional references to the deleterious effects of a difficult labour and to sinking of the lungs (which is discussed later), most of Farr's signs were rarely mentioned by medical witnesses in the eighteenth century. In practice, the likelihood that a child had been born dead was determined by assessing the child's maturity and viability.

In 1762, John Browne, a surgeon in Sheffield, told an inquest jury that the body that he had examined 'appeared to this Informant to be of Maturity for Birth not only from its size but from the great quantity of

Hair on its head, and from the Nails of its fingers and Toes'.[28] Such evidence was generally taken as evidence of a child's maturity, but, in the absence of corroborating evidence, was not usually taken as proof that the child had been born alive. As the surgeon Stephen Cleasby testified at the inquest investigating the death of Ruth Peacock's child in 1792, 'the said Child appears to him to be or to have been at or near her full Time but whether the said Child had been born alive he does not pretend to say with certainty'.[29]

In contrast, evidence that a child had been born prematurely was regularly admitted as proof of still-birth. Prematurity was signified by the absence, or imperfect development, of a child's nails and hair, and by its small size. Thus, at a trial in 1725, a midwife testified that 'to the best of her Judgment, the Prisoner did not go her full time, for the Toe-Nails of the Infant were not perfect'.[30] Opinions on this type of evidence were not the exclusive preserve of medical practitioners. Non-medical witnesses sometimes offered opinions about a child's maturity. In 1761, for example, John Atkinson, a rugmaker of Holbeck in Leeds, testified before an inquest jury that 'to the best of this Informant's Judgment he believes the said female Infant Child to be a perfect and compleat Child and born in full time according to the usual course of Nature'.[31] The same evidence from unskilled witnesses was admitted in the trial courts.[32] In addition, inquest juries were capable of deciding that a child had been born prematurely and dead apparently without hearing medical testimony.[33] However, it is clear from the records that, in most cases, evidence of prematurity and opinions about the probability of still-birth were presented by midwives and, increasingly frequently, by male medical practitioners.

Medical evidence of prematurity and still-birth had some influence in the courts. In the north of England, a number of investigations into suspicious infant deaths did not proceed beyond the coroner's court because the inquest jury found that the child had been born prematurely and dead. At an inquest in Morpeth in 1790, for example, the jury echoed the opinion of the surgeon involved by concluding that 'the said Child was Born Dead; and that it appeard also to them not to have been Born at, or to have come to its full or due time of Birth'. No further legal action was taken against the child's mother.[34] In addition, some coroners' juries directly acknowledged the influence of medical evidence in their inquisitions, and it may be significant that most inquest verdicts concurred with the opinions given by midwives and surgeons.[35]

Similar evidence of prematurity contributed to acquittals in the trial courts, a factor which may itself have encouraged the acceptance of such evidence at inquests. The Old Bailey Sessions Papers summed up the evidence at the trial of Jane Todd in 1727 in the following words:

but no Marks appearing of any Violence offered, besides, she did not go her full Time, the Child's Nails not being in their full Proportion, and she having made Provision for its Birth, it was the Opinion of the Court, from the strict Examination of the Evidences, that it was Still-born, (as she affirm'd) and that she flattered herself with concealing her Shame, by carrying it off with so much Privacy: Upon the whole the Jury acquitted her.[36]

At the beginning of the eighteenth century, Daniel Defoe warned that evidence about the prematurity of a child, even from a midwife present at the birth, was being admitted too readily by credulous jurors, who were unaware of the double meanings in the evidence presented to them. 'Old-Bedlams [*sic*], or pretended Midwives', he pointed out, had 'got the ready rote of swearing the Child was not at its full Growth, for which they have a hidden Reserve, that is to say, the Child was not at Man's or Woman's Growth'.[37] Although rare attempts to bribe midwives appear in the court records,[38] there is little evidence to justify Defoe's concern. Most evidence presented by medical practitioners and midwives at inquests in the north of England in fact confirmed that the child had been born at full term. Moreover, inquest juries sometimes ignored medical evidence that a child had been born prematurely when they felt that the circumstances merited a verdict of murder, such as when violence had been inflicted on the child's body.[39] In addition, local suspicions of murder were sufficiently potent in some cases to override evidence that a child had been still-born. A number of single women were committed for trial by a magistrate, or even by the coroner himself, even though an inquest jury had found that their children had been born dead.[40]

It does appear, however, that evidence relating to prematurity and still-birth, whether in support of the prosecution or defence, stimulated far less debate in coroners' and trial courts than other tests for live- and still-birth. Only rarely did a witness express any doubt about the validity of conclusions based on the presence or absence of hair and nails,[41] and even when medical writers agreed that children born after at least seven months gestation could live,[42] the courts generally accepted that incomplete development of hair and nails signified a degree of prematurity sufficient to prove that the child had been born dead.

The regular, and largely unquestioned, acceptance of prematurity as a sign of still-birth in cases of suspected new-born child murder may have been due to two factors. First, an association between the growth of hair and nails, the degree of maturity, and the probability of still-birth, had been used in the courts for many years prior to the passage of the 1624 statute. The validity of the association was therefore established by precedent.[43] Second, the admission of such evidence to exempt a woman from the 1624 statute had the unqualified, and influential, approval of Hale:

> If upon the view of the child it be testified by one witness by apparent probabilities, that the child was not come to its *debitum partus tempus*, as if it have no hair or nails, or other circumstances, this I have always taken to be a proof by one witness, that the child was born dead, so as to leave it nevertheless to the jury, as upon a common law evidence, whether she were guilty of the death of it or not.[44]

Significantly, judicial acceptance of this type of evidence throughout the seventeenth and eighteenth centuries created a space in the legal process for medical testimony and facilitated the further acceptance of evidence derived from a view of the body in the last half of the eighteenth century.

The lung test

During the eighteenth century, support for the 1624 statute declined and an increasing number of trials were conducted using common law rules of evidence. In these circumstances, it became increasingly important for the prosecution to prove that a dead child had been born alive if it was to prove that the child had been murdered. Tests for live-birth therefore became critical. A number of signs indicating live-birth received attention in both coroners' and trial courts in the eighteenth century: evidence that a child had cried; the clenched (or sometimes unclenched) position of a child's hands; the passage of meconium (the distinctive first bowel movement of a new-born infant); and the warmth of the child's body.[45] But the test that attracted the most interest, and stimulated the most heated discussions, was the removal of a child's lungs to see if they floated in water, a procedure referred to as the lung test. In theory, if the lungs floated in water, it was assumed that the child had breathed and had, therefore, been born alive; if the lungs sank, it was supposed that the child had been still-born. Although used occasionally in the early decades of the eighteenth century, the lung test came to prominence in the middle years of the century precisely when the courts were returning to common law rules of evidence. As well as illustrating the extent of medical interest in this crime and the medico-legal problems faced by the courts, the lung test also exemplifies the novel concern with the body as a source of evidence.

The differences between fetal and adult lungs had been known since Galen's comments in *De Usu Partium*.[46] The potential application of such differences to distinguish between live- and still-birth was pointed out by the seventeenth-century physician William Harvey in 1653: 'And by this observation of the different complexion, you may discover whether a Mother brought her Childe alive or dead into the world; for instantly after inspiration the Lungs change colour: which colour remains, though the fetus dye immediately after.'[47] In 1668, an English translation of

Bartholin's work on anatomy included the observation that the substanceof fetal lungs was 'compact and thick; so that being cast into Water it sinks, which the lungs of grown persons will not do'.[48]

However, the sinking or swimming of the lungs in water does not appear to have been used in England until the early decades of the eighteenth century. There is no mention of the test in the first edition of William Cheselden's *The Anatomy of the Humane Body*, published in 1713, but the second edition of 1722 includes the following discussion of the test:

> The Lungs of Animals before they have been dilated with Air, are specifically heavier than Water, but upon inflation they become specifically lighter and swim in Water; which experiment may be made to discover whether a Dead Child was Still Born or not; but if the Child has Breath'd but a little, and the experiment is made long after, the Lungs may be Collaps'd, and grow heavier than Water, as I have experimented, which may lead a Man to give a wrong Judgment in a Court of Judicature; but then it will be on the Charitable side of the Question.[49]

The origins of the forensic use of the test in Cheselden's time are unclear. The courts and medical practitioners may have been influenced by the extensive employment of the test in continental courts since the end of the seventeenth century,[50] or they may have been prompted to pursue the suggestions of Harvey and Bartholin as common law trials became more frequent. By the 1730s, the test was being performed at inquests and presented in evidence at the Old Bailey: in 1737, a surgeon testified in court that 'The Coroner desired me to try the Experiment on the Lungs, which is commonly done on such Occasions'.[51] There is, however, no record of the test being used in the northern courts until the 1760s. In that decade, it was employed by nearly seventy-five per cent of medical practitioners appearing as witnesses, but thereafter it appears slightly less frequently in the Northern Circuit records.[52] But in spite of Bartholomew Parr's opinion, in 1809, that 'English courts do not admit this experiment as evidence',[53] the lung test was performed at inquests, and discussed in trial courts and in medical and legal literature, throughout the late eighteenth and nineteenth centuries. It remains a topic of debate in modern textbooks of forensic medicine.[54]

Opinions differed about the conclusions that could be drawn from the lung test. Some surgeons were convinced that swimming of the lungs in water was certain proof of live-birth. In 1765, Richard Ferrly, giving evidence at an inquest in Westminster, stated that 'the lungs of the said child were inflated, and floated entirely upon the surface of the water, which is an incontestable proof that the child was born alive'.[55] Similarly, sinking of the lungs was interpreted by some surgeons as proof that the child had died before birth. An inquisition from 1775 stated that 'Mr William Robinson Surgeon in Otley opened the Body of the said Child and took out the Lungs which immediately Sunk in Water from which Circumstance together with the Putrified appearance of Body he believes that the said Child had been dead some time before it was born'.[56]

In spite of the certainty expressed by some witnesses, the nature of the test and the validity of its conclusions were always subject to controversy. Even Cheselden's early discussion of the test was qualified by a warning about circumstances that could lead to an error of judgement in the courts. When the 1624 statute lost its force and the test became more widely used, an increasing number of medical practitioners expressed the opinion that the test should be interpreted with caution. In 1774, a correspondent to *The Gentleman's Magazine* quoted a lecturer's opinion that although the lung test 'may sometimes prove true, upon the whole it should be regarded no other ways than as a very uncertain and precarious proof of the fact in question'.[57] At an inquest in Newcastle in 1775, the surgeon and man-midwife William Smith testified that 'though he agrees with the general opinion of the Lungs swimming in Water as a sign of Air having been inflated into the Lungs and consequently that the Child was borne alive yet declares that he does not look upon this as an infallable Criterion'.[58] And in his *Elements of the Practice of Midwifery*, published in 1775, Alexander Hamilton suggested that a number of circumstances 'should make us cautious in giving judgement in such cases'.[59]

Although Giovanni Battista Morgagni (whose work was published in English in 1769) and Samuel Farr, in 1788, both discussed circumstances in which the lungs of a live-born infant might sink in water,[60] concern about a mistake of this nature was limited by the knowledge that such an error would, as Cheselden indicated, 'be on the Charitable side of the Question'. Given the reluctance to convict accused women in this period, far more effort was expended in debating 'the material question, viz. in suspicious cases, how far may we conclude that the child was born alive, and probably murdered by its mother if the lungs swim in water?'[61]

All writers on the subject accepted that if lungs swam in water, they must contain air. However, the presence of air in the lungs was not conclusive evidence that the child had respired. The lungs could have been inflated by respiration, by putrefaction, by efforts to resuscitate the child, or, according to Erasmus Darwin, a physician in Lichfield, by the child simply falling 'on its side' at delivery.[62] Provided the test was confined to normal lungs, putrefaction need not pose a problem; close inspection and dissection of the corpse would determine whether the lungs or the rest of the body had undergone any decomposition and would distinguish between inspired air and the large collections of gas found in putrefied lungs. This principle was recognised at several inquests. In 1771, in a case in which the lungs floated, the coroner's jury commented that 'as the Body is turned into a State of Putrifaction the experiment is very Uncertain and not to be depended upon'.[63] In 1795, James Shaw, a surgeon in Otley, deposed that 'Upon Opening the Body and taking out the Lungs they floated in Water, from all which Appearances (the Child being perfectly fresh without the smallest Appearance of Putrefaction) It is my opinion the said Child was born alive'.[64]

In his dissertation on drowning, published in 1746, Rowland Jackson suggested that the 'last Method of restoring still-born Children to Life is, to blow into their Mouths'.[65] In 1752, William Smellie agreed that the lungs of a still-born child could be expanded by blowing into its mouth with a cannula, having apparently successfully resuscitated a child himself by that method.[66] Although a number of eighteenth-century writers were convinced that the lungs of a still-born child would swim in water if the child's mother had attempted to resuscitate it,[67] at the turn of the nineteenth century there was some reluctance to accept that resuscitation attempts could inflate lungs sufficiently to cause them to float unless the child had already made some respiratory effort.[68] In 1800, Christopher Hodgson, a reverend magistrate, also echoed local prejudices by doubting whether a mother would ever want to resuscitate a bastard child whose birth and death had been concealed.[69] To a large extent, the question appears to have been academic in the eighteenth century. The matter only appears once in the northern court records, when, in 1764, a surgeon, finding that the lungs of Jane Stuart's child swam in water, concluded that the child had been born alive. Jane testified to the magistrate that 'so soon as she was able after the birth of the said Child which might be two or three Minutes she Blew into the Mouth of the said Child but could not perceive any signs of Life in it'.[70]

In the absence of putrefaction, and of any attempt to resuscitate the child, many surgeons inferred that a child whose lungs floated in water had been born alive. This conclusion was complicated, however, by the fact that in English law a child had not been born, and therefore could not be murdered, until its body (excluding the umbilical cord and placenta) had been completely expelled from its mother.[71] In the context of new-born child murder this had two important implications. First, it meant that a mother who killed her child in the birth (that is, before complete expulsion) could not be found guilty of murder. Second, it followed that a child that had breathed in the birth but died before complete expulsion had legally been born dead. It was, therefore, feasible that a child whose lungs were found to float in water could nevertheless have been still-born. The significance of this was not lost on medical witnesses. At the trial of Mary Wilson at the Old Bailey in 1737, a surgeon testified that:

> On trying the Experiment upon the Lungs of this Child, they floated on the Water: But I think the Certainty of this Experiment may have Objections to it. As for instance, where a Child hath stuck in the Birth a few Minutes, if it comes in the natural Way, it may respire and breath a little; which Respiration may make the Lungs specifically lighter than the Water, yet the Child may die before 'tis born.[72]

This aspect of the lung test was extensively discussed in the courts, particularly in the middle decades of the century. It led some witnesses to limit their conclusions to the opinion that a child had breathed, without affirming that this constituted live-birth. In the early years of the nineteenth century, the idea that a child strong enough to breath in the birth might die before complete expulsion was regarded by Parr as 'a fancy within the verge of possibility only, but too improbable to induce us to enlarge on it'.[73] But in the eighteenth century, most medical witnesses, when examined by the courts, acknowledged the possibility and were reluctant to conclude that a child had been born alive solely on the basis of the lung test.

William Hunter, an anatomist, surgeon, physician and man-midwife, also doubted whether even evidence of live-birth should be accepted as evidence of murder. In his paper 'On the uncertainty of the signs of murder, in the case of bastard children', published posthumously in 1784, he suggested that many new-born children 'from circumstances in their constitution, or in the nature of the labour, are but barely alive; and after breathing a minute or two, or an hour or two, die in spite of all our attention. And why may not that misfortune happen to a woman who is brought to bed by herself?'[74] Inquest juries in the north of England often returned verdicts of natural death or still-birth at the end of the eighteenth century, and the possibility of a child dying naturally in the birth or soon afterwards further weakened the force of the lung test.

In general, the courts' handling of the medical evidence, and the caution advised by medical writers, demonstrate a reluctance to accept the lung test as conclusive when the life of an accused woman was in the balance. At the trial of Mary Wilson in 1737, for example, the surgeon testified that 'without some other Circumstances to corroborate this Experiment, I should be loth to determine thereby positively. I think the Experiment (where a Person's Life is at Stake) too slight to be built upon.'[75] Although some medical witnesses did conclude that swimming of the lungs indicated live-birth, and although some writers, particularly at the end of the century, were critical of arguments put forward against the test, the test was never established as anything more than 'very inconclusive evidence'.[76] In 1755, one surgeon even refused to perform the test at an inquest because the coroner expected a 'final answer' from it:

> The coroner asked me whether I thought the child was born alive? I said it was very difficult to distinguish that. After that he said, will you try the experiment upon the lungs? And there was water brought up. I asked him what he did expect upon that? He said, for me to give a final answer, whether it was born alive or not. Then I declined it, as looking upon it not conclusive.[77]

To a large extent, the lung test's inability to provide the courts with the requisite certainty about live- and still-birth stemmed from the sentiments that had encouraged its use in the courts in the first place. Dissatisfaction with the severity of the 1624 statute and growing reluctance to convict accused women under the statute, had prompted the courts to require common law standards of evidence before convicting for murder. The same reluctance prompted medical practitioners to object to swimming of the lungs being taken as certain proof of live-birth when a capital sentence might depend upon it. Letters and articles arguing for cautious use of the lung test in the 1760s, 1770s and 1780s, were written from the same viewpoint as those arguing for cautious use, or repeal, of the 1624 statute, and for more sympathetic treatment of pregnant single women and unmarried mothers.[78] Although inspired by the prosecution's need to prove live-birth, the lung test almost invariably assisted the defence by increasing the court's doubts about live-birth, and by providing some justification for juries' reluctance to convict women on the basis of circumstantial evidence alone.

It would be a mistake, however, to ascribe the test's inability to clarify the issue of live-birth solely to leniency, either on the part of medical practitioners performing the test or on the part of the courts. Beattie's suggestion, for example, that medical evidence only 'carried weight when it supported an acquittal' and that it was then decisive even 'when its validity was clearly questionable at best', should be modified.[79] In the coroners' courts, where the life of an accused woman was not immediately at stake, where the evidential problems were probably less well appreciated,[80] and where local concern about the poor rates was prominent, many medical witnesses believed, along with the rest of the neighbourhood, that accused women had indeed murdered their children. In 1782, one medical practitioner, for example, ignored his own observations on the lungs when speculating about the possibility of a child having been born alive and murdered: 'he examined the Lungs of the said Child which from their specific Gravity and Colour led him to conclude that they had never been fully inflated and consequently that the Child had not breathed; he is nevertheless of Opinion that it might be alive about the time of Birth and thrown into the River at the same time'. The inquest jury concluded that the child had been murdered.[81]

Doubts about the test's conclusiveness were also generated by legal problems inherent in establishing guilt at common law. Inexplicit legal definitions of birth, live-birth, and still-birth, and the absence of any legal protection of a child during birth,[82] rendered even the clearest medical evidence doubtful. Medical discussions of live-birth were also inconsistent. While evidence of respiration was viewed as a sign of live-birth,[83] a child that had respired in the birth and then died before complete expulsion could nevertheless be taken to have been still-born. Although some writers and witnesses insisted that deaths in the birth should still be viewed as murder,[84] the difficulties of accurately identifying the time of birth and the time of death were not resolved by medical witnesses in the eighteenth century. Such indecision or uncertainty on the part of medical witnesses could be rapidly exposed by the court or by counsel.

Uncertainties associated with the problems of distinguishing between live- and still-birth, and with the results of the lung test, were sometimes reflected in inquest verdicts. In addition to verdicts of still-birth and murder, a number of apparently indeterminate verdicts were reached, such as 'found dead', 'killed in the birth', 'Death by Misfortune', and so on.[85] Drawing on inquests held in Westminster between 1761 and 1866, Greenwald and Greenwald have argued that the rising number of such verdicts between these dates 'made clear the jurors' fear of condemning a woman for disposing of an unwanted infant'.[86] However, the fact that some women were tried, and that one woman was found guilty and hanged, in the eighteenth century after such inquest verdicts suggests that leniency on the part of jurors was not the sole reason for inquest verdicts being framed in these ways.[87] The variety of verdicts may also reflect jurors' attempts to identify the cause of death as accurately as possible in the face of uncertainties inherent in the medical evidence presented to them in court.

Acceptance of the lung test was also hampered by the lack of a standard procedure for its performance. Different surgeons performed the test in different ways, any of which could apparently lead to errors of judgement. While some medical practitioners in the north of England immersed the whole lungs in water, sometimes with the heart attached, others immersed them separately, or divided them into lobes or smaller sections before testing them. Although the advantages and disadvantages of performing the test in different ways were discussed in various works by continental authors, some of which were available in English,[88] no attempts were made to develop a standard procedure for the test (or to pursue alternative tests on the lungs such as that introduced by Ploucquet in the 1780s)[89] during the eighteenth century, and it is not surprising that practitioners differed in their assessment of the test's validity.

In spite of doubts about the lung test's validity, both coroners and trial courts regularly employed medical witnesses to perform the test and to interpret its results. In addition, the test was acknowledged and discussed by legal writers as well as medical practitioners. In 1766, Daines Barrington, then Recorder of Bristol, referred to the test in a footnote to his comments on the 1624 statute:

> The experiment of trying whether the lungs of the dead child will float in water, is generally admitted as evidence in these trials. There is certainly ingenuity in the experiment, and arguments very properly deducible from it in a matter of less importance than the life of a criminal. It appears by the Sessions Papers, however, that surgeons have differed in opinion with regard to this point.[90]

In the 1791 edition of Gilbert's *Law of Evidence*, Capel Lofft, a barrister, discussed surgical opinion on the lung test as an example of 'Proof by Experts'.[91] Although Lofft recognised the inability of the lung test to prove that a child had been born alive, his comments highlight the extent to which the lung test, and medical testimony, had become accepted by the courts by the end of the eighteenth century.

Evidence of violence

In addition to searching for signs of prematurity and performing the lung test, medical practitioners examined the bodies of dead children for any evidence that violence had been inflicted on the child. Like the lung test, evidence of violence became particularly important as accused women were tried under common law rules of evidence, since according to legal authorities, if 'there be no concealment proved [and the 1624 statute could not be applied], yet it is left to the jury to inquire, whether she murdered it or not, by those circumstances, that occur in the case, as if it be wounded or hurt, &c'.[92]

Marks of violence were a major focus for neighbours who found and examined the body. Witnesses frequently commented on the state of the corpse and interpreted manifest evidence of violence, such as a severed limb or head, neck wounds, bruises and fractures, as proof that the child had been murdered. At an inquest in 1744, for example, Elizabeth Cooper testified that she had seen Elizabeth Conney's dead child and that 'such marks of violence appeard upon the body of the said Male Child as put it out of doubt of its being Murdered'.[93] Many midwives and male medical practitioners viewed marks of violence in the same light. In 1762, Sarah Weatherhead, midwife, testified at an inquest 'that she see no Marks of Violence whatsoever upon it save a little Bruses about its Neck which she this Witness imagined something bad'.[94] And in 1780, William Pawlett, a surgeon, deposed that 'from some Marks which he observed around the Neck of the said Child, there is too much reason to believe the said Child had been wilfully Strangled'.[95] The association between such marks on a child's body and murder prompted some accused women to insist, even before the body had been found, that they had not inflicted any violence on the child.[96]

The presence or absence of marks of violence could certainly influence a jury's verdict. In 1749, for example, an inquest jury in Emley in Yorkshire found that 'the Child Scull was broke and other suspistious marks of Violence of the inside of its Right Ear, And so the jurors on their Oath say that the Male Child was Feloniously Murdered by some person or persons as yet unknown'.[97] In some cases, marks of violence could overcome both evidence of prematurity and the problems of convicting married women. Mary Morgan, although married, was found guilty of murder at the Old Bailey in 1724 apparently because she was unable to give a satisfactory account of two stab wounds in her child's belly.[98] Conversely, the lack of evident violence was frequently noted by witnesses and appears to have contributed to acquittal on occasions. According to the report of Sarah Nicholson's trial at the Old Bailey in 1719, since there 'appeared no Marks of Violence upon the Child the Jury acquitted her'.[99]

Although evidence of violence on a child's body could result in conviction, there were several problems concerning this type of evidence that became more apparent in the last half of the eighteenth century. The first problem concerned the difficulties of relating the time of injury to the time of death. In law, neither the infliction of violence after death nor the destruction of a child in the birth were criminal. Evidence of violence could therefore be negated by the inability of a medical witness to establish to the court's satisfaction that the child had been born alive and that the injury had been received after birth. In 1771, a surgeon at the Old Bailey gave his opinion that a deep neck wound, almost severing a child's head from its body, had been a mortal wound. However, he could not say with certainty that the child had been alive after birth. When he was cross-examined by the prisoner's counsel,[100] he further admitted that if the child had been born alive and then wounded, 'there must have been ten or twenty times more blood than I perceived'. The small amount of blood present raised the possibility that the wounds had in fact been inflicted on a still-born child and, therefore, could not have caused the child's death. The woman was acquitted.[101]

The second problem that surfaced in court was the possibility that a child's injuries, in particular those to the head and neck, had been sustained accidentally during labour, especially if the labour had been difficult or if the woman had been so surprised by delivery that the child had fallen on to the floor or into the privy. The possibility of accidental injury was acknowledged by medical witnesses, particularly in cases of precipitous labour and delivery.[102] Although bruises, swellings, and skull fractures aroused suspicions of murder in the neighbourhood (or at least suspicions that the woman had been negligent in failing to call 'proper Assistance'),[103] they were increasingly attributed by medical writers and witnesses to birth trauma or to sudden delivery. Thus, in the early years of the nineteenth century, Christopher Johnson quoted the testimony of a surgeon and physician who had examined the body of a new-born child: '"Proceeding to remove the scalp, the bones of the skull were covered with clotted blood, this being removed, both parietal bones were found fractured across; these are phenomena, however, sometimes produced by the violence of a woman in labour."'[104] 'It is needless to say', Johnson commented, 'that the woman was acquitted.'[105]

The final problem relating to violence concerned the state of the child's umbilical cord or navel string, which attracted increasing comment in the Northern Circuit courts in the 1760s when medical evidence of live-birth and murder was becoming increasingly important. A torn or cut, but untied, navel string was regarded by some medical witnesses not only as a cause of death but also as evidence of violence. In 1799, at the inquest into the death of Susanna Staniforth's new-born child, John Moorhouse, a surgeon from Sheffield testified 'that he can discover no marks of violence upon the Body excepting that the Navel String has been separated by some sharp Instrument and was not afterwards tied up, the want of which wou'd in his opinion produce the death of the Child by Bleeding'.[106] According to some commentators, it was important for medical witnesses to note whether the cord had been cut or simply torn since, as Erasmus Darwin maintained, if 'it is rent or torn off, or bit off, I believe it will cease to bleed spontaneously, as in other Animals'.[107] It was also important, according to Farr, to recognise that a failure to tie the umbilical cord could only be the cause of death if 'a mortal haemorrhage' had ensued.[108] Lack of evidence for such a haemorrhage, and the possibility that the cord might break spontaneously as the child fell from the woman in labour, reduced the weight of this evidence in both coroners' and trial courts. As in the case of most other marks of violence, an untied umbilical cord was insufficient evidence of violence on the part of the mother to prove murder even though it was often interpreted as evidence of neglect and murder by the woman's neighbours.[109]

Conclusion

In his work on crime and the courts, Beattie suggested that medical evidence 'became less rather than more important in eighteenth-century infanticide cases, for in itself it could not generally prove that a mother had murdered her newborn child'.[110] Although signs of a child's maturity, the results of the lung test, and evidence of violence appeared unable to resolve certain problems facing the courts, Beattie's opinion underestimates the significance of, and the changing regard for, medical testimony during the eighteenth century. Particularly in the last half of the century, medical evidence derived from a close inspection of the body of a dead child constituted a critical component of local investigations and forensic discussions of the crime.

Locally, a woman's neighbours routinely called in medical practitioners in order to confirm their suspicions about the cause of a child's death and to persuade a suspect to confess at least to having been pregnant. Perhaps encouraged by the force of local suspicions, coroners and their juries routinely summoned medical practitioners to examine dead bodies and medical opinion clearly influenced the form and content of subsequent inquest verdicts. Although medical evidence generally failed to withstand the greater scrutiny to which it was subjected in the trial courts, its importance was nevertheless acknowledged especially in the last half of the century. In 1781, one of the judges at the Old Bailey criticised a coroner and his jury for failing to send for a surgeon to examine a child's body.[111] And the Old Bailey Sessions Papers demonstrate that in many trials in the last half of the century, the court expended considerable time and effort considering medical evidence. Medical witnesses were examined and cross-examined in great depth by court and counsel. By the end of the eighteenth century, court practice and the works of legal and medical writers had not only ensured that medical evidence and the coroner's inquest were established constituents of investigations into the suspected murders of new-born children, but also that medical testimony in these cases was regarded as the paradigm of medical involvement in the court room.[112] In this way, the ready acceptance of medical testimony in these cases may have facilitated the inclusion of medical witnesses in other trials.

Perhaps paradoxically, uncertainties in the medical evidence may well have proved useful to the courts. Throughout the eighteenth century, most women were acquitted of new-born child murder. In the north of England, there were no convictions for murder after 1760 until the law changed in 1803. Doubts about medical evidence both reflected and contributed to the courts' general reluctance to convict women accused of this crime. In addition to raising doubts about the cases presented by prosecutors and many witnesses, uncertainties in medical testimony provided courts with a legitimating rationale for acquitting defendants. The equivocal nature of medical evidence furnished judges and juries with the necessary evidential and interpretative flexibility to steer a middle course not only between the conflicting accounts of events offered by suspects and their accusers but also between the rigours of statute law and emerging humanitarian concerns. Thus, while persistent prosecutions and occasional convictions appeased local demands for some form of public retribution, frequent acquittals, legitimated by medical opinion, satisfied humanitarian concerns (and the claims of accused women themselves) that suspects were guilty of little more than concealing their pregnancies.

Notes

1 See the case of Martha Gleadhill, 1749, ASSI 45/24/1/37-8A. According to Burn, a general warrant to apprehend all persons suspected, at least in the case of robbery, was void – Richard Burn, *The Justice of the Peace, and Parish Officer*, (3rd ed., London, 1756), p. 725. However, Martha Gleadhill's case and the description of such investigations in printed broadsheets and newspapers suggest that a general search could be used to identify suspects – see *Albertus the Second: or, the Curious Justice*, (n. d.), and *The Times*, (4 June 1787), p. 3. On a number of occasions, neither local knowledge nor a search of local single women uncovered the mother's identity and the inquest verdict of murder 'by person or persons unknown' was pursued no further. As well as reflecting local ignorance of the mother's identity, these verdicts may also indicate a reluctance on occasions to accuse certain members of the community.

2 An inquest could only be held *super visum corporis*, that is upon view of a body.

3 Some of the arguments presented in this chapter first appeared in Mark Jackson, 'Suspicious infant deaths: the statute of 1624 and medical evidence at coroners' inquests', in Michael Clark and Catherine Crawford (eds.), *Legal Medicine in History*, (Cambridge, Cambridge University Press, 1994), pp. 64-86. I am grateful to Michael and Cathy for their constructive comments on early drafts of that article.

4 See, for example, J. D. J. Havard, *The Detection of Secret Homicide*, (London, Macmillan and Co. Ltd., 1960), pp. 11-36.

5 Ibid., pp. 28-32.

6 Matthew Hale, *History of the Pleas of the Crown*, ed. Sollom Emlyn, (2 vols., London, 1736), vol. II, p. 222; Edward Umfreville, *Lex Coronatoria: Or, The Office and Duty of Coroners*, (London, 1761), p. v.

7 Hale, *Pleas of the Crown*, vol. II, p. 57; Hale's opinion was repeated by Umfreville, *Lex Coronatoria*, pp. 208-14. The case referred to by Hale, and Hale's influence, are discussed by Havard, *Secret Homicide*, pp. 39-42.

8 The development of legal medicine in England, compared to that on the continent, is discussed in: Havard, *Secret Homicide*, pp. 1-10; Thomas Rogers Forbes, *Surgeons at the Bailey*, (New Haven, Yale University Press, 1985); C. Crawford, 'The emergence of English forensic medicine: medical evidence in common-law courts, 1730-1830', (D.Phil. thesis, Oxford, 1987); and Catherine Crawford, 'Legalizing medicine: early modern legal systems and the growth of medico-legal knowledge' in Clark and Crawford (eds.), *Legal Medicine in History*, pp. 89-116.

9 'An Act for the Attendance and Remuneration of Medical Witnesses at Coroners' Inquests', 6 & 7 Will.IV c.89, 1836.

10 For more detailed discussion of these issues, see Forbes, *Surgeons at the Bailey*, pp. 1-48; Crawford, 'Legalizing medicine'.

11 On the speedy responses of coroners in investigating homicides in the early nineteenth century, see R. W. England Jr., 'Investigating homicides in Northern England, 1800-1824', *Criminal Justice History*, VI (1985), 105-23. The coroner and his jury also remained active in the investigation of suicides throughout the seventeenth and eighteenth centuries – see Michael MacDonald, 'The secularisation of suicide in England 1660-1800', *Past and Present*, 111 (1986), 50-97.

12 Umfreville, *Lex Coronatoria*, pp. 177-8. According to Umfreville, an inquisition taken on a Sunday was void.

13 For early English publications on medico-legal issues, see Forbes, *Surgeons at the Bailey*, pp. 3-7.

14 Havard, *Secret Homicide*, pp. 6-7.

15 For wider perspectives on this, see L. J. Jordanova, 'Gender, generation and science: William Hunter's obstetrical atlas', in W. F. Bynum and R. Porter (eds.), *William Hunter and the Eighteenth-century Medical World*, (Cambridge, Cambridge University Press, 1985), pp. 385-412; L. J. Jordanova, *Sexual Visions: Images of Gender in Science and Medicine between the Eighteenth and Twentieth Centuries*, (Harvester Wheatsheaf, 1989).

16 Jordanova, *Sexual Visions*.

17 Between 1720 and 1759, coroners and magistrates were involved in investigating the following number of cases respectively: 1720s – 6/8; 1730s – 21/13; 1740s – 15/13; 1750s – 15/15. In some cases, both coroners and magistrates were involved. On one occasion in this period, the inquest was acknowledged to be a more appropriate form of inquiry when, in 1724, a justice of the peace in Yorkshire advised John Storrey to call a coroner to investigate the suspicious death of Elizabeth Cunny's child - Elizabeth Cunny, 1725, ASSI 45/18/2/18-20

18 Between 1760 and 1799, coroners and magistrates investigated the following number of cases respectively: 1760s – 27/13; 1770s – 22/8; 1780s – 18/2; 1790s – 17/4.

19 The statute was 25 Geo.II c.29.

20 Throughout the eighteenth century, there were far fewer coroners than magistrates in each county. There were usually one or two coroners for each of the counties of Cumberland, Northumberland, and Westmorland, and a further one or two for each county town. In Yorkshire, there were usually six or seven coroners in the West Riding, four in the North, two in the East, two for the City of York, and a few others in particular liberties. Between July 1793 and March 1794, John Wrightson, coroner in the North Riding, presided over at least thirty-six inquests. He travelled between three and forty-nine miles, at an average of twenty-five miles per inquest, for which he could be reimbursed at the rate of 9d/mile.

21 Umfreville, *Lex Coronatoria*, pp. 216-17, 218.

22 Many county coroners held office for many years. In Cumberland, for example, Thomas Dixon was one of the coroners for the county for over twenty years from 1765 until 1787. Pennock Ward was one of two coroners for the East Riding of Yorkshire from the summer of 1732 until 1756. Coroners for towns such as Newcastle-upon-Tyne, however, were elected on a yearly basis. The Northern Circuit records demonstrate that many coroners convened inquests into the deaths of new-born children on more than one occasion. For example, between August 1790 and December 1795, John Wrightson, one of the coroners for the North Riding of Yorkshire, held inquests into the deaths of at least five new-born children.

23 William Smith, surgeon and man-midwife, for example, testified at inquests and appeared in court in at least three cases: Mary Hills, 1775, ASSI 45/32/1/121; Elizabeth Bryson, 1775, ASSI 45/32/1/38; and Mary Stolker, 1778, see the indictment and recognizances in ASSI 44/93i-iii.

24 Samuel Farr, *Elements of Medical Jurisprudence*, (London, 1788). Faselius' work was originally published in 1767. Farr's book seems to have sold well in this country. According to Christopher Johnson in the preface to his translation of Mahon's work,

Farr's book was 'now out of print' - Christopher Johnson, *An Essay on the Signs of Murder in New Born Children*, tr. from the French of Dr. P. A. O. Mahon, (Lancaster, 1813), p. ix. Chapter V of Farr's work, 'Of the Murder of Infants', set out a systematic approach to the investigation of suspected murders, based on examination of both the mother and the child. In his conclusion (pp. 68-9), Farr complained 'that although so much is required, so little is generally done in these cases' and expressed the hope that his work would 'meet the attention of judges and lawyers in this particular circumstance, which so often comes before them, to the shame and scandal of humanity; and that they will be enabled to correct the errors of coroners, or ignorant surgeons, who may have been misled in the depositions they give in'.

25　Percivall Willughby, *Observations in Midwifery*, ed. H. Blenkinsop, (S. R. Publishers Ltd., Yorkshire, [1863] 1972), pp. 11-12.

26　For an inquisition acknowledging that an injury had caused a premature delivery, see Mary Bains, 1755, ASSI 44/70i.

27　Farr, *Medical Jurisprudence*, pp. 55-9.

28　Hannah Frost, 1762, ASSI 45/26/6/22-3.

29　Ruth Peacock, 1793, ASSI 45/38/1/141-2. Sometimes, two medical witnesses agreed that a child had been born at full time but disagreed as to whether it had been born alive - see Mary Gough, Old Bailey Sessions Papers (OBSP), September 1719, p. 4.

30　Deborah Greening, OBSP, February 1725, p. 1.

31　Ann Grosier, 1761, ASSI 45/26/5/31-8. See also Mary Robinson, 1791, ASSI 45/37/2/155.

32　For example: Pleasant Bateman, OBSP, February 1723, p. 3; Martha Busby, OBSP No. VI, July 1731, p. 8; Mary Robinson, OBSP No. III, February-March 1768, pp. 106-7.

33　In Sarah Warburton's case (1755, ASSI 44/70ii and ASSI 45/25/3/114-16), the inquest jury found the child to have been 'Born dead and Two Months before its Time'. It is possible that the jury in this and other cases heard medical evidence of which there is no record.

34　The inquisition and depositions are in ASSI 44/106iii.

35　The influence of medical opinion was acknowledged in the inquisitions concerning Mary Little (1755, ASSI 44/70i), and Martha Morton/Thomas Hardman (1767, ASSI 44/80).

36　Jane Todd, OBSP, July 1727, pp. 2-3.

37　Daniel Defoe, *The Generous Protector, or a Friendly Proposal to Prevent Murder and Other Enormous Abuses, By Erecting an Hospital for Foundlings and Bastard-Children*, (London, 1731), p. 9.

38　At the trial of Grace Usop otherwise Tarras, James Leger and Magdalen Leger at the Old Bailey in 1745 (OBSP No. VIII, October 1745, pp. 245-8), Eleanor Johnson testified that James Leger had told her to 'go up and tell Tarras's mother to bribe the midwife, or else Tarras will be hanged'.

39　See: Dorothy Henderson, 1789, ASSI 45/36/3/84, ASSI 44/104ii; Dorothy Smith, 1779, ASSI 45/33/3/122, ASSI 44/94i.

40　In 1739, for example, an inquest jury in Westmorland found that Sarah Leigh's child 'was dead at the time she bore it'. Four days later, a magistrate re-examined the witnesses and committed Sarah to gaol 'on Suspition of haveing Murthred a Feemale Bastard Child borne on her Body without the Assistance of any Middwife or any other Aid'. The second inquiry may have been prompted by the inquest's conclusion that Sarah had buried her child 'in order to preserve her Credit and Reputation, and to conceal the said Child from the knowledge of the Neighbourhood' – the gaol calendar and inquisition are in ASSI 44/54.

41　At Frances Palser's trial (OBSP No. VI, July 1755, p. 238), when asked if the child was at its full growth, the midwife replied: 'There is no certainty as to that; it had nails on its fingers, and hair on its head. I thought it was at full growth.' On the problems of relating maturity to the presence or absence of hair or nails, see Johnson, *Signs of Murder in New Born Children*, p. 86.

42 William Smellie, *A Treatise on the Theory and Practice of Midwifery*, (London, 1752), pp. 124-6; Farr, *Medical Jurisprudence*, pp. 25-6. In 'The Third Medicolegal Response of Giovanni Battista Morgagni: On whether an infant can be born alive and perfect seven months after conception?', Morgagni concluded that a seven month fetus could live. (English translation in *Archives of the Forensic Sciences*, 1 (1972), 384-7.) In 1737, at the Old Bailey (Mary Wilson, OBSP, April 1737, pp. 89-91), a midwife testified that she had only once seen a child survive after being born two or three months premature. In the same context, the midwife also commented on the difficulty of accurately establishing the length of pregnancy: 'I have been mistaken six Weeks in my own Reckoning my self'.

43 For an example of the recognised association between hair, nails and prematurity in 1574, see Alan Macfarlane, 'Illegitimacy and illegitimates in English history', in Peter Laslett, Karla Oosterveen and Richard M. Smith (eds.), *Bastardy and its Comparative History*, (London, Edward Arnold, 1980), p. 76.

44 Hale, *Pleas of the Crown*, vol. II, p. 289.

45 See: Ann Pabs, OBSP, March 1718, p. 3; Mary Inman, OBSP, July 1721, p. 4; Eleanor Sikes, 1737, ASSI 45/21/1/111-15; Mary Jackson, 1742, ASSI 45/22/2/73-85A; Hannah Frost, 1762, ASSI 45/26/6/22-3; the information of Isabell Allinson in the case of Ruth Peacock, 1793, ASSI 45/38/1/141-2; Willughby, *Observations in Midwifery*, p. 98; Farr, *Medical Jurisprudence*, p. 65.

46 Galen, *De Usu Partium*, tr. Margaret Tallmadge May, (2 vols., New York, 1968), vol.II, Book 15, p. 670. Galen's comments were referred to by Giovanni Battista Morgagni in his discussion of the lung test in *The Seats and Causes of Diseases*, tr. Benjamin Alexander, (3 vols., London, 1769), vol. I, p. 536.

47 William Harvey, *Anatomical Exercitations, Concerning the Generation of Living Creatures*, (London, 1653), p. 435.

48 *Bartholinus Anatomy; Made from the Precepts of his Father*, (London, 1668), p. 117.

49 William Cheselden, *The Anatomy of the Humane Body*, (London, 1722), p. 156. This passage was repeated in subsequent editions of the work in the eighteenth century. Cheselden was a surgeon and anatomist at St Thomas's Hospital in London.

50 On the use of the test on the Continent, see R. P. Brittain, 'The hydrostatic and similar tests of live birth: a historical review', *Medico-Legal Journal*, 31 (1963), 189-94.

51 Mary Wilson, OBSP No. IV, April 1737, p. 90. The test was also used in the Surrey courts in the 1730s: Mary Mills, Surrey Assize Proceedings, Lent 1739, p. 17.

52 There are, however, too few recorded uses of the test in the north of England to draw any definite conclusions. Lungs were examined or tested in water by 9 out of 13 medical practitioners in the 1760s, by 5 out of 15 in the 1770s, by 3 out of 17 in the 1780s, and by 4 out of 16 in the 1790s.

53 Bartholomew Parr, *The London Medical Dictionary*, (3 vols., London, 1809), vol. II, p. 181. According to some historians, the test was used far more often in Westminster coroners' courts in the middle of the nineteenth century than in the eighteenth century – Gary I. Greenwald and Maria White Greenwald, 'Medicolegal progress in inquests of felonious deaths: Westminster, 1761-1866', *The Journal of Legal Medicine*, 2 (1981), 193-264.

54 Alan A. Watson, *Forensic Medicine: A Handbook for Professionals*, (Aldershot, Gower, 1989), pp. 273-4.

55 Quoted in Greenwald and Greenwald, 'Medicolegal progress in inquests', 248-9.

56 From an inquisition taken before Thomas Parkinson in Yorkshire, 6 November 1775, in ASSI 44/91i.

57 *The Gentleman's Magazine*, (October 1774), 462-3.

58 Mary Hills, 1775, ASSI 45/32/1/121. Smith gave the same opinion at another inquest that year – Elizabeth Bryson, 1775, ASSI 45/32/1/38.

59 Alexander Hamilton, *Elements of the Practice of Midwifery*, (London, 1775), p. 62; see also Thomas Percival's doubts about the test in his *Medical Ethics*, (Manchester, 1803), p. 86.

60 Morgagni, *The Seats and Causes of Diseases*, pp. 536-7; Farr, *Medical Jurisprudence*, p. 59.

61 William Hunter, 'On the uncertainty of the signs of murder, in the case of bastard children', *Medical Observations and Inquiries*, 6 (1784), 284.

62 Erasmus Darwin discussed the signs that might incriminate an unmarried mother in a letter written in 1767, reproduced in *The Letters of Erasmus Darwin*, ed. Desmond King-Hele, (Cambridge, Cambridge University Press, 1981), pp. 41-2.

63 From an inquisition taken in Yorkshire, before Thomas Parkinson, in ASSI 44/86ii.

64 Ann Gibson, 1795, ASSI 45/38/3/45-6.

65 Rowland Jackson, *A Physical Dissertation on Drowning*, (London, 1746), p. 79.

66 Smellie, *Treatise on Midwifery*, p. 226; William Smellie, *A Treatise on the Theory and Practice of Midwifery*, (2 vols., 1762-4), vol. II, p. 384.

67 Hunter, 'On the uncertainty of the signs', p. 285; Morgagni, *The Seats and Causes of Diseases*, p. 538; Farr, *Medical Jurisprudence*, p. 59.

68 Parr, *Medical Dictionary*, vol. II, p. 181. Parr did, however, admit that humanity should take the possibility into consideration when life was at stake.

69 C. Hodgson, *A Letter from a Magistrate in the Country, to his Medical Friend at Peterborough*, (Peterborough, 1800), p. 13.

70 Jane Stuart, 1764, ASSI 45/27/2/142-4.

71 See Stanley B. Atkinson, 'Life, birth, and live-birth', *Law Quarterly Review*, LXVIII (1904), 134-59.

72 Mary Wilson, OBSP No. IV, April 1737, pp. 90-1.

73 Parr, *Medical Dictionary*, vol. II, p. 181.

74 Hunter, 'On the uncertainty of the signs', pp. 287-8. A similar point was made by Daines Barrington, *Observations on the Statutes, Chiefly the More Ancient*, (London, 1766), p. 425.

75 Mary Wilson, OBSP No. IV, April 1737, p. 91.

76 The words of Mr Patch, surgeon, at the trial of Mary Robinson, OBSP No.III, February-March 1768, p. 107.

77 Frances Palser, OBSP No. VI, July 1755, p. 239.

78 For further discussion of these arguments, see the next chapter.

79 J. M. Beattie, *Crime and the Courts in England 1660-1800*, (Oxford, Clarendon Press, 1986), p. 121.

80 See, for example, the illuminating comments in 'A short View of the remarkable Difference in the State of the Defence made use of at the Coroner's Inquest from that which was afterwards brought and made use of at the Old Bailey', in the British Library, 515.l.2(237).

81 Ann Goodair, 1782, ASSI 45/34/3/51-2.

82 See Atkinson, 'Life, birth, and live-birth'.

83 Farr, *Medical Jurisprudence*, pp. 52-3.

84 According to Farr (*Medical Jurisprudence*, p. 48), killing a child 'at the time of delivery, and immediately or soon after they are brought into the world' both constituted 'child murder'.

85 See the inquisitions concerning: Phebe Watkinson's child, 1778, in ASSI 44/93iii; unknown infant, 1787, ASSI 44/102i; Susan Sedgewick's child, 1745, ASSI 44/59.

86 Greenwald and Greenwald, 'Medicolegal progress in inquests', p. 263.

87 Although Isabella Hailes was found by an inquest jury to have murdered her child 'in its birth', she was later found guilty and hanged at the Northumberland assizes – Isabella Hailes, 1757, ASSI 45/26/1/69, ASSI 44/72, ASSI 42/5.

88 Morgagni, *The Seats and Causes of Diseases*, p. 537; M. Portal, 'Memoire dans lequel on demontre l'action du Poumon sur l'Aorte, pendant le temps de la Respiration; et ou l'on prove que dans l'Enfant qui vient de naitre, le Poumon droit respire avant le gauche', (1769), reviewed in *Medical and Philosophical Commentaries*, vol. I, part IV (London, 1773), 409-12.

89 Ploucquet's test, first used in Germany in the 1780s, involved determining the ratio between the weight of the lungs and that of the whole child. Because of the inflow

of blood on respiration, the body:lung ratio would be about 35:1 in a live-born child, compared with 70:1 in a still-born child. The test was discussed by Johnson, *Signs of Murder in New Born Children*, pp. 62-74.

90 Barrington, *Observations on the Statutes*, p. 424.

91 Geoffrey Gilbert, *The Law of Evidence*, enlarged by Capel Lofft, (2 vols., London, 1791), vol. I, p. 301.

92 Hale, *Pleas of the Crown*, vol. II, p. 289; William Hawkins, *A Treatise of the Pleas of the Crown*, (2 vols., London, 1716-21), vol. II, p. 438.

93 Elizabeth Conney, 1744, ASSI 45/22/4/31-33A.

94 Ann Bailey/John Sharp/Elizabeth Sharp, 1762, ASSI 45/26/6/6-7.

95 Ann Holt, 1780, ASSI 45/34/1/55-6.

96 See Hannah Dodd, 1788, ASSI 45/36/2/38-9.

97 Martha Gleadhill, 1749, ASSI 44/64.

98 Mary Morgan, OBSP, March 1724, p. 7.

99 Sarah Nicholson, OBSP, Dec. 1719, p. 2.

100 Defence counsel were in practice uncommon in these cases. The defendants usually simply spoke for themselves. On the increasing involvement of defence counsel in eighteenth-century trials, see: John H. Langbein, 'The criminal trial before the lawyers', *The University of Chicago Law Review*, 45 (1978), 263-316; J. M. Beattie, 'Scales of justice: defense counsel and the English criminal trial in the eighteenth and nineteenth centuries', *Law and History Review*, 9 (1991), 221-67.

101 Elizabeth Packins, OBSP No. IV, April 1771, pp. 200-4.

102 See the midwife's testimony in Hannah Bradford, OBSP No. IV, April 1732, p. 109. See also Ann Ridoubt (OBSP, August 1728, p. 4), on the impossibility of a child surviving a difficult labour, and Mary Radford (OBSP, January 1723, p. 6), for the court's opinion that a jaw fracture was sustained when the child fell into a chamber pot at delivery. Elizabeth Warner (OBSP No. II, January 1760, pp. 68-73), was 'Acquitted, as delivered by surprise.'

103 See the depositions of the midwife and surgeon in Elizabeth Ormston, 1763, ASSI 45/27/1/61B-D.

104 Johnson, *Signs of Murder in New Born Children*, p. 104, fn. Deventer and Roederer both suggested in the eighteenth century that skull fractures could occur spontaneously in labour; see Erwin H. Ackerknecht, 'Legal medicine in transition (16th–18th centuries)', *Ciba Symposia*, 11 (1950), 1296.

105 Johnson, *Signs of Murder in New Born Children*, p. 104, fn.

106 Susanna Staniforth, 1799, ASSI 45/40/1/118. The state of the navel string was in fact commented on once prior to the 1760s, in 1742, but interest only blossomed in the last decades of the century.

107 *The Letters of Erasmus Darwin*, pp. 41-2.

108 Farr, *Medical Jurisprudence*, p. 62.

109 In 1781, an inquisition (in ASSI 44/97i) concluded that an unknown woman 'did neglect and refuse to tie and secure ... that part of the said funis or navel string'.

110 Beattie, *Crime and the Courts*, pp. 120-1.

111 Elizabeth Harris, OBSP No. V, May 1781, p. 269.

112 When Umfreville, for example, outlined the form of a summons for the assistance of a surgeon at an inquest, the case he chose was the investigation of the death of a new-born child; *Lex Coronatoria*, p. 510. And Lofft chose surgical opinion on the lung test as his example of 'proof by experts' - Gilbert, *Law of Evidence*, vol. I, p. 301.

5

Virtuous or vicious: conflicting accounts of accused women

Introduction

On 13 March 1777, *The Cumberland Pacquet* reported the discovery of the dead body of a new-born female child 'upon the sand near Bransty'. Two women, the report continued, had subsequently been confined to gaol, 'for committing the horrid and most unnatural crime of murder upon the body of an infant'.[1] Such forceful condemnation of the act of new-born child murder was commonplace. Throughout the eighteenth century, the murders of new-born children were regularly denounced as barbaric and unnatural crimes.

While contemporary writers and witnesses agreed that new-born child murder was 'a crime of the blackest dye',[2] there was disagreement about precisely how the character and conduct of suspects should be interpreted and to what extent accused women should be held criminally responsible for their actions. In line with hostile attitudes expressed by suspects' neighbours, some writers reiterated a belief, redolent of six-teenth- and seventeenth-century discussions of the crime, that single women who concealed the births and deaths of bastard children were lewd and unnatural murderers.[3] During the eighteenth century, however, such preconceptions about the character and conduct of accused women were increasingly challenged by writers, particularly medical writers, who sought to account for suspects' behaviour and responsibility in broader terms. In many later eighteenth-century discussions of new-born child murder, accused women were no longer portrayed as cruel and barbaric murderers, but as modest and virtuous victims of circumstances beyond their control.

In this chapter, I shall examine the features and implications of these conflicting accounts of the character and conduct of accused women in detail, and explore the extent to which they influenced discussions in court and contributed to debates about the 1624 statute. In the process, I shall argue that the promotion of a novel, ostensibly more humanitarian, account of the intentions and actions of accused women by medical practitioners in this period not only contributed to and legitimated the courts' reluctance to convict but also held discrete professional and personal benefits for its advocates.

Suspects as wicked murderers

In 1701, Matthew Henry, a presbytarian minister, preached a prison sermon in the Castle of Chester 'where three Women were under Sentence of Death for murthering their Bastard Children'. According to his biographer, Henry delivered 'a very aweful and awakening Discourse, from *James*. i.15. *"Then when Lust hath conceived, it bringeth forth Sin, and Sin when it is finished bringeth forth Death"*'.[4] Henry's depiction of the path of female ruin from lust through to death was reiterated in discussions of new-born child murder throughout the eighteenth century. The notion that single women inevitably progressed from one crime to the next is evident, for example, not only in the testimony of witnesses and prosecutors, but also in some discussions of the law. In 1766, the coroner Edward Umfreville concluded his comments on new-born child murder with the opinion that: '*"Peccatum, peccati causa est & poena"*, for in this Crime of Incontinency, we observe Fornication and Adultery, then the Birth of a Bastard, which to hide the Shame, begets Murder and Murder Execution.'[5]

Underlying such accounts of the persistent transgressions of single women was an assumption that women accused of this crime were indeed guilty of murder. This assumption was frequently accompanied by strong condemnation not only of the act of murder itself but also of the character of women supposed to have murdered their bastard children. Harsh judgements of suspects are evident in a variety of contemporary sources throughout the century. In 1713, the author of comments in *The Guardian* described accused women as 'Monsters of Inhumanity' who were being inappropriately acquitted 'for want of Legal Evidence' against them.[6] In his proposal to prevent such murders by erecting an hospital for foundlings, Daniel Defoe also denounced such women as 'merciless Mothers' and 'wicked Murderers' who were escaping 'the Vengeance due to shedders of Innocent Blood'.[7]

Similarly critical epithets appear in court records and in newspaper reports of suspected murders. In 1746, an inquest jury in Cumberland found that a new-born child had been thrown into a river by 'some unnatural mother'.[8] According to the Old Bailey Sessions Papers, in 1760, Elizabeth Warner was asked by a constable sent to take her into custody 'how she could be so great a brute as to murder her child'.[9] And a report in *The Times* in 1790, in which Elizabeth Rushmere was referred to as an 'inhuman mother' for abandoning her new-born child in Norfolk, was one of many disparaging descriptions of women accused of murder that appeared in both local and national newspapers.[10]

The character and conduct of suspects were also ruthlessly scrutinised and exposed by authors of broadsheets, ballads and criminal biographies. These pamphlets, which characteristically described the lives and deeds of criminals in minute detail, were published and sold for popular entertainment and often conveyed distinct moral and political messages. The circumstances and consequences attending the concealment of pregnancy and the supposed murders of illegitimate children were extensively explored in a variety of eighteenth-century pamphlets. Although the accuracy of such publications is clearly questionable on occasions, they provide an informative source of contemporary representations of women accused of this crime.[11]

Many broadsheets reiterated the harsh assessment of suspects evident elsewhere. In 1711, for example, 'A full and true Account of a most horrid and barbarous Murder' recounted the actions of Elizabeth Smith, a servant in London, who having 'play'd the Harlot', concealed her pregnancy, and given birth in secret, was suspected of having murdered the child 'by running of a Penknife into its Heart'.[12] Similarly sensational descriptions of 'barbarous and bloody murders', and demands that the 'inhuman' perpetrators of such acts be brought more readily to justice, appeared regularly throughout the eighteenth and early nineteenth centuries.[13]

The message to be learned from such pamphlets was often made explicit. According to 'The Lamentation of Mary Butcher', single women would be wise to resist the 'treach'rous Tongue' of a 'false Man', but, if they did yield to temptation and become pregnant, they should rather confess their condition than conceal pregnancy and risk further censure.[14] Other broadsheets offered similar warnings to single women. In 'The Last Speech and Dying Words of Ellinor Sils', published in 1725, Ellinor apparently expressed the hope that her 'untimely Death may be a Warning to Young and Old, for realy the Sin of geting a Child by a deluding Man is enough but far more greater is the Murdering of it'.[15]

Melancholy accounts of the pathetic lives and deaths of women convicted of new-born child murder, and supposedly *verbatim* reports of their despondent reflections while in gaol or of their gallows confessions, were intended not only to entertain the public but also to prevent other women from suffering similar fates. Significantly, although they starkly contrasted the cruel and unnatural behaviour of supposedly brutal and inhuman women with the natural affection felt by most mothers for their children, such broadsheets contained the seeds of a novel, more humanitarian, account of suspects' behaviour. By drawing attention to the potential for all single women to be lured from the path of virtue by the seductive power of men, published ballads and broadsheets highlighted the extent to which even modest and virtuous women could find themselves suspected of murder.

Humanitarian accounts of suspects

In Remark C of *The Fable of the Bees*, first published in 1714, the physician Bernard Mandeville challenged a common notion that 'she who can destroy her Child, her own Flesh and Blood, must have a vast stock of Barbarity, and be a Savage Monster, different from other Women'. Supposed murderers, he argued, could in fact be 'Diligent, Faithful and Obliging, have abundance of Modesty, and if you will, be Religious'. If, having preserved her chastity for many years, such a woman at last surrendered 'her Honour to a Powerful Deceiver' and proved to be with child, her situation could be intolerable:

> the fear of Shame attacks her so lively, that every Thought distracts her. All the Family she lives in have a great opinion of her Virtue, and her last Mistress took her for a Saint. How will her Enemies, that envied her Character, rejoice! how will her Relations detest her! The more modest she is now, and the more violently the dread of coming to Shame hurries her away, the more Wicked and more Cruel her Resolutions will be, either against her self or what she bears.[16]

According to Mandeville, modesty and the fear of shame derived not from female nature, as was commonly supposed, but from female education: 'The Multitude will hardly believe the excessive Force of Education, and in the difference of Modesty between Men and Women ascribe that to Nature, which is altogether owing to early Instruction'.[17] In *A Modest Defence of Publick Stews*, published in 1724, Mandeville similarly stressed that the natural desires of young women were counterbalanced by 'strong Notions of Honour carefully inculcated into them from their Infancy'.[18] Apparently intended to protect the marriage interests of single women, such 'artificial Chastity' paradoxically contributed to their ruin by encouraging them to conceal and murder their children: 'the Destruction of Bastard Infants ... is almost unavoidable, especially in modest Women, who will be guilty of this Cruelty as long as Female Chastity carries that high Reputation along with it, which it really deserves'.[19] Conversely,

Mandeville argued, 'Common Whores, whom all the World knows to be such, hardly ever destroy their Children; ... not because they are less Cruel or more Virtuous, but because they have lost their Modesty to a greater degree, and the fear of Shame makes hardly any Impression upon them'.[20]

Significantly, although he acknowledged that women accused of this crime might at one stage have been modest, virtuous women, Mandeville was of the opinion that they should, in these circumstances, nevertheless be found guilty of murder. In *The Fable*, he had carefully stressed that the value of modesty depended upon its consequences: 'Because Impudence is a Vice, it does not follow that Modesty is a Virtue; it is built upon Shame, a Passion in our Nature, and may be either Good or Bad according to the Actions perform'd from that Motive.'[21] Accordingly, Mandeville dismissed any notion that suspects should be treated with pity, insisting that 'the Law is justly severe in this Particular, as rightly judging that a Mind capable of divesting itself so intirely of Humanity, is not fit to live in a civiliz'd Nation'.[22]

In practical terms, the notion that modesty might precipitate concealment and murder was instrumental in establishing the Foundling Hospital, which although firmly based on principles of utility nevertheless appealed to humanitarian convictions that poor and needy unfortunates should be treated with compassion rather than hostility.[23] Although Thomas Coram had apparently been prompted to establish the Hospital in order to save the lives of deserted infants lying in the streets of London, he was well aware that single mothers concealed and abandoned or murdered such children simply to hide their shame, or because there was no remedy for the disgrace of their condition.[24] By offering such women the opportunity to escape from their predicament, the Foundling Hospital challenged the view that these women were necessarily profligate and vicious. The Hospital's policies were based upon an assumption that the mothers of bastards were in fact virtuous victims who would respond better to being relieved of their burden than to being exposed to further shame and punishment. Similarly sympathetic attitudes towards the plight of fallen women underlay the efforts of the Magdalen Hospital, established in 1758, to rehabilitate penitent prostitutes.[25]

In the second half of the eighteenth century, such sympathetic approaches to the dilemmas faced by expectant single women became increasingly conspicuous. Significantly, while later writers adopted Mandeville's emphasis on the causal role of modesty, they rejected his belief in the criminal responsibility of accused women. In 1767, for example, Erasmus Darwin, a medical practitioner in Lichfield, received a letter requesting advice about a case of suspected new-born child murder. In his reply,

Darwin reassured the sender that his request for help needed no apology because it was in the 'Cause of Humanity', and, having discussed the pertinent medical evidence, presented his own impression of the character and behaviour of accused women:

> The Women that have committed this most unnatural Crime, are real Objects of our greatest Pity; their education has produced in them so much Modesty, or Sense of Shame, that this artificial Passion overturns the very Instincts of Nature! – what Struggles must there be in their Minds, what agonies! – and at a Time when, after the Pains of Parturition, Nature has designed them the sweet Consolation of giving Suck to a little helpless Babe, that depends upon them for its hourly Existance!
>
> Hence the Cause of this most horrid Crime is an excess of what is really a Virtue, of the Sense of Shame, or Modesty. Such is the Condition of human Nature![26]

Although he acknowledged that the crime was unnatural, Darwin insisted (contrary to Mandeville) that the excessive modesty that led women to contemplate this crime was 'really a Virtue' and that women in this situation were worthy of 'our greatest Pity' rather than condemnation. In the last half of the eighteenth century, Darwin's formulation of the character of suspects appeared more appropriate than Mandeville's. During a debate in the House of Commons in 1772, supporters of the motion to repeal the 1624 statute stressed that repeal would serve the interests of both justice and humanity and claimed that a woman's attempts to conceal the birth of her bastard child 'might proceed from the best causes, from real modesty and virtue'.[27] Two years later, a correspondent to *The Gentleman's Magazine* echoed Darwin's belief that suspects should be treated with pity by referring to them as 'poor unhappy women'.[28]

Towards the end of the century, the implications of this new approach to the character and conduct of accused women were most extensively elaborated by William Hunter in an essay 'On the uncertainty of the signs of murder, in the case of bastard children'. Like Darwin, Hunter had been approached for his advice on a particular case. His informant believed that the woman was innocent but 'understanding that the minds of the people in that part of the country were much exasperated against her, by the popular cry of *a cruel and unnatural* murder, he feared, though innocent, she might fall a victim to prejudice and blind zeal'. Hunter's views were apparently instrumental in securing the young woman's acquittal and the case provided the seeds for Hunter's essay, which was delivered as a lecture in 1783 and published posthumously the following year.[29]

Throughout the essay, Hunter rehearsed a number of the arguments previously put forward by Mandeville, Darwin and others. Women 'who are pregnant without daring to avow their situation,' he asserted, 'are commonly objects of the greatest compassion; and generally are less criminal than the world imagine'.[30] While acknowledging that in some instances new-born children were wilfully murdered by their mothers contrary to 'the most universal dictates of humanity', Hunter insisted that in most cases the woman simply 'has an unconquerable sense of shame, and pants after the preservation of character; so far she is virtuous and amiable'. Such women might be tempted to destroy themselves, if they did not know 'that such an action would infallibly lead to an inquiry, which would proclaim what they are so anxious to conceal'.[31] As the dangers of child-birth approached, therefore, women might devise schemes for concealing the birth and perhaps for murdering the child. Hunter was emphatic, however, that whatever a woman's intent during this time, she was usually surprised by delivery and in her distress was deprived of 'all judgment, and rational conduct'. When she recovered, the child, 'whether still-born or not, is completely lifeless'.[32]

Significantly, Hunter's account suggests that, unlike Mandeville, he did not believe that most accused women were guilty of murder. Indeed, he was openly concerned that innocent women had been sentenced to death as a result of 'equivocal proofs and inconclusive reasoning', and hoped that the 'facts' presented in his essay would save such 'unhappy and innocent women' from the gallows.[33] Whereas Mandeville had simply suggested a motive for the behaviour of murderers without questioning the fact that they were guilty, Hunter was intent on encouraging a more considerate, less hasty and less prejudiced assessment of suspects with the aim of removing them from public suspicion. Clearly aimed at provoking sympathy and prompting acquittal, Hunter's use of the novel explanatory account of women was explicitly humanitarian.

The development of this humanitarian approach was necessarily associated with a reappraisal of much of the evidence against accused women. In particular, it prompted discussion of both the weight to be given to concealment and the responsibility of men. In the first instance, if single women concealed their pregnancies, and the births and deaths of their children, because they were modest and virtuous (and not because they were cruel and unnatural), then concealment should no longer be regarded as 'undeniable evidence' of murder, as it had been by Lord Chief Justice Kelyng in 1664.[34] According to Hunter, for example, concealment could not 'amount to more than a ground of suspicion, and therefore should not determine a question, otherwise doubtful, between an acquittal, or an ignominious death'.[35] As Thomas Percival, a physician in

Manchester, pointed out shortly before the 1624 statute was repealed, the statutory emphasis on concealment failed to distinguish between the innocent and the guilty:

> The statute, indeed, which makes the concealment of the birth of a bastard child full proof of murder, confounds all distinctions of innocence and guilt, as such concealment, whenever practicable, would be the wish and act of all mothers, virtuous or vicious, under the same unhappy predicament.[36]

The new approach to the character of accused women therefore generated doubts about the probative value of concealment and, by undermining the presumption of the 1624 statute, contributed to the humanitarian attempts of Hunter and others to prevent convictions. The new approach also drew attention to social pressures that encouraged women to conceal and possibly murder their children. In addition to criticising both a traditional emphasis on the preservation of female chastity and the legislation that inflicted shame on unmarried mothers, writers stressed the part played by the seducers of women, that is by the fathers of dead children. The strategies employed by men to avoid maintaining bastard children were well known. On occasions, they were accused of murdering their pregnant lovers or of attempting to procure a miscarriage, or were implicated in the abduction or murder of the child itself.[37] In many cases of suspected murder, however, the reputed fathers of dead children had simply refused to honour a promise of marriage and left the parish, or had bribed a woman to filiate her child on another man.[38]

The lack of responsibility shown by men for the consequences of their sexual behaviour was strongly criticised during the eighteenth century. Public appeals advocating male chastity and increased male responsibility were part of widespread efforts to diminish vice, encourage marriage, and expand the population.[39] Similar appeals were made by writers seeking to reassess the criminality of single women accused of murder. Early in the century, Mandeville had recognised that many women later accused of murdering their children had been deceived and neglected by men.[40] The same point was made in broadsheets and ballads. Although the majority of broadsheets continued to rebuke such women for their behaviour, they also acknowledged the extent to which deceitful men were to blame at least for having initiated a tragic sequence of events:

> Ah! cruel the Swain, to betray thus the Fair
> To sin against Nature, when urg'd by Despair
> Or the Nymph, or the Swain, which the guiltier was?
> She murder'd, 'tis true, but his Vice was the Cause.[41]

Similar conclusions as to the moral, if not criminal, responsibility, of men were reached elsewhere. In 1774, members of the Conversation Society in Manchester, debating the question of whether men were more to blame for tempting than women for yielding, apparently concluded that men were indeed the offenders.[42] Significantly, Hunter made use of contemporary preoccupations with male responsibility for the consequences of seduction in his attempt to re-apportion blame for the deaths of new-born children:

> In most of these cases the father of the child is really criminal, often cruelly so; the mother is weak, credulous, and deluded. Having obtained gratification, he thinks no more of his promises; she finds herself abused, disappointed of his affection, attention, and support, and left to struggle as she can, with sickness, pains, poverty, infamy; in short, with compleat ruin for life![43]

In spite of such eloquent emphases on the responsibility of men, it is clear that neither the actions nor the criminality of men figured prominently in legal investigations. Few of the reputed fathers of dead new-born children were implicated in suspected murders in the Northern Circuit courts and none of those that were indicted were found guilty. Morover, the identity of a child's father was mentioned by suspects in only approximately thirty per cent of cases from which examinations survive.[44] Suspects may well have revealed the fathers' identities in these cases under pressure from their neighbours or from an examining coroner or magistrate who would be eager to identify potential begetters of bastards in the parish. In addition, some suspects may have attempted to generate sympathy for their condition by pointing out the manner in which they had been cruelly treated by the men concerned.

Although debates about the responsibility of men seem to have had little practical impact on the generation of suspicion and the process of prosecution, there is some evidence that attempts to recast accused women as the passive, compassionate, pitiable, and innocent victims of society's heathen principles and of men's criminally cruel behaviour were already being acknowledged in part by a wider public. Some witnesses in the north of England, for example, were appreciative of suspects' characters and acknowledged the incentive for a modest woman to conceal her condition. Having heard evidence that Sarah Leigh had never 'behav'd otherwise than very modestly', the inquest jury investigating the death of her child in 1739 concluded that Sarah had borne the child alone and buried it 'in order to preserve her Credit and Reputation'.[45] Similarly, witnesses called at the Old Bailey as character references testified to the modest and virtuous nature of suspects. In 1781, for example, Rebecca

Cowley was described by one witness as 'an honest, modest, simple girl' and by her mistress as 'a very honest, sober, well-behaved girl' who had never been seen 'in company with a man'.[46]

The practical impact of a more tolerant appraisal of suspects' characters, which gained significance from the extensive use of character evidence in eighteenth-century courts,[47] is particularly apparent at the trial of Mary Wilson at the Old Bailey in 1737. In the first instance, Mary's reputation for modest behaviour allayed suspicions that she might be pregnant. As her master, Mr Jodrell, testified: 'She having behav'd in this Manner, gave me less Reason of any Suspicion that she was with Child.' Second, when her condition became known, it prompted Mary's employer to conclude that she had been '*seduced* by this Servant left in the Family with her'. Finally, and perhaps most importantly, some witnesses did not believe that a woman who had always 'behaved soberly and virtuously, and was a diligent and industrious Servant' was likely to have murdered her child. When Mr Jodrell and his wife were asked directly (probably by the judge) as to whether from 'the Character and Behaviour of the Prisoner' they thought Mary 'would be guilty of the Murder of her Child', they agreed that 'she would not, on any Account whatever'. After speaking in her own defence, Mary Wilson was acquitted.[48]

New interpretations of the behaviour of women accused of murdering their new-born children represented a discrete change in attitudes to female sexual and criminal responsibility. A significant feature of the new approach was the development of a particular narrative form in which it could be expressed. According to Thomas Laqueur, in the eighteenth century 'a new cluster of narratives came to speak in extraordinarily detailed fashion about the pains and deaths of ordinary people in such a way as to make apparent the causal chains that might connect the actions of its readers with the suffering of its subjects'.[49] Including realistic novels, autopsies, clinical reports, and social inquiries, Laqueur refers to this new form as 'the humanitarian narrative'. The distinctive features of this narrative form were 'its reliance on detail as the sign of truth', its use of the human body as an object of scientific discourse, and its exposition of 'the lineaments of causality and of human agency'. By describing suffering, the narrative also offered 'a model for precise social action'.[50]

As Laqueur demonstrates, Hunter's essay on the signs of murder exemplifies the concerns and techniques of the new narrative form. Hunter (like Erasmus Darwin), for example, legitimated his authority in such cases by reference to detailed case histories taken from his extensive clinical experience. Moreover, Hunter not only focused on scientific evidence derived from examining the bodies of dead children and the minds and bodies of accused women, but also on eliciting sympathy for accused women in order to save them from execution. The force of his argument was increased by his use of a narrative form, linking social commentary with forensic medicine, that was prevalent elsewhere, in broadsheets, ballads, and textbooks.[51]

While the express aim of Hunter and others was to encourage a reassessment of the character of accused women, it is clear that the consequences of humanitarian narratives were complex. Laqueur suggests that such narratives were not exclusively altruistic, and that they carried rhetorical arguments distinct from their humanitarian aims. He points out, for example, that medical practitioners in the eighteenth century 'subscribed explicitly to the "party of humanity" as an element of their professional self-definition'. By drawing attention to the natural weaknesses and frailties of modest women in conjunction with a discussion of forensic aspects of these cases, medical practitioners like Hunter were, according to Laqueur, 'staking out professional turf against the laity in general, against ignorant magistrates, and against the legal profession'.[52] Significantly, by emphasising the innocent credulity of women and the contribution of men, Hunter and other writers were also reaffirming traditional views of male agency and female passivity.

These complex features of ostensibly humanitarian analyses of suspected new-born child murderers are particularly apparent in discussions about the mental state of suspects at the time of birth, in which the natural weaknesses of pregnant and parturient women occupied a central position. Although it was not until the nineteenth century that the insanity defence (and, more particularly, the importance of puerperal insanity) became a major medico-legal issue,[53] the possibility that a defendant could have been sufficiently unbalanced at the time of birth in order to mitigate her culpability for her child's death had been occasionally acknowledged in the sixteenth and seventeenth centuries.[54] In the eighteenth century, the issue was discussed extensively by a number of writers, and evidence about state of mind was presented and debated at several trials.

Throughout the century, both the general public and medical practitioners acknowledged that pregnancy and labour were associated with physical and emotional stress. Local newpapers carried stories of women performing bizarre acts while pregnant.[55] Women suspected of murdering new-born children were often unfit to be transferred to gaol immediately after the birth, and both hasty and prolonged labours were known to be mentally and physically debilitating.[56] It was also recognised that the distress of labour could render women practically incapable at the birth or precipitate a temporary phrenzy or insanity. This raised the possibility that certain women might not be entirely responsible for the deaths of their children. A small number of women accused of murder in the

Northern Circuit courts indeed explained their children's deaths in terms of their own incapacity at the birth. In 1773, for example, Margaret Hedley testified that, 'the Pains and Agony of her Labour were so sudden and great at the time, that it occasion'd her to take several fits and deprived her so farr of her senses, that she knows not nor does she now recollect whether the Child was born alive or dead, but she remembers that as soon as she came to her senses she found the said Child lying dead upon the Ground and observed that the Child had lost a quantity of blood from the Navel String'.[57] Similar claims were very occasionally supported by expert opinion. At the Old Bailey in 1728, a midwife had testified that, in the extremity of labour, Ann Ridoubt 'might not be sensible of' the fact that the navel string had broken.[58]

On occasions, witnesses also testified that a defendant had been 'out of her senses' or that she was of such limited intelligence that she was incapable of looking after herself at the birth. At the trial of Ann Terry in 1744, for example, witnesses testified not only that Ann was out of her senses after her delivery but also that she was '*non compos mentis*' and a 'very silly foolish girl, not capable of taking care of herself'.[59] Similarly, when Mary Rayner was tried for the murder of her bastard child at Chelmsford in 1751, her mistress apparently spoke 'much in her Favour, as being underwitted, as she term'd it, and call'd five other Witnesses to prove her a Fool; and it being imagined the Child might die in the Birth, she was acquitted'.[60] And in 1781, a midwife testified that when she first examined Elizabeth Harris she found her to give 'very odd answers at times, as if she was not quite right in her head'.[61]

The potential benefit of such evidence for the defence was occasionally acknowledged by counsel.[62] However, its influence on judges and juries clearly varied. In Mary Rayner's case, the evidence was apparently instrumental in securing acquittal. Evidence of insanity also apparently contributed to the acquittal of a woman at Castletown on the Isle of Man in 1774: 'In the course of the trial, the woman was found insane, and no proof appearing that the child was alive when born, she was acquitted.'[63] There were, however, a number of cases in which evidence of mental or physical incapacity was disregarded by the judge or jury. In 1723, for example, Mary Radford was found guilty in spite of evidence that she was a 'very silly Creature; that she was a half natural, and that her Mother was so before her'.[64] Ann Terry was convicted and sentenced to death in 1744, and at Chelmsford in 1754, the judge apparently directed jurors to find a woman guilty of murder after they had initially found her to be insane.[65]

There is insufficient evidence in the court records to assess the precise influence of incapacity or insanity defences on juries' verdicts. The inability of defences based upon incapacity to guarantee acquittal may simply be an expression of the variable acceptance of insanity defences by eighteenth-century courts in general.[66] It may also be the product of persistent prejudices against the bearers of bastards. In the trial at Aylesbury in 1668, in which a married woman was accused of killing her infant while in a 'temporary phrenzy', the jury was advised that 'had there been any occasion to move her to this fact, as to hide her shame, which is ordinarily the case of such as are delivered of bastard children and destroy them ... these had been evidences, that the phrenzy was counterfeit'.[67] Public recognition that single women possessed strong motives for concealing and murdering their bastard children may have continued to undermine their claims of insanity or incapacity.

It may also be significant that, apart from the occasional testimony of a midwife, evidence about mental incapacity was introduced by suspects themselves or was presented to juries by lay witnesses, by neighbours, relatives and employers of the accused. Unlike discussions of the lung test, in which medical opinion was prominent, medical testimony was not required to clarify questions of insanity or incapacity at the birth in the eighteenth century.[68] This should not be taken to imply that there was no medical framework within which claims about the insanity or incapacity of accused women could be interpreted in this period. On the contrary, it is clear that psychological issues were generally discussed and interpreted within the context of eighteenth-century physiology. Within this framework, women's proneness to irrationality and insanity was directly linked to their reproductive capacity:

> The natural processes which women undergo, of menstruation, parturition, and of preparing nutriment for the infant, together with the diseases to which they are subject at these periods, and which are frequently remote causes of insanity, may, perhaps, serve to explain their greater disposition to this malady [insanity].[69]

Significantly, it was precisely this physiological appraisal of women as naturally weak, passionate, irrational and potentially insane that William Hunter used, together with case histories, to support his ostensibly humanitarian claims about the lack of responsibility of accused women. In the first place, Hunter claimed that pregnant single women who committed suicide should not be held responsible either for their own deaths or for those of their unborn children because they acted 'under a phrenzy from despair' created by the unfortunate situation in which they found themselves. Hunter observed:

> It is only murder when it is executed with some degree of cool judgment, and wicked intention. When committed under a phrenzy from despair, can it be more offensive in the sight of God, than under a

phrenzy from a fever, or in lunacy? It should therefore, as it must raise our horror, raise our pity too.[70]

Hunter's second point was that the death of a healthy new-born child should be attributed not to the mother's intent to kill the child but to her inability to cope in the extremity of labour: 'An unhappy woman delivered by herself, distracted in her mind, and exhausted in her body, will not have strength or recollection enough to fly instantly to the relief of the child.'[71] Of course, for many writers and witnesses who remained suspicious of concealment, giving birth in secret itself constituted the essence of the crime. Such reasoning, argued Hunter, was mistaken because it failed to take account of the suspect's state of mind:

> In most of these cases we are apt to take up an early prejudice; and when we evidently see an intention of concealing the birth, conclude that there was an intention of destroying the child: and we account for every circumstance upon that supposition, saying, why else did she do so and so? and why did she not do so and so? Such questions would be fair, and draw forth solid conclusions, were the woman supposed at the time to be under the direction of a calm and unembarrassed mind; but the moment we reflect that her mind was violently agitated with a conflict of passions and terror, an irrational conduct may appear very natural.[72]

The humanitarian aims of Hunter's emphasis on the irrational and phrenzied behaviour of accused women were clear: 'The insane are not held to be responsible for their actions.'[73] As Laqueur has suggested, however, Hunter was also making epistemological claims. By highlighting the tendency for women's passionate and irrational natures to cause mental instability during pregnancy and delivery, Hunter was appropriating knowledge of women's behaviour to medical discourse and restricting the involvement of lay and legal understanding in the determination of guilt. By providing a natural explanation for an apparently unnatural crime, he was therefore 'declaring epistemological sovereignty over the bodies and minds' of suspects.[74] In doing so, however, he was reaffirming a traditional male dominance that was in part responsible for the suspects' predicament. Accused women were not only the passive victims of male seduction (a situation criticised by Hunter himself) but also pawns in the struggle for male medical superiority.

Opposition to humanitarian accounts

New assessments of the behaviour and culpability of accused women were not universally accepted. Hunter himself acknowledged the strength of popular prejudice in these cases and court records and printed broadsheets provide ample evidence that local opinion generally remained hostile. Certain central elements of the new approach, particularly lenient interpretations of concealment, were also criticised in a number of other locations. In debates on repeal of the 1624 statute in the Commons in the 1770s, opponents of repeal justified the construction of the statute on the grounds that concealment 'might justly be compared to the case of a man possessed of a poison, so fatal in its nature, so secret in its operation, that no human prudence could guard against its effects'.[75] Just as it was reasonable, they argued, for possession of such poison to be a capital crime, so it was acceptable for concealment to be made proof of murder. Although supporters of repeal suggested that this analogy was inappropriate, largely because concealment, unlike possession of a poison, did not necessarily imply a vicious motive, the argument reappeared in William Paley's *The Principles of Moral and Political Philosophy*, first published in 1785. Paley, archdeacon of Carlisle and an acknowledged opponent of criminal law reform, favourably compared the legal presumption of the 1624 statute with that created by the 1697 statute on coining, both of which were intended to facilitate conviction and increase the certainty of punishment:

> The offence of counterfeiting the coin could not be checked by all the terrors and the utmost severity of law, whilst the act of coining was necessary to be established by specific proof. The statute which made the possession of the implements of coining capital, that is, which constituted that possession complete evidence of the offender's guilt, was the first thing that gave force and efficacy to the denunciations of law upon this subject. The statute of James the First, relative to the murder of bastard children, which ordains that the concealment of the birth should be deemed incontestible proof of the charge, though a harsh law, was in like manner with the former, well calculated to put a stop to the crime.[76]

Although Thomas Percival later criticised this analogy for being 'not fully conclusive',[77] the conservative opinions of Paley and others were sufficiently influential to challenge humanitarian interpretations of concealment and to delay repeal of the 1624 statute.[78]

At the turn of the nineteenth century, the new approach was also questioned by writers who accepted that women concealed the deaths of their bastard children in order to conceal their shame, but who refused to accept that a woman's shame was the product of virtuous modesty, or that the desire to avoid shame was sufficient to absolve a suspect from her guilt. In 1803, for example, Thomas Percival (who himself disagreed with the use of concealment as evidence of murder) criticised William Hunter for having 'exalted the sense of shame into the principle of virtue'.[79] A similar point had already been made by Christopher Hodgson, a reverend magistrate from Castor who, in 1800, published an extensive refutation of Hunter's arguments. In a passage reiterating a view of fallen women expressed frequently throughout the eighteenth century, Hodgson questioned Hunter's vision of suspects as virtuous women:

> He speaks of a woman with child of a bastard as possessing a respectable virtue and a high sense of shame: it is more than probable, perhaps, that this shame and that virtue were lost a little before she became pregnant.[80]

Hodgson was not the only writer at the turn of the century to single out Hunter for particular criticism. Christopher Johnson, a surgeon from Lancaster, also challenged Hunter's exposition of the behaviour of accused women. While both Hodgson and Johnson acknowledged Hunter's professional reputation, neither was impressed by his excursion into matters of morality. 'But when Doctor William Hunter quits the theatre of the Surgeon for the Chair of the Casuist,' wrote Hodgson, 'he then occupies a situation for which I do not think him qualified.'[81] Johnson further felt that Hunter's essay had derived 'from the reputation of its author a degree of importance, to which it would not otherwise be entitled'.[82]

The two writers based their objections on different premises. While Hodgson relied heavily on biblical quotes to substantiate his arguments, Johnson, quoting Paley, used historical and cultural evidence to argue that the murder of new-born children had not only occurred in the past but also that it was still prevalent. The two authors also differed in their assessment of Hunter's clinical experience. From Hunter's implication that even a good woman could not be completely virtuous and chaste, Hodgson concluded that 'his connexion with women has been only or chiefly with those of easy virtue or doubtful morals'.[83] Johnson, on the other hand, suggested that Hunter had 'moved only in the highest circles of society ... and his delineation of the female character proves that he had only the virtuous in contemplation'.[84] Both writers, however, refused to accept Hunter's 'favourable view of human nature'.[85] Johnson insisted that a mother's behaviour, even in the circumstances described by Hunter, amounted 'to little less than murder, and ought to be punished as an aggravated act of manslaughter'.[86] In terms strongly reminiscent of the spirit of the 1624 statute and representative of a renewed emphasis on christian morality at the turn of the nineteenth century, Hodgson emphasised the dangers of Hunter's humanitarian concerns for the maintenance of moral and social order:

> To endeavour to save the life of an innocent woman is a generous, noble and manly effort. But if the foregoing Probabilities and conjectures

were to be always admitted in a court of Justice without any kind of proof whatever to support them, the effect of a very material evidence would be thereby destroyed, and every guilty woman perhaps escape with impunity... . Our duty requires that we should do justice to the Country as well as to the Individual. If the Law be capitally violated, the law then demands capital satisfaction.[87]

Not surprisingly, Hodgson also fiercely contested Hunter's opinions on insanity. In the first place, he disagreed with Hunter's opinion that despair exculpated a pregnant woman from the blame of committing suicide.

Frenzy or Lunacy proceeds, I apprehend, chiefly if not altogether from natural evil – despair generally from moral. Moral evil is engendered by moral depravity, and moral depravity proceeds from A WANT OF THE FEAR OF GOD.[88]

Second, Hodgson criticised both the logic and the practical consequences of Hunter's claim that even women who had indeed killed their children had probably done so in a state of temporary insanity.

Such a construction is certainly both charitable and fair when anything can be brought in evidence to countenance, even but a little, the real existence of such supposed distraction of mind: but thus to suppose away such wilful murders without this restriction, would be very injurious to the public welfare. We might as well, in that case, at once reckon it impossible for a woman ever to be guilty of so black a crime except in a state of madness. This would at once save the Country the trouble and expense both of Prosecution and Indictment. What it might save to the morals of the people, can only be known by experience, which often comes too late to be of any real advantage either to the Public, or the Individual.[89]

The general thrust of this argument was not new. In 1716, the serjeant-at-law William Hawkins had referred to 'a strange Notion, which has unaccountably prevailed of late, That every one who kills himself must be *Non compos* of Course; for it is said to be impossible, that a Man in his Senses should do a Thing so contrary to Nature and all Sense and Reason'.[90] Hawkin's objections to the implications of such reasoning were reiterated by Richard Burn in the 1750s: 'if this doctrine were allowable, it might be applied in excuse of many other crimes as well as this; as for instance that of a mother murdering her child, which is also against nature and reason; and this consideration, instead of being the highest aggravation of a crime, would make it no crime at all'.[91] Like Hawkins and Burn, Hodgson refused to accept the implications of this argument. He therefore rejected the inevitability of Hunter's link between the concealment and supposed murder of a bastard child on the one hand, and a woman's insanity and lack of culpability on the other.

Hodgson's final objection to Hunter's thesis concerned the question of intent. According to Hunter, most women, even if they had contemplated killing the child during pregnancy, were in fact surprised and incapacitated by the delivery to such an extent that the child died in the birth or shortly afterwards. For Hodgson, this was not sufficient to remove responsibility for the death.

> That the child in this case died by accident, is but a poor extenuation of the Mother's guilt; for its death was, by the supposition, already predetermined if it had unfortunately survived its mother's recovery from the effects of her fright and confusion. The poor unhappy Innocent was doomed to die; its life was determined to be made a sacrifice to the preservation of its mother's character and reputation in the world - a character wilfully intended to have been stained with infant blood, and preserved by secret murder. The horrid intention contracts the guilt, and the inhuman act confirms it.[92]

Hodgson's argument, based on the biblical text of Matthew 5.28 and rooted in the evangelical morality prevalent at the turn of the nineteenth century, was incompatible with legal theory. In 1685, in his guide for magistrates, for example, Bond had advised that, 'Intent to Commit Murder or Felony is not punishable, unless the Act be done'.[93] Nearly a century later, the barrister and statesman William Eden similarly argued in his *Principles of Penal Law* that 'mere speculative wantonness of a licentious imagination, however dangerous, or even sanguinary in its object, can in no case amount to a crime'.[94] Consequently, while evidence of incapacity at the birth may not always have ensured acquittal, Hunter's account of the irrational conduct of women during pregnancy and child-birth remained central to the courts' efforts to determine both the intent and the precise actions of accused women.

Conclusion

The fate of women accused of murdering their new-born children constituted a popular literary theme throughout the eighteenth century.[95] Authors of broadsheets and ballads recounted the lives, characters and actions of defendants in intimate detail. Local and national newspapers reported the discovery of bodies, the arrest of suspects and the outcome of inquests and trials. Printed trial reports narrated the presentation and discussion of evidence and the nature of the verdicts reached by juries. Medical and legal authors in particular debated the character and conduct of suspects and the vagaries of the evidence on which they were to be tried.

Some years ago, Hoffer and Hull suggested that public attitudes to women accused of new-born child murder softened substantially throughout the eighteenth century.[96] Evidence from contemporary literature and from court records suggests that eighteenth-century attitudes to accused women were more heterogeneous, and often more hostile, than Hoffer and Hull's analysis suggests. Many writers (as well as many witnesses) continued to condemn women who concealed the births and deaths of their children as lewd, unnatural, and inhuman murderers. Indeed, at the turn of the nineteenth century, a number of writers reiterated many of the harsh presumptions about accused women that had been embodied in the 1624 statute.

However, it is clear that more sympathetic assessments of the character and conduct of accused women did become more prevalent in the eighteenth century. Medical writers in particular attempted to characterise suspects not as wilful murderers but as virtuous, compassionate, and above all innocent, victims of their circumstances. Although such endeavours to reassess maternal responsibility for infant deaths failed to dispel local suspicions of murder, novel humanitarian constructions of the behaviour of defendants clearly had a number of significant consequences both in and out of court. First, it is possible that the opinions of Hunter and others contributed directly to acquittal in some cases.[97] Second, new approaches to suspects, together with doubts about medical evidence (to which novel interpretations of character and conduct contributed), encouraged the courts to temper the severity of the 1624 statute and legitimated their reluctance to convict. This aspect of the courts' behaviour became a central issue in parliamentary debates about repeal of the 1624 statute in the last decades of the century. More broadly, medical articulations of the new approach, in particular debates about temporary insanity, facilitated the appearance of 'puerperal insanity' as a new disease category and contributed to the emergence of new-born child murder as predominantly a medical issue in the nineteenth century.[98]

Notes

1 *The Cumberland Pacquet*, (13 March 1777), p. 3.

2 The phrase used in *The Times*, (3 August 1786), p. 3.

3 See, for example: Daniel Defoe, *The Generous Protector, or a Friendly Proposal to Prevent the Murder and Other Enormous Abuses, By Erecting an Hospital for Foundlings and Bastard-Children*, (London, 1731), p. 9; *The Guardian*, 105 (11 July 1713). On sixteenth- and seventeenth-century attitudes, it is important to note that the 1624 statute itself, in line with other bastardy legislation of the period, was directed at the 'lewd Mothers' of bastards. See also William Gouge's reference to the 'lewd and unnaturall women' who abandoned their children in *Of Domesticall Duties*, (London, 1622), p. 507.

4 W. Tong, *An Account of the Life and Death of Mr. Matthew Henry*, (London, 1716), p. 177.

5 Edward Umfreville, *Lex Coronatoria: Or, The Office and Duty of Coroners*, (London, 1761), pp. 46-7.

6 *The Guardian*, 105 (11 July 1713).

7 Defoe, *The Generous Protector*, p. 9.

8 The inquisition is in ASSI 44/60. The mother was later identified by a jury of women as Elizabeth Pruddam, 1746, ASSI 45/23/2/81-3.

9 Elizabeth Warner, Old Bailey Sessions Papers (OBSP), No. II, January 1760, p. 72.

10 *The Times*, (2 February 1790), p. 3.

11 For a detailed discussion of criminal biographies in this period, see Lincoln B. Faller, *Turned to Account: The Forms and Functions of Criminal Biography in Late Seventeenth- and Early Eighteenth-century England*, (Cambridge, Cambridge University Press, 1987).

12 'A full and True Account of a most horrid and barbarous Murder committed Yesterday, April 24th in St James's-House by Eliz. Smith, upon the Body of her own Male Child', (London, 1711).

13 The numerous examples in the British Library include: 'The Lamentation of Mary Butcher, Now confined in WORCESTER-CITY-GAOL, On Suspicion of murdering her Male Bastard Child, in April last', (n.d.); 'God's Judgment against False Witnesses. To which is added. An Account of the Execution of Mary Shrewsbury, for the Murder of her Bastard Child', (n.d.); 'The Apprehending and Taking of Phoebe Cluer, On Suspicion of the Murder of her Bastard Child', (n.d.); 'A Trophy of Christ's Victory; Or, The great Mercy of God in Christ, Examplified, in the speedy and seasonable Repentance of Elizabeth Blackie, who was Executed for Child Murder, at Jedbergh, 27th of May, 1718', (Dumfries, 1719).

14 'The Lamentation of Mary Butcher'.

15 'The Last Speech and Dying Words of Ellinor Sils, who is to be Burn't alive this present Wednesday being the 19th, of this Instant May 1725. For Murdering her own Child', (n. d.).

16 Bernard Mandeville, *The Fable of the Bees; or, Private Vices, Publick Benefits*, (2 vols., Oxford, [6th ed., 1732] 1924), vol. I, Remark C, p. 75.

17 Ibid., pp. 71-2.

18 Bernard Mandeville, *A Modest Defence of Publick Stews: or, an Essay upon Whoring, As it is Now Practis'd in these Kingdoms*, (Augustan Reprint Society, No. 162, [1724] 1973), p. 42.

19 Ibid., p. 26.

20 Mandeville, *The Fable of the Bees*, pp. 75-6. Cases in which prostitutes did apparently murder or abandon their new-born children were not in fact unknown; see, T. R. Forbes, 'Crowner's Quest', *Transactions of the American Philosophical Society*, 68 (1978), 41.

21 Mandeville, *The Fable of the Bees*, p. 74.

22 Mandeville, *A Modest Defence*, p. 4.

23 For a discussion of factors influencing the founding of, and support for, the Hospital, see Donna Andrew, 'London charity in the eighteenth century', (PhD thesis, Toronto, 1977).

24 John Brownlow, *The History and Objects of the Foundling Hospital*, (4th ed., London, 1881), p. 3; R. H. Nichols and F. A. Wray, *The History of the Foundling Hospital*, (London, Oxford University Press, 1935), p. 14. See also Coram's petition to the King, reproduced in Nichols and Wray, *Foundling Hospital*, pp. 16-17.

25 W. A. Speck, 'The harlot's progress in eighteenth-century England', *British Journal for Eighteenth-Century Studies*, 3 (1980), 127-39; Andrew, 'London charity', pp. 139-48.

26 *The Letters of Erasmus Darwin*, ed. Desmond King-Hele, (Cambridge, Cambridge University Press, 1981), p. 42.

27 *The Parliamentary History of England*, (1771-4), XVII, col. 453.

28 *The Gentleman's Magazine*, (October 1774), 463.

29 William Hunter, 'On the uncertainty of the signs of murder, in the case of bastard children', *Medical Observations and Inquiries*, 6 (1784), 266-90. According to

Christopher Johnson, Hunter's essay reposed 'in comparative oblivion for almost thirty years' until it 'recently re-appeared before the public in various forms': in a . republication of Volume 6 of *Medical Observations and Inquiries*; as a paper reprinted in Lancaster 'for gratuitous distribution'; and 'advertised for separate sale in London'. See Christopher Johnson, *An Essay on the Signs of Murder in New Born Children*, translated from the French of Dr. P. A. O. Mahon, (Lancaster, 1813), p. xii.

30 Hunter, 'On the uncertainty of the signs', p. 269.

31 Ibid., pp. 272, 273.

32 Ibid., pp. 273-4.

33 Ibid., pp. 280, 290.

34 Sir John Kelyng, *A report of divers cases in Pleas of the Crown, adjudged and determined in the reign of . . . Charles II*, (London, 1708), pp. 32, 33.

35 Hunter, 'On the uncertainty of the signs', p. 285.

36 Thomas Percival, *Medical Ethics*, (Manchester, 1803), pp. 84-5. See also Daines Barrington, *Observations on the Statutes, Chiefly the More Ancient*, (2nd ed., London, 1766), p. 425.

37 In a notorious case in Yorkshire in 1775, John Bolton was committed to gaol for the murder of his apprentice Elizabeth Rainbow, 17 years old and pregnant by him. For an account of the trial, see *The Trials at Large of the Felons in the Castle of York, 1775-8*, in York City Reference Library. In 1788, Jonas Broadbent, a weaver in Yorkshire, was found guilty of assaulting Sarah Cowling with an intent to procure a miscarriage – the gaol calendar entry and indictment are in ASSI 44/103iv. For men implicated in a child's abduction and death, see Joseph Barnfather and Edward Robinson, 1760, ASSI 45/26/4/5E-J, ASSI 44/75.

38 In 1766, for example, Ann Usher claimed that she 'was often entreated by the said [John] White to filiate the Child on Joseph Sharp'. John Hutchinson also gave evidence that White had asked him, at the coroner's inquest, to tell Ann Usher 'that if she did but keep her own Council, they coud not all hurt her' – see Ann Usher (1766, ASSI 45/28/2/146-8) and John White (1767, ASSI 45/28/3/183-7). A man's failure to honour a promise of marriage apparently led some women to commit suicide – see, for example, *The York Courant*, (17 April 1733), p. 4.

39 Andrew, 'London charity', p. 74. Such emphasis on men was not new. In the early seventeenth century, certain Puritan writers had demanded a single standard of sexual morality – see Ivy Pinchbeck and Margaret Hewitt, *Children in English Society*, (2 vols., London, Routledge and Kegan Paul, 1969-73), vol. I, p. 205.

40 Mandeville, *The Fable of the Bees*, p. 75.

41 From *Albertus the Second: or, the Curious Justice*, (n.d.).

42 Reported in *The Cumberland Pacquet*, (22 December 1774), p. 3.

43 Hunter, 'On the uncertainty of the signs', pp. 269-70.

44 Of the seventy-four women for whom examinations survive, twenty-three identified the father on formal examination; a further five apparently informed their neighbours. In twenty cases, the suspects also revealed the father's occupation: six men were, or had been, fellow servants; six were described as the woman's master or his son; the occupations of the remainder were given as clothier, mariner, husbandman, shoemaker, soldier, collier, schoolmaster, and staymaker.

45 Sarah Leigh, 1739, ASSI 45/21/3/94-97A, ASSI 44/54.

46 Rebecca Cowley, OBSP No. V, May 1781, pp. 306-8.

47 On the importance of character evidence, see: John H. Langbein, 'The criminal trial before the lawyers', *The University of Chicago Law Review*, 45 (1978), 263-316; and Peter King, 'Decision-makers and decision-making in the English criminal law, 1750-1800', *The Historical Journal*, 27 (1984), 25-58.

48 Mary Wilson, OBSP No. IV, April 1737, pp. 89-91 (my emphasis).

49 Thomas Laqueur, 'Bodies, details, and the humanitarian narrative', in Lynn Hunt (ed.), *The New Cultural History*, (Berkeley, University of California Press, 1989), pp. 176-7.

50 Ibid., pp. 177-8.

51 As Laqueur suggests (ibid., p. 187), the 'narrative form for "humanitarian" sympathy and action' was widely disseminated.

52 Ibid., pp. 184, 187-8. Significantly, medical practitioners were indeed prominent in promoting the new approach to accused women, in challenging local prejudices, and in combating the severity of the law.

53 On the development of the insanity defence in infanticide cases in the nineteenth century, see the discussions in: N. Walker, *Crime and Insanity in England :Vol. I The Historical Perspective*, (Edinburgh, Edinburgh University Press, 1968); Roger Smith, *Trial by Medicine: Insanity and Responsibility in Victorian Trials*, (Edinburgh, Edinburgh University Press, 1981); Shelley Day, 'Puerperal insanity: the historical sociology of a disease', (PhD thesis, Cambridge, 1985); Joel Peter Eigen, *Witnessing Insanity: Madness and Mad-Doctors in the English Court*, (New Haven, Yale University Press, 1995).

54 Day, 'Puerperal insanity', pp. 80-2, 111.

55 See, for example, the account of 'a very melancholy Affair' in which a pregnant woman 'rip'd her Womb open, which done, she took out the Child, and cut it in Pieces' – *The York Courant*, (8 June 1742).

56 In 1739, the churchwardens ordered John Thackery, beadle of Isleworth, to find Elizabeth Harrard a bed 'because she was not in a fit Condition to be sent to Newgate' after her delivery – OBSP No. VII, September 1739, p. 135.

57 Margaret Hedley, 1773, ASSI 45/31/1/119-24.

58 Ann Ridoubt, OBSP, August 1728, p. 4.

59 Ann Terry, OBSP No. V, May 1744, p. 116.

60 The case was reported in *The York Courant*, (13 August 1751), p. 1.

61 Elizabeth Harris, OBSP No. V, May 1781, p. 268.

62 At the trial of Elizabeth Sturt in Kingston-upon-Thames in 1751, the defence counsel expressly cross-examined witnesses about the possibility that Elizabeth was 'weak in her understanding', or that she could have been out of her senses during labour - Surrey Assize Proceedings, August 1751, p. 25.

63 *The Cumberland Pacquet*, (22 December 1774), p. 3.

64 Mary Radford, OBSP, January 1723, p. 6.

65 The Chelmsford case is quoted by Douglas Hay in 'Property, authority and the criminal law', in Douglas Hay, Peter Linebaugh, John G. Rule, E. P. Thompson, Cal Winslow, *Albion's Fatal Tree: Crime and Society in Eighteenth-Century England*, (Allen Lane, 1975), p. 29.

66 For a discussion of this, see: Eigen, *Witnessing Insanity*, pp. 12-30; Joel Peter Eigen, 'Intentionality and insanity: what the eighteenth-century juror heard', in W. F. Bynum, Roy Porter and Michael Shepherd (eds.), *The Anatomy of Madness*, vol. II, (London, Tavistock, 1985), pp. 34-51.

67 Matthew Hale, *History of the Pleas of the Crown*, ed. Sollom Emlyn, (2 vols., London, 1736), vol. I, p. 36.

68 A similar pattern is evident in other trials – Eigen, *Witnessing Insanity*, pp. 24-5; ibid., 'Intentionality and insanity', p. 42.

69 John Haslam, *Observations on Insanity*, (London, 1798), p. 108. Haslam also discussed the case of a woman, admitted to Bethlem in 1795, who had destroyed her infant during an attack of insanity following delivery (ibid., pp. 51-3). See also William Battie's opinion that 'Madness frequently succeeds or accompanies Fever, Epilepsy, Child-birth and the like muscular disorders', in *A Treatise on Madness*, (London, 1758), pp. 52-3.

70 Hunter, 'On the uncertainty of the signs', p. 271. Similar sentiments had been expressed in discussions of suicide since the late seventeenth century. In 1672, William Ramesey suggested that those who killed themselves 'should rather be objects of our greatest pity than condemnation', on the grounds that many of them were mentally disturbed – quoted in Michael MacDonald, 'The secularization of suicide in England 1660-1800', *Past and Present*, 111 (1986), 81.

71 Hunter, 'On the uncertainty of the signs', pp. 288-9.

72 Ibid., p. 278.

73 Ibid., p. 268.

74 Laqueur, 'The humanitarian narrative', p. 188.

75 *The Parliamentary History of England*, (1771-4), XVII, col. 452.

76 William Paley, *The Principles of Moral and Political Philosophy*, (2nd ed., London, 1786), pp. 549-50. The statute making possession of the implements of coining high treason was 'An Act for the better preventing the counterfeiting the current Coin of this Kingdom', 8 & 9 W.III c.26, 1697.

77 Percival, *Medical Ethics*, p. 81.

78 See the discussion of this below, Chapter 7.

79 Percival, *Medical Ethics*, p. 84.

80 C. Hodgson, *A Letter from a Magistrate in the Country, to his Medical Friend at Peterborough*, (Peterborough, 1800), p. 2.

81 Hodgson, *A Letter from a Magistrate*, p. 1.

82 Johnson, *An Essay on the Signs of Murder*, p. xii. This work, translated from the French of Mahon, contained an introductory discussion of the subject by Johnson himself.

83 Hodgson, *A Letter from a Magistrate*, p. 2.

84 Johnson, *An Essay on the Signs of Murder*, p. xii.

85 Ibid., p. xii.

86 Ibid., p. xix.

87 Hodgson, *A Letter from a Magistrate*, p. 13.

88 Hodgson, *A Letter from a Magistrate*, p. 4. Hodgson also admonished Hunter for not using his privileged position with his female patients to counsel them against suicide.

89 Ibid., p. 7.

90 William Hawkins, *A Treatise of the Pleas of the Crown*, (2 vols., London, 1716-21), vol. I, p. 67. Similar comments on the use of this argument to support *non compos mentis* verdicts in suicide cases were common in the early eighteenth century – see MacDonald, 'The secularization of suicide', p. 76.

91 Richard Burn, *The Justice of the Peace, and Parish Officer*, (3rd ed., London, 1756), p. 382.

92 Hodgson, *A Letter from a Magistrate*, pp. 9-10.

93 J. Bond, *A Complete Guide for Justices of Peace*, (London, 1685), p. 116.

94 William Eden, *Principles of Penal Law*, (2nd ed., London, 1771), p. 84.

95 Preoccupations with unmarried motherhood and the fate of illegitimate children were not unique to England in this period. The same theme preoccupied German writers, particularly in the Storm and Stress period. See: Oscar Helmuth Werner, *The Unmarried Mother in German Literature*, (New York, AMS Press Inc., [1917] 1966); Johanna Geyer-Kordesch, 'Infanticide and medico-legal ethics in eighteenth-century Prussia', in Andrew Wear, Johanna Geyer-Kordesch and Roger French (eds.), *Doctors and Ethics: The Earlier Historical Setting of Professional Ethics*, (Amsterdam, Rodopi, 1993), pp. 181-202; Mary Nagle Wessling, 'Infanticide trials and forensic medicine: Württembergs, 1757-93', in Michael Clark and Catherine Crawford (eds.), *Legal Medicine in History*, (Cambridge, Cambridge University Press, 1994), pp. 117-44.

96 Peter C. Hoffer and N. E. H. Hull, *Murdering Mothers: Infanticide in England and New England 1558-1803*, (New York, New York University Press, 1981), pp. 65-91.

97 According to Hunter himself, his comments on the original case referred to him led to the woman concerned being acquitted – Hunter, 'On the uncertainty of the signs', p. 267. In the nineteenth century, some writers apparently attributed the courts' leniency to Hunter's work – see the comment in Day, 'Puerperal insanity', p. 87. It is noticeable that convictions were extremely rare in the last half of the eighteenth century, when humanitarian accounts gained prominence.

98 See: Smith, *Trial by Medicine*, pp. 143-60; Day, 'Puerperal insanity'.

6

Evidence in court:
the verdicts of inquest,
grand and trial juries

Introduction

Conflicting accounts of pregnancy, birth and death and competing interpretations of the character and conduct of women accused of murdering
their new-born children gained practical significance in the courtroom.
Contradictory interpretations of the evidence presented by suspects, witnesses and prosecutors were thrown into sharp relief not only by the
adversarial nature of legal proceedings but also by an awareness of the
severe penalties that could be inflicted on accused women. Coroners' and
grand juries possessed the power to inflict on women the ignominy of a
public trial. Trial juries, frequently referred to as juries of 'life and death',
possessed the power to send women to the gallows or to ensure their
transportation.

There are two outstanding features of the verdicts returned by these
juries in the eighteenth century. First, the further a case moved from its
local context, the more likely was the jury to find in favour of the accused.
Thus, while most inquest juries (that is, local juries drawn from the
immediate neighbourhood) returned verdicts of 'wilful murder' against
the child's mother, grand juries (hearing cases in the assize courts) in the
north of England discharged nearly one quarter of the women presented
to them during the course of the century.[1] More critically, trial juries in
the north of England acquitted over ninety-five per cent of women sent to
trial. Although the conviction rate may have been slightly higher in some
jurisdictions,[2] the infrequency of convictions was clearly not confined to
the Northern Circuit.[3] In general, evidence that had generated local
suspicions and initiated prosecution was insufficient to secure convictions
in the assize courts.

The second general feature of jury verdicts in this period is that
during the course of the eighteenth century, juries became increasingly

reluctant to find against the defendant. Not only were coroners' juries increasingly prepared to return verdicts of natural death or still-birth in the last few decades of the century, but the percentage of accused women discharged by grand juries in the north of England increased steadily throughout the century.[4] More strikingly, it became increasingly rare for women to be convicted by a trial jury and hanged in the last half of the century. In the north of England, for example, there were no convictions for new-born child murder in the eighteenth century after 1757.[5]

Both of these features of jury verdicts can be understood in part as a product of the courts' general tendency to mitigate the severity of statute law in this period. During the course of the century, courts responded to the extension of capital punishment to a wide variety of newly-created or previously non-capital crimes by adopting increasingly merciful interpretations of the law. As Douglas Hay suggested in an influential essay on the criminal law in this period, 'most penal statutes were interpreted by judges in an extremely narrow and formalistic fashion', generally in favour of the defendant.[6] In the absence of comprehensive criminal law reform, such strategies provided courts with opportunities to limit the severity of the penal code at their discretion.

However, evidence that both grand and trial juries were more likely to find in favour of the defendant in cases of new-born child murder than in other murder cases suggests that factors peculiar to this particular crime also contributed to high rates of discharge and acquittal.[7] In part, the courts' increasing reluctance to convict can be explained in terms of doubts about the certainty of medical evidence and the emergence of more sympathetic constructions of the character of accused women. The manner in which these factors operated in court was, however, clearly complex, influenced not only by debates about these particular issues but also by a wide variety of factors that could determine the extent to which such debates were acknowledged by judges and juries. Thus, the admission and weight of certain evidences was determined by rules governing, or at least used to legitimate, the actions and decisions of the various juries, and by changing laws of evidence and standards of proof in this period.

In this chapter, I shall explore the extent to which jury composition and function, judicial authority, rules governing the admission of evidence, and the standards of proof adopted by the courts influenced jury verdicts. In the process, I shall argue that the influence of these factors in these particular cases was linked to the manner in which they imposed specific restrictions on the application of the 1624 statute.

Inquest juries

An inquest jury was the first jury to consider the evidence against an accused woman. As I suggested in Chapter 4, during the course of the eighteenth century, the inquest became the major form of pre-trial inquiry in these cases, replacing the magistrate's hearing. Comprising at least twelve 'good and lawful' men summoned from '4, 5, or 6 of the next adjacent Towns' usually within one or two days of the discovery of a body, coroners' juries were closer than other juries to the circumstances surrounding alleged murders, in terms of both time and place.[8] Such proximity to events was traditionally believed to facilitate inquiry, since, as Umfreville pointed out in his extensive work on the coroner's office in 1761, 'the Neighbourhood is supposed to be the best Judge of the Fact to be inquired into'.[9] However, as the judge and jurist William Blackstone indicated in his *Commentaries on the Laws of England* published in the 1760s, there could be problems associated with local juries:

> A jury coming from the neighbourhood is in some respects a great advantage; but is often liable to strong objections: especially in small jurisdictions, as in cities which are counties of themselves, and such where assises are but seldom holden; or where the question in dispute has an extensive local tendency; where a cry has been raised and the passions of the multitude been inflamed; or where one of the parties is popular, and the other a stranger or obnoxious ... In all these cases, to summon a jury, labouring under local prejudices, is laying a snare for their consciences.[10]

This problem of jury partiality was particularly acute at the inquest. Although there was no official property qualification governing inclusion in a coroner's jury, it is likely that most jurors were householders selected from men of middling status in the parish.[11] In spite of Umfreville's direction that interested parties should not appear on a coroner's jury, it is clear that as contributors to the parish rates, and as members of the neighbourhood already prejudiced against women accused of this crime, jurors in these cases were unlikely to be impartial to the outcome of the inquiry.[12] Indeed, in rare cases, there is evidence that the dead child's father himself served on the jury and attempted to manipulate proceedings.[13]

Statutory rules governing the admission of evidence may also have influenced inquest verdicts. According to the Marian statute of 1554, coroners were to record 'the Effect of the Evidence given to the Jury before him, being material'.[14] This was interpreted by legal writers as a direction for inquest juries to hear evidence both for and against accused women, largely on the grounds that the inquest was not for accusation but 'rather for information of the truth of the fact as near as the jury can assert it'.[15] However, although the inclusion of evidence for the defence may have raised doubts about the case against accused women, the force of such doubts may have been limited not only by the strength of local suspicions but also by the fact that inquest jurors did not need to be unanimous in their verdict. If an inquest jury failed to agree on a verdict, the coroner was to 'collect the Numbers and declare the Majority, into which the Minority sinks, and the Verdict or Finding (which is to be given by the Foreman) is from Necessity; as "*ex dicto majoris partis juratorum*" taken and considered as the Verdict of all'.[16] This procedure, which would conceal doubts about ambiguous evidence, might explain why medical evidence supporting a suspect was sometimes disregarded in favour of a guilty verdict.[17]

In this context, the coroner himself may also have influenced inquest verdicts, or at least determined the action that was to be taken against an accused woman. In some cases, jurors were clearly informed of the terms of the 1624 statute by the coroner or his clerk.[18] In others, the decision to commit a woman to trial may have been taken by the coroner rather than by the jury. In 1765, for example, an inquest jury in Yorkshire failed to agree on whether Ann Peirson's two new-born children had been still-born or not, even though a surgeon had testified to probable still-birth. The coroner, George Petch, nevertheless bound several witnesses to give evidence, and committal proceedings were later completed by a magistrate.[19]

There is some limited evidence that coroners' juries in the north of England became increasingly reluctant to find accused women guilty of murder during the last decades of the eighteenth century. Inquest verdicts of natural or accidental death, or of still-birth, certainly appear more regularly in the court records after 1770.[20] The increasing prevalence of such verdicts might suggest that, as in the case of inquest juries investigating possible suicides, coroners and their juries played a central role in transforming public attitudes to certain types of behaviour or, at least, in translating changing attitudes into official verdicts.[21] However, it would be a mistake to read too much into such verdicts in these cases without further study. The scarcity of coroners' records from the first half of the century and their inconsistency in the last half of the century make it difficult to draw conclusions about the pattern of verdicts during this period without more extensive information from a wide variety of coroners' jurisdictions. Moreover, since the majority of surviving inquisitions in the Northern Circuit records are from cases that subsequently reached the trial courts because the inquest jury had found a verdict of wilful murder against a particular woman, it is also clear that for most of the eighteenth century, local opinion in these cases continued to be hostile rather than sympathetic.

Grand juries

Grand juries were alternative juries of presentment to inquest juries.[22] Comprising at least twelve but not more than twenty-three men of the county, the grand jury was regarded as an essential part of the system protecting people from frivolous accusations. As freeholders and rate-payers, as members of local governing elites, and, in some cases, as justices of the peace, grand jurors probably shared many of the interests of inquest jurors. Significantly, many grand jurors were likely to have been involved locally in managing the problems associated with the behaviour of women accused of bearing, concealing and murdering bastard children. However, their distance from the alleged events (in terms of both the time between the initial accusation and the assize session and the lack of personal involvement in the cases before them) may have encouraged grand juries to find in favour of the accused more often than coroners' juries.

After receiving instructions from one of the circuit judges at assizes, grand jurors withdrew to hear the indictments drawn up against the prisoners. If the jurors believed that there was sufficient evidence for the prisoner to be tried, the bill of indictment would be marked 'true bill' (or *billa vera* prior to 1732) and forwarded to the trial court. However, if the evidence was regarded as insufficient, the bill would be marked 'not found' (previously *ignoramus*) and the prisoner would be 'discharged by proclamation'. Grand juries therefore served to filter the accusations preferred by a neighbourhood before they were heard by a trial jury. The manner in which they were to do this was the subject of considerable disagreement among legal writers. In particular, opinion differed on two issues both of which influenced juries' verdicts: first, whether the grand jury ought to hear evidence from both the prosecution and defence; and, second, the degree of certainty required for a grand jury to find a 'true bill'.

According to the seventeenth-century jurist Sir Matthew Hale, the grand jury was only to consider evidence for the crown.[23] This view was supported by a number of legal writers in the late seventeenth and eighteenth centuries, notably by Zachary Babington, an associate clerk of assize on the Oxford circuit, and by Blackstone.[24] The reason for limiting evidence to one side of the matter derived from the fact that the grand jury was a jury of accusation and presentment, not determination. Thus, according to Blackstone, grand jurors were 'only to hear evidence on behalf of the prosecution: for the finding of an indictment is only in the nature of an enquiry or accusation, which is afterwards to be tried and determined; and the grand jury are only to enquire upon their oaths, whether there be sufficient cause to call upon the party to answer it'.[25]

This argument was rejected by writers who, in response to the political trials of the late seventeenth century, emphasised the grand jury's role as a safeguard against false and malicious accusations. In *The Security of Englishmen's Lives*, first printed in 1681 but subsequently published at intervals throughout the eighteenth century, Lord Somers (who was appointed as Lord Chancellor in 1697) argued that the grand jurors' oath to 'present the truth, the whole truth, and nothing but the truth' obliged them 'to be diligent in their inquiries, that is, to receive no suggestion of any crime for truth, without examining all the circumstances about it, that fall within their knowledge'.[26] Although Somers gave preference to evidence for the prosecution, he did not rule out the use of any testimony that would enable jurors to make an accurate presentment of the matter before them.[27] In 1699, the author of *A Guide to Juries* was more insistent that grand juries should consider all sides of an issue before reaching a conclusion:

> Thus one would admire how it comes to pass, that they of the Grand Jury should often hear but one side: Their Oath, it's apparent, is against this: It says, 'Present the whole Truth', not concealing or omitting any part of it; which implies as well all one side can inform them as the other … It proceeds, and says, And 'nothing else but the Truth', which how can possibly, or any Jury-man be satisfied in, unless hear both Parties?[28]

In spite of these objections to the practice, it is likely that grand juries generally heard only evidence for the prosecution during the eighteenth century. In addition to Blackstone's opinion on the matter, it is significant that although Sollom Emlyn (the editor of Hale's *History of the Pleas of the Crown*) and the legal writer William Nelson both suggested that the grand jury's practice of hearing only one side of the evidence was 'repugnant to Reason and Law', they nevertheless acknowledged the existence, and cited precedent in support, of the general rule.[29]

The second, closely related, aspect of grand jury procedure that may have contributed to jurors' assessment of a case concerned the degree of certainty that was required before a bill was to be endorsed and sent forward to the trial jury. On the basis that a bill was to be endorsed a '*true* bill', both Somers and the author of *A Guide to Juries* believed that grand jurors should be thoroughly persuaded of the guilt of the accused before finding the indictment true. Both writers rejected the notion that bills should be found true simply on the basis of probability, because then 'the whole proceedings would be brought to depend upon the fancies of men'.[30] While probability might be sufficient grounds for gambling, Somers argued, it was insufficient for the administration of justice. The clarity of evidence required for an indictment to be endorsed should be the same as that required for a trial jury verdict of guilty.[31] The author of *A Guide to Juries* believed that any uncertainty should lead the grand jury to reject the bill: 'So that one must know beyond all doubt, before say *Billa vera*, else say, *Ignoramus*, which is in English, we doubt, we do not know, we are not certain if it be true.'[32]

This interpretation of grand juries' responsibilities was not universally accepted. Hale and Babington, both writing before Somers and, perhaps significantly, before the notorious political trials of the late 1670s and 1680s, were of the opinion that 'in case there be *probable* evidence, they ought to find the bill'.[33] Babington indeed asserted that endorsing a bill 'true' simply designated the case as 'meet' or 'fit' for further inquiry by another jury.[34] However, although the third edition of Nelson's *The Law of Evidence*, published in 1739, cautiously supported Hale and Babington,[35] most legal writers in the eighteenth century appear to have preferred Somers' opinion that a grand jury should be as certain of the truth of an indictment as a trial jury. In a footnote to Hale's comments on the grand jury, Sollom Emlyn approvingly referred to Sir John Hawles' remarks on the trial of the Earl of Shaftesbury, in which Hawles 'unanswerably shews, that a grand jury ought to have the same persuasion of the truth of the indictment, as a petty jury, or a coroner's inquest'.[36] Similar conclusions were drawn by other legal writers. Blackstone, for example, pointed out the danger of finding indictments on the basis of probabilities: 'A grand jury however ought to be thoroughly persuaded of the truth of an indictment, so far as the evidence goes; and not to rest satisfied merely with remote probabilities: a doctrine, that might be applied to very oppressive purposes.'[37] And William Eden insisted that grand juries were certainly 'not authorized to expose a fellow-citizen to the shame, expence, and danger of a public trial, upon the vague suggestion of a mere probability'.[38]

It is difficult to determine the extent to which these factors influenced grand jury decisions. Apart from the marking of bills 'true' or 'not found', court records provide few clues as to how grand juries functioned or on what grounds they made decisions. It is certainly possible that an increasing emphasis on the certainty, or at least the strong probability, that was to accompany a true bill encouraged grand juries to discharge an increasing number of women accused of new-born child murder in the eighteenth century. However, it would appear that the percentage of bills not found at the end of the eighteenth century in these cases exceeded the percentage not found in other crimes in the same period.[39] It is possible, therefore, that grand jury procedure was not of primary importance and that factors peculiar to this crime were largely responsible for this trend. Although there is no clear evidence that grand jurors were fully aware of changes in the laws of evidence, or of changing views towards the evidence admitted in trials of women accused of murdering new-born children, they were charged by Westminster judges conversant with current legal opinion. In addition, although in general there was a sharp distinction between grand jurors and those who served as trial jurors, it is clear that some grand jurors had already served on trial juries in these cases, an experience that would have provided them with a knowledge of the laws of evidence and standards of proof employed in the trial courts.[40] In this way, changes in legal opinion could have been incorporated into grand jury decisions. Whether or not grand jurors were directly influenced by such factors, they would nevertheless have known that trial juries, for whatever reasons, increasingly acquitted women accused of murdering new-born children. This fact alone may have encouraged grand juries to reject an increasing percentage of indictments.

Trial jury verdicts

Women accused of new-born child murder reached the trial courts by two routes: as the result of an inquest verdict of wilful murder; and/or as the result of a grand jury finding a true bill. Once in court, it is unlikely that many trials for new-born child murder lasted more than an hour. Trial juries generally heard several cases each day and rarely left the courtroom before returning their verdicts.[41] However, although accounts in the Old Bailey Sessions Papers suggest that in most trials the jury heard much the same range of evidence as that presented by witnesses before magistrates and coroners,[42] it is clear that in the trial court, evidence was subjected to much greater scrutiny than in previous stages of investigations into these cases. In particular, the judge played a critical role in this period, examining witnesses in depth and directing jurors on the law when necessary.[43]

The trial jurors themselves were freeholders selected from a list of suitable men in the county.[44] Although they were generally of lower social and financial status than grand jurors in the eighteenth century, trial jurors were nevertheless also accustomed to administering local affairs. Recent research on the precise composition of juries indicates that the majority of trial jurors also served as overseers of the poor, church-wardens, and constables.[45] Significantly, these were the men most likely to be involved actively in the arrest and prosecution of women accused of murdering their new-born children. In this context, the high acquittal rate for this crime is even more striking.

It is difficult to determine precisely why eighteenth-century trial juries acquitted such a large majority of women accused of murdering their new-born children or, indeed, why they chose to convict certain defendants. Printed trial reports from the Old Bailey, from Surrey and Sussex assizes and from York, rarely recorded juries' reasons for their decisions. The majority of reports simply concluded with an unqualified verdict of 'Not Guilty' or 'Guilty', or simply with the word 'Acquitted'. In some cases, the reports' conclusions were more expansive, but usually no more informative.[46] In only a handful of cases was any particular piece of evidence detailed as instrumental in determining the verdict. However, printed trial reports and other contemporary sources suggest that certain types of evidence could be influential in the courts in terms of both regulating the application of the 1624 statute and determining verdicts, notably: evidence of marriage; signs of still-birth; evidence, or the lack of evidence, of intent to kill the child; marks of violence on the child's body; and, as I discussed in the previous chapter, the woman's reputation and evidence of temporary insanity.

A small number of women indicted under the 1624 statute were certainly acquitted because they produced witnesses to prove that they were married. Once exempted from the statute, the evidence against them was rarely sufficient to convict these women at common law. The report of Mary Bristow's trial at the Old Bailey in 1718, for example, concluded that, 'it not being a Bastard Child, the Evidence, if true, could not support the Indictment, therefore the Jury acquitted her'.[47] Significantly, the authors of the Sessions Papers sometimes expressed their frustration at what they saw as the inadequacies of common law in these cases, particularly in the early years of the century. At the trial of Ann Masie in 1717, for example, the defendant apparently proved to the court's satisfaction that she had been married to Edward Wingate, who had died when she was only six weeks pregnant. Consequently, after the 1624 statute had been read in court, 'she was deemed not to be affected by that Statute' and it became 'the Prosecutors' business to prove the child was born alive and that she murthered it'. The prosecution failed to prove live-birth and murder, and the trial report concluded with a complaint that 'tho' the Action was so unaccountably inhuman, for which she gave but little Satisfaction, the Jury acquitted her of the Indictment'.[48]

As I have already suggested, evidence of still-birth could also clearly influence juries. Some Old Bailey Sessions Papers explicitly referred to a jury's finding of still-birth, although it is not clear whether the juries' findings in these particular cases accurately reflected the evidential impact of still-birth. In all three cases, the defendants had already been acquitted on a grand jury indictment, and the children were found to have been born dead 'on the Coroner's Inquisition'.[49] It is possible, therefore, that a verdict of still-birth was employed as the simplest way in which to stop proceedings against a woman who had already been acquitted.

There is, however, some clearer evidence of the manner in which judges and juries were prepared to accept evidence of still-birth and the extent to which the statutory clause concerning still-birth was increasingly interpreted in favour of the defendant. At the trial of Sarah Scott at the Surrey assizes in 1741, one of the witnesses gave evidence that Sarah 'always deny'd that she had been deliver'd of a Child, only said a Lump of Flesh came from her'. Sarah had apparently also insisted 'that she never heard the Child cry, nor that it was a Child that she knew of. She said she had committed a Fault in doing as she had done, but that she had not committed Murder, for it was not a Child.' Basing his arguments on legal opinion that confessions should be taken in their entirety (that is both for and against the defendant),[50] and demonstrating the variable interpretation of the developing hearsay rule in this period,[51] the judge recommended that Sarah's claims ought to have some weight in her favour, and since 'there was no Proof that the Prisoner was delivered of a Child, the Jury acquitted her'.[52]

At the end of the century, Justice Heath imposed similar restrictions on the prosecution's use of a woman's initial testimony. According to the evidence of John Dunbar, Ann Perry had confessed that she had given birth but insisted that the child had been still-born. 'If you make use of this confession', Justice Heath warned the prosecution, 'you must take it altogether, unless you can contradict it.' Since the prosecution counsel admitted that he could not contradict her statement that the child had been still-born, and since medical evidence failed to establish live-birth, Ann Perry was acquitted.[53] Such judgements demonstrate precisely how much legal opinion had altered in favour of the defendant in these cases. In spite of the 1624 statute's incitement to disregard such claims, judges and juries were clearly prepared simply to take the defendant's word that the child had been still-born.

Evidence of intent to conceal and murder (or, conversely, the lack of intent) was also critical in trials under the 1624 statute, and printed trial reports suggest that judges and juries paid considerable attention to this point. For example, evidence that a mother had prepared clothes or linen for her child (or sometimes that she had asked for assistance at the birth) was routinely allowed to show that she had not intended to conceal its death, thereby exempting her from trial under the statute. In most cases, evidence of this nature (which had been admitted since the late seventeenth century),[54] encouraged the courts to acquit. Thus, according to the report of Ann Seabrook's trial in 1756, since it had been 'prov'd that she (the said Ann Seabrook) had been seen making Preparations for a Child, the Jury without going out of Court brought her in not Guilty'.[55] Similarly, in a report in *The Times* in 1788, Ann Green's provision of baby linen 'sufficient for any new born child' was recognised as a 'favourable' circumstance in her case and she was found not guilty.[56] Conversely, the absence of preparations could contribute to conviction. In 1722, for example, Ann Morris was found guilty at the Old Bailey after admitting that she had not prepared clothes for her child.[57] The success with which women pleaded 'benefit-of-linen' in eighteenth-century trials may explain both frequent references to this line of defence in the pre-trial examinations of accused women in the north of England and contemporary fears that such exemptions from the 1624 statute were being abused.[58] It may also explain why, when an experienced coroner, George Petch, and a constable, Robert Proud, admitted that they had not confirmed Frances Harrison's testimony that she had some child's clothes in her box, the comment 'The greater Fools you' was added to the foot of Petch's note on the matter.[59]

Evidence that a defendant had informed somebody of her pregnancy or that she had attempted to call for assistance during labour was also taken as proof that she had not intended to conceal the child's death. Such an interpretation of the evidence, which had found judicial support in the ruling of Lord Chief Justice Kelyng and his associates at the trial of Ann Davis in 1664,[60] served to exempt women from trial under the statute and may explain why some accused women insisted that they had informed the child's reputed father of the pregnancy at their pre-trial examinations. In a similar vein, by the end of the eighteenth century, the presence of an accomplice at the birth (usually the child's father or the defendant's mother) also took the case out of the statute. In 1793, Justice Heath apparently held that Jane Peat, whose mother had been present at the birth, was exempted from the statute 'for if any person be present, although privy to the guilt, there can be no concealment by the mother within the statute, and the case stands as at common law'.[61] As in the case of judicial opinion on still-birth, this judgement demonstrates the extent to which judges in the eighteenth century were interpreting the 1624 statute in favour of defendants, since, according to the statute, the legal presumption was applicable to any woman who had concealed the death of her child 'by herself or the procuring of others'.

The question of intent may have operated to encourage acquittals in another way. In most murder trials, if a jury considered that the defendant had been responsible for the victim's death but that the evidence did not sustain a charge of murder because there had been no intent to kill, it could return a partial verdict of manslaughter. Cases in which this verdict was commonly reached included homicides following quarrels and those resulting from unlawful acts. The significance of reducing the charge from murder to manslaughter was that the lesser crime was within the benefit of clergy and therefore not necessarily punishable with death.[62] Since there were no clear grounds (such as provocation) for reducing the charge in trials of new-born child murder, no partial verdict was available to the jury in these cases.[63] The absence of this option may have encouraged the courts to acquit rather than convict women on the basis of what was increasingly regarded as ambiguous evidence.[64]

On occasions, other factors were clearly instrumental in determining verdicts. Although marks of violence on a child's body were increasingly challenged as evidence of murder, it is clear that in some cases, such evidence contributed to conviction. In 1724, Mary Morgan, a married woman, was found guilty of murdering her child because she could give 'no Account how it came by the two Stabs in the Belly, one of which was deposed to be such an one that the Bowels came out'.[65] In 1760, Ann Hullock admitted to a constable that she had cut her child's throat with a knife. Although she insisted in court that she had not intended to do it, she was found guilty of murder.[66] And in the Northern Circuit courts, the convictions of Anne Milburne in 1728 and Elizabeth Conney in 1744 may have been linked to evidence that violence had been inflicted on their children's bodies.[67] Conversely, the absence of marks of violence appears to have been instrumental in securing a reprieve for Margaret Evans in 1763.[68]

It appears then that the lack of preparation for the birth, the presence of marks of violence that could not be attributed to the trauma of birth, and the absence of a defence,[69] could provide a jury with sufficient reason to convict. Conversely, evidence of still-birth, doubts about the possibility of live-birth, evidence that the defendant had made preparations for the birth, the absence of marks of violence, and the testimony of witnesses to the defendant's good character may all have worked in favour of the accused. However, the fact that very similar evidence had routinely resulted in conviction in the seventeenth century, and that apparently very similar evidence could result in either conviction or acquittal in the eighteenth century,[70] suggests that the precise nature of the evidence, or at least of that recorded in the Old Bailey Sessions Papers, was not the only, or even the primary, factor in determining the high (and rising) acquittal rate.

It is possible that the trial jury's power over life and death and a growing sensitivity to the number of capital statutes constrained the zeal of men who, within a local context, were eager to harass suspects. A reluctance to employ capital punishment may have been accentuated in these cases by the fact that the majority of defendants were women (who were traditionally treated less severely by the courts),[71] and by the fact that the alleged victim was usually an illegitimate child, legally regarded as '*nullius filius*', or the 'child of no-one'.[72] It may well be that the deaths of children who remained legally and socially disadvantaged throughout the century failed to excite men of middling status sufficiently to consign the children's mothers to the gallows.[73] Moreover, from the point of view of local rate-payers, the ignominy of the trial itself may have been seen as sufficient punishment and as a suitable deterrent to other potential offenders.[74] However, while prosecution itself may have satisfied the needs of neighbours and local officials in this way, other factors determined the context in which such attitudes were expressed and contributed to the rising acquittal rate. In particular, developments in the law of evidence and in standards of proof accentuated growing doubts about the evidential basis for conviction in these cases.

Laws of evidence and standards of proof

Prior to the eighteenth century, there were few explicit rules of evidence and no clearly formulated standards of proof to be employed in the courts. During the eighteenth century, however, this situation was radically altered by the publication of a number of texts concerned solely with the law of evidence, and by increasingly clear formulations of maxims relating to the admissability of evidence, the credibility of witnesses, and the required standard of proof. This process was so extensive that, by the end of the century, the law of evidence was viewed by at least one legal writer as central to British liberty: 'The law of evidence is of the utmost importance to every member of the British state. It may be said, with great propriety, that the liberty, the life, and the property of every individual depend upon this law'.[75]

Developments in the law of evidence in this period were stimulated by a number of factors. In the first place, discussions that followed the political and religious upheavals of the late 1670s and 1680s highlighted the problems associated with trial by jury and stressed the need to guarantee the safety of subjects against malicious prosecutions and wrongful convictions. One of the consequences of these discussions was the Treason Act of 1696 which, among other provisions, granted defendants the right to counsel in cases of treason.[76] Although arguments against the use of defence counsel other than in points of law persisted with respect to capital crimes other than treason, it is clear that, by the 1730s, judges were allowing both prosecution and defence counsel to examine and cross-examine witnesses at the Old Bailey in a variety of cases.[77]

The presence of defence counsel in court was by no means guaranteed.

The employment of counsel may have been beyond the means of many defendants, and, even if hired, their involvement remained at the discretion of the judge. In new-born child murder trials, for example, the majority of defendants continued to conduct their own defence throughout the century. However, as John Langbein and J. M. Beattie have separately argued, the advent of lawyers served to change the dynamics of jury trial in a significant way, eventually dislodging judges from their commanding role in court and making the jury more dangerous.[78] According to Langbein, it was the intrusion of lawyers into the courtroom that stimulated the development of rules governing the admission of certain types of evidence.[79]

New legal discourses on evidence and proof were also shaped by the cultural and intellectual environment of the seventeenth and eighteenth centuries. As Barbara Shapiro has argued, the language and concepts employed by legal writers were shared by influential scientist philosophers of the period.[80] In addressing problems concerning the certainty of evidence and the credibility of witnesses, John Locke, Robert Boyle, and others had proposed a probabilistic theory of knowledge. A similar approach was adopted by lawyers such as Sir Matthew Hale and Sir Geoffrey Gilbert (Lord Chief Baron of the Court of Exchequer at the time of his death in 1726) in their attempts to establish a systematic treatment of legal evidence and proof. Gilbert himself acknowledged Locke's influence on his work.[81] Later in the eighteenth century, John Morgan, a barrister and the author of a series of legal essays, also noted Locke's contribution to the subject.[82]

Several features of the emergent laws of evidence merit attention in the present context. In the first place, a number of legal writers began to place increasing emphasis on degrees of certainty and probability in legal deliberations. In *The Law of Evidence*, which served as an influential model for subsequent treatises on evidence after its posthumous publication in 1754, Gilbert indicated that since most human actions were 'not capable of strict Demonstration therefore the Rights of Men must be determin'd by Probability', which was itself 'founded upon obscure and indistinct Views, or upon Report from the Sight of others'.[83] Reliance on the testimony of others generated the need for rules determining the evidence heard by the jury and the rules of probability by which that evidence was to be considered.

In the absence of direct demonstration that an offence had been committed, the courts were to rely upon the testimony of witnesses to circumstances that might enable a jury to presume the fact in question. Thus, according to Gilbert, when 'the Fact itself cannot be proved, that which comes nearest to the Proof of the Fact is, the Proof of the Circumstances that necessarily and usually attend such Facts, and these are called Presumptions and not Proofs, for they stand instead of the Proofs of the Fact till the contrary be proved'.[84] Circumstantial, or presumptive, evidence was to be carefully evaluated by the courts. First, grounds of probability were to be assessed by determining whether the evidence conformed with the jurors' own knowledge and experience of life.[85] Second, evidence was to be interpreted in the context of the witnesses' credibility. Factors affecting the credit to be afforded to witnesses included their number, their integrity, knowledge and skill, and their indifference to the issue.[86]

Credible testimony to circumstances known to attend certain facts created a presumption that the fact was so. Just as Locke had described the several degrees of probability giving rise to several degrees of assent, so legal writers referred to presumptions as violent, probable and light according to the weight they carried in law. '*Violent presumption* is many times equal to full proof; for there those circumstances appear which necessarily attend the fact. *Probable presumption*, arising from such circumstances as usually attend the fact, hath also its due weight. *Light* or rash presumptions have not any weight or validity.'[87] According to Capel Lofft's edition of Gilbert's work, a violent presumption was required to convict in capital cases.[88]

This account of how jurors were to assess witnesses and draw conclusions from the evidence presented to them was not accepted unreservedly in the eighteenth century. It would appear, for example, that some juries remained reluctant to accept circumstantial evidence as a basis for conviction. Towards the end of the eighteenth century, William Paley complained about 'two popular maxims, which seem to have a considerable influence in producing the injudicious acquittals of which we complain'. One of these mistaken maxims was 'that circumstantial evidence falls short of positive proof'. Paley countered this misconception by insisting that 'a chain of circumstantial evidence' was less likely to be false and more amenable to discussion than the uncorroborated testimony of a single eyewitness.[89] On occasions, judges certainly needed to remind juries (and lawyers) of the significance of chains of circumstantial evidence. At the trial of Robert Fawthorp for murder in 1749, Sir Thomas Burnet, one of the judges of the Court of Common Pleas, countered the defence counsel's request that the jury 'be very careful not to add Blood to Blood, by convicting the Prisoner upon Circumstances only', by informing the jury that 'the Law does admit a Series of Circumstances, where they are sufficiently clear and connected, to be proper Evidence of Murder: For that if it did not, Murders might be so secretly committed as wholly to preclude all positive Proof'.[90]

However, jurists were also aware of the dangers of accepting circumstantial evidence, not only in terms of the decision-making process in court but also in terms of the effective administration of justice. As Hale, one of the first legal writers to approach legal evidence in terms of probability and certainty, warned at the end of his discussion of the 1624 statute:

> In some cases presumptive evidences go far to prove a person guilty, tho' there be no express proof of the fact to be committed by him, but then it must be very warily presumed, for it is better five guilty persons should escape unpunished, than one innocent person should die.[91]

Hale's caution about the use of circumstantial evidence was not only repeated in eighteenth-century treatises on evidence (albeit in different mathematical terms),[92] but it was also a critical issue for members of parliament advocating repeal of the 1624 statute in the 1770s.[93]

Debates about determining the probability of guilt on the basis of circumstantial evidence raised a further issue in the courts. If verdicts were to be reached on the grounds of probability, that is on the ability of the evidence to induce a presumption of guilt, how certain was the trial jury to be in order to convict? What standard of proof was to be employed in criminal trials? Traditionally, the burden of proving a fact rested with the prosecution. More particularly, according to the eminent seventeenth-century jurist Edward Coke, 'the testimonies and the proofs of the offence ought to be so clear and manifest, as there can be no defence of it'.[94] Indeed, this was one of the reasons why it was not thought necessary to allow defendants the use of counsel. During the course of the eighteenth century, this requirement for clear evidence was increasingly expressed as a need for the prosecution to remove all doubt of the defendant's guilt before the jury should convict. Thus, at Robert Fawthorp's trial in 1749, the judge concluded his summing up with the following remarks:

> You will therefore (says he) consider whether the Circumstances in the present Case, are such as leave no Manner of Doubt in your Minds, as to the Prisoner's having actually committed these Murders; and if you are thoroughly persuaded thereof in your own Consciences, you may find him guilty upon Circumstantial Evidence only ... But tho' the Probability of his Guilt should appear to you ever so great, yet if you have any the least Doubt whether these Murders might not possibly have been committed, notwithstanding, by some other Person; in that Case you ought to acquit him.[95]

Such assessments of the certainty (or lack of doubt) necessary to return a guilty verdict were eventually expressed in the legal maxim that a jury should be persuaded of a defendant's guilt 'beyond a reasonable doubt' before convicting.[96] This concept was coupled with the emergence of what became known as the 'presumption of innocence'. Essentially, this presumption amounted to no more than a belief that guilt should be proved by the prosecution beyond reasonable doubt, and, as such, it did not become established as a legal maxim until the nineteenth century.[97] However, it is clear that similar phrases in favour of the accused were employed from the late seventeenth century. The author of *A Guide to Juries*, for example, insisted that 'Every Jury must always remember, they may presume nothing but Innocency; and Innocency &c. they ought, until the contrary be proved'.[98] In the eighteenth century, Gilbert similarly stated that 'in Criminal Prosecutions the Presumption is in Favour of the Defendant, for thus far is to be hoped of all Mankind, that they are not guilty in any such Instances, and the Penalty inhances the Presumption'.[99] Significantly, William Hunter endorsed this particular presumption (appropriately enforced by judges) as a means of protecting women accused of new-born child murder from local prejudices:

> Most of these reflexions would naturally occur to any unprejudiced person, and therefore upon a trial in this country, where we are so happy as to be under the protection of judges, who by their education, studies, and habits, are above the reach of vulgar prejudices, and make it a rule for their conduct to suppose the accused party innocent, till guilt be proved. With such judges, I say, there will be little danger of an innocent woman being condemned by false reasoning.[100]

During the late seventeenth and eighteenth centuries, the gradual development of a law of evidence, clearer formulations of the standard of proof in criminal cases, and the increasing use of defence counsel all operated in favour of defendants facing capital charges. The effects of these changes were transmitted to defendants through the knowledge and intervention of judges and lawyers in the trial courts, and were enhanced by the fact that many trial jurors were experienced jurors who were likely to be aware both of the evidential requirements in particular cases and of general developments in the laws of evidence.[101] These developments may also have encouraged grand juries to discharge an increasing proportion of suspects.

Although developments in the laws of evidence operated in favour of all defendants, there are several reasons why women accused of murdering their new-born bastard children in particular benefited from these changes. First, extensive debates about accepting circumstantial evidence raised doubts about the validity of presuming that concealment signified murder. If concealment constituted no more than 'the lowest degree of presumptive evidence of felonious homicide', as Thomas Percival suggested at the turn of the nineteenth century,[102] then it clearly failed to create the 'violent Presumption' increasingly required in capital cases. Together with forceful humanitarian objections to the prosecution's reliance on evidence of concealment, concerns about circumstantial evidence undermined the terms of the

1624 statute. By encouraging the courts to allow exemptions from the statute, this process facilitated acquittal.

Second, the 1624 statute's inability to distinguish between innocence and guilt on the basis of concealment appeared to encourage the conviction of seemingly innocent women. In 1772, proponents of repeal of the statute complained that although 'it was infinitely better that ten guilty persons should escape, than one innocent person should suffer; that this law, on the contrary, asserted it to be better, that ten innocent persons should be hanged, than one guilty person should escape'.[103] The statute was therefore seen to be at odds with increasingly clearly articulated standards of proof and at variance with an emerging presumption of innocence that operated in favour of the accused.[104]

By the 1760s, such restrictions on the use of the 1624 statute had become so extensive that trials under the statute appear to have been uncommon. Although texts published in the first half of the eighteenth century make no mention of the statute's severity nor of its replacement by common law, in 1766, Daines Barrington advised that 'no execution should be permitted, unless the criminal, convicted under this act, would have been guilty of murder by the common law'.[105] At the end of the decade, William Blackstone suggested that the courts were by that time requiring evidence at common law that the child had been born alive and murdered before they would convict:

> it has of late years been usual with us in England, upon trials for this offence, to require some sort of presumptive evidence that the child was born alive, before the other constrained presumption (that the child, whose death is concealed, was therefore killed by it's parent) is admitted to convict the prisoner.[106]

There is no clear evidence from the Northern Circuit court records about the relative use of the statute and common law in this period. Fletcher Rigge, clerk for the northern courts from 1772, continued to draw up indictments 'against the form of the Statute'. However, indictment against the statute did not exclude trial at common law. Given the general attitude to the statute by this time, and the absence of convictions from these courts after 1760, it is likely that even those women indicted under the statute were tried by common law rules of evidence.

By the early 1770s, the statute's demise appears to have been complete, a situation welcomed by William Eden, a proponent of criminal law reform, in 1771:

> The modern exposition of this statute is a good instance, that *cruel laws have a natural tendency to their own dissolution in the abhorrence of mankind*. It is now the constant practice of the courts to require, that the body of the child shall be found, before any conviction can take place; and if it

should happen, that the mother had any child-bed linen, or other preparatives in her possession, prior to her delivery, it is generally admitted as a proof, that no concealment was intended. Moreover, it is not unusual to require some degree of evidence that the child was actually born alive, before the ungenerous presumption, that the mother was the wilful author of the death of her new-born infant, is permitted to affect her. These humane deviations from the harsh injunction of the statute have nearly amounted to a tacit abrogation of it.[107]

Significantly, explicit rejection of the 1624 statute, and the subsequent return to common law rules of evidence, ensured that medical testimony was subjected to increasingly rigorous scrutiny. As use of the statutory presumption declined, medical evidence became increasingly important as a means of determining whether a child had been born alive and murdered. As I have already suggested, medical witnesses were rarely able to provide the courts with any certainty about the cause of death, especially when they were meticulously examined by circuit judges and lawyers who were not only aware of developing concerns about circumstantial evidence, probability, certainty, and doubt, but who were also conversant with contemporary medical literature on the subject.[108] In particular, in adopting new approaches to evidence and proof, the bench increasingly exposed the uncertainty inherent in medical testimony and, by undermining the evidential core of the prosecution's case, facilitated acquittal.[109]

Conclusion

During the eighteenth century, developing laws of evidence and standards of proof, together with emergent humanitarian constructions of the character and conduct of accused women, imposed specific restrictions on the application of the 1624 statute. As the courts increasingly interpreted the statute in favour of the defendant, allowing exemptions from the statute's presumption and giving credence to suspects' own accounts of events, it became usual for defendants, even if they were unmarried, to be tried at common law. With the prosecution once more dependent on medical evidence of live-birth and murder, it became increasingly common for coroners', grand and trial juries to discharge or acquit women accused of murdering their new-born children. Although the attitudes embodied in the 1624 statute remained uppermost in the minds of rate-paying parishioners and were responsible for the persistent accusation and prosecution of single women thought to have murdered their children, in the courts such attitudes were no longer sufficient to justify conviction and hanging. As William Hunter maintained, in 1784, 'surely the only crime is the having been pregnant, which the law does not mean to punish with death'.[110]

The courts' exercise of their discretionary powers in this way was not of course unique. As a number of historians have suggested, not only was there a growing popular resistance to capital punishment itself but it was also customary for judges and juries to mitigate the severity of statute law in the eighteenth century by interpreting capital statutes in favour of the defendant.[111] Although the move away from the 'bloody code' was widespread, it would appear that judicial attitudes towards the 1624 statute represent a particularly early example of the restrictive tendencies of the courts in this respect.[112] Significantly, it was the administrative and ideological implications of restrictive interpretations of the 1624 statute, as much as humanitarian sentiment, that prompted debate about repeal of the statute in the last decades of the eighteenth century.

Notes

1 Between 1720 and 1800, grand juries in the north of England discharged approximately twenty-four per cent of the women presented before them. This figure is comparable to the figure given by Beattie for Surrey, where about twenty-seven per cent of accused women were discharged by proclamation between 1660 and 1800 – see J. M. Beattie, *Crime and the Courts in England 1660-1800*, (Oxford, Clarendon Press, 1986), p. 402.

2 In the sixty-three Old Bailey cases that I have studied, 12 per cent of women indicted were convicted. According to Malcolmson, however, forty-six of the sixty-one women tried at the Old Bailey between 1730 and 1774 were acquitted, giving a conviction rate of nearly 25 per cent – see R. W. Malcolmson, 'Infanticide in the eighteenth century', in J. S. Cockburn (ed.), *Crime in England 1550-1800*, (London, Methuen, 1977), p. 197. According to Hunnisett's figures, approximately 14 per cent of women accused of new-born child murder in Wiltshire between 1752 and 1796 were convicted – see R. F. Hunnisett (ed.), *Wiltshire Coroners' Bills 1752-1796*, (Wiltshire Record Society, 1981).

3 It appears, for example, that in Staffordshire, not one of thirty-nine women tried between 1742 and 1802 was sentenced to death – see Malcolmson, 'Infanticide in the eighteenth century', p. 197. None of the twenty-four women tried at the Lancaster assizes in the reign of George II were found guilty – see David Harley, 'Rape, bastardy and infanticide: the midwife as investigating agent in pre-industrial England', unpublished paper, 1990. And according to Beattie, of thirty-five women indicted in Surrey between 1722 and 1802, only one woman was convicted – Beattie, *Crime and the Courts*, p. 119.

4 The percentage of women discharged by Northern Circuit grand juries in each decade was approximately: 1720s – 0; 1730s – 9; 1740s – 12; 1750s – 20; 1760s – 33; 1770s –25; 1780s – 24; 1790s – 48.

5 Dorothy Gatenby in 1754 and Isabella Hailes in 1757 were the last women to be hanged for this crime in the Northern Circuit until the turn of the nineteenth century. Hoffer and Hull drew similar conclusions about the pattern of trial jury verdicts at the Old Bailey – Hoffer and Hull, *Murdering Mothers: Infanticide in England and New England 1558-1803*, (New York, New York University Press, 1981), pp. 71-5.

6 Douglas Hay, 'Property, authority and the criminal law', in Douglas Hay, Peter Linebaugh, John G. Rule, E. P. Thompson, Cal Winslow, *Albion's Fatal Tree: Crime and Society in Eighteenth-Century England*, (London, Allen Lane, 1975), p. 32.

7 Beattie's figures suggest that roughly fifteen per cent of murder suspects were discharged by the grand jury compared with twenty-seven per cent of women accused of new-born child murder – Beattie, *Crime and the Courts*, p. 402. For his figures on conviction rates in murder trials, see ibid., p. 411. For a comparison of the conviction rates for 'infanticide' and adult homicide, see also Hoffer and Hull, *Murdering Mothers*, pp. 75-8.

8 For the laws governing the summoning of jurors see Edward Umfreville, *Lex Coronatoria: Or, the Office and Duty of Coroners*, (London, 1761), p. 179. In the north of England, most juries inquiring into the deaths of new-born children contained between twelve and sixteen members.

9 Ibid., p. 179.

10 William Blackstone, *Commentaries on the Laws of England*, (4 vols., Oxford, 1765-9), vol. III, p. 383.

11 Although Umfreville acknowledged that the 'common Law sets no Value on [coroners'] Jurors', he nevertheless asserted that jurors should be 'of sufficient Understanding and competency of Estate, and least suspitious' - Umfreville, *Lex Coronatoria*, pp. 186-7. See also Michael MacDonald's assessment of the status of inquest jurors in 'The secularization of suicide in England 1660-1800', *Past and Present*, 111 (1986), 50-100.

12 Umfreville himself refused to admit a prejudiced neighbour as a juror - Umfreville, *Lex Coronatoria*, p. 186.

13 In 1766, John White was on the jury inquiring into the death of his own child born to Ann Usher. White was later accused of persuading Ann not to reveal his identity at the inquest. The inquisition is in ASSI 44/81. The full details emerged a year later, during investigations into White's involvement in the child's death – John White, 1767, ASSI 45/28/3/183-7.

14 'An Act touching Bailment of Persons', 1 & 2 Ph.& M. c.13, 1554.

15 Matthew Hale, *History of the Pleas of the Crown*, ed. Sollom Emlyn, (2 vols., London, 1736), vol. II, pp. 60-2; see also Umfreville, *Lex Coronatoria*, pp. 205-6.

16 Umfreville, *Lex Coronatoria*, pp. 306-7.

17 See Dorothy Henderson (1789, ASSI 45/36/3/84, ASSI 44/104ii), in which medical evidence of prematurity was ignored, although in this instance evidence of violence might have precipitated the verdict of live-birth and murder. Any doubt on the part of a medical practitioner that a child had been born alive was also generally overruled by the coroner's jury; see, for example, Mary Windas, 1786, ASSI 45/35/3/233-4, ASSI 44/101i.

18 See, for example, the inquisition in the case of Susannah Stephenson, 1741, ASSI 44/56.

19 Ann Peirson, 1765, ASSI 45/28/1/69-74, ASSI 44/80.

20 In the 1750s, the first decade from which records from cases not reaching court survive, there were 13 verdicts of murder and 4 other verdicts, mostly of still-birth. In the following four decades, the figures were: 1760s, 28 murder and 5 others; 1770s, 20 and 13; 1780s, 26 and 12; 1790s, 16 and 17.

21 For comments on the role of coroners and their juries in suicide, see MacDonald, 'The secularization of suicide'.

22 The jury was named 'grand' because it regularly contained more than twelve members, because the jurors were to be of greater estate and quality than trial jurors, and because it was also known as the 'The King's Jury' – see Zachary Babington, *Advice to Grand Jurors in Cases of Blood*, (London, 1677), pp. 4-5.

23 Hale, *Pleas of the Crown*, vol. II, p. 157.

24 Babington, *Advice to Grand Jurors*, preface, and pp. 63, 71; William Blackstone, *Commentaries on the Laws of England*, (4 vols., Dublin, 1770), vol. IV, p. 300.

25 Blackstone, *Commentaries*, (1770), vol. IV, p. 300.

26 Lord Somers, *The Security of Englishmen's Lives: or the Trust, Power and Duty of Grand Juries of England*, (London, 1766), pp. 22-3.

27 Ibid., pp. 25-6. Jurors were first to enquire what they themselves knew of the matter, then hear witnesses for the prosecution, and finally any other testimony that might help.

28 *A Guide to Juries: Setting Forth their Antiquity, Power, and Duty, From the Common Law and Statutes*, by a Person of Quality, (London, 1699), pp. 54-6.

29 Hale, *Pleas of the Crown*, vol. II, pp. 61, 157; William Nelson, *The Law of Evidence*, (3rd ed., London, 1739), p. 17.

30 Somers, *The Security of Englishmen's Lives*, pp. 88-92; The author of *A Guide to Juries* (pp. 40-1) was of the opinion that court clerks encouraged grand juries to find bills true only on 'a probability of the thing being true' in order to increase their fees from drawing up indictments.

31 Somers, *The Security of Englishmen's Lives*, pp. 90, 100. This opinion was complicated by the fact that the certainty required for a guilty verdict at the trial was not itself clearly established in this period - see the discussion later in this chapter.

32 *A Guide to Juries*, p. 52.

33 Hale, *Pleas of the Crown*, vol. II, p. 157.

34 Babington, *Advice to Grand Jurors*, pp. 124-5.

35 The 3rd edition of Nelson's *Law of Evidence*, p. 17, stated that 'Probable Evidence may be sufficient for a Grand Jury to find a Bill'.

36 Hale, *Pleas of the Crown*, vol. II, p. 157 fn.

37 Blackstone, *Commentaries*, (1770), vol. IV, p. 300.

38 William Eden, *Principles of Penal Law*, (2nd ed., London, 1771), p. 322 note; see also Richard Burn, *The Justice of the Peace, and Parish Officer*, (3rd ed., London, 1756), p. 392.

39 In the first decade of the nineteenth century, apparently only one in five or six bills was not found by grand juries. The comparison between this and the number of bills not found in new-born child murder cases may be misleading, however, since the early nineteenth century figures cover all crimes and allow no analysis of the figures for particular categories of offences. See Leon Radzinowicz, *A History of English Criminal Law and its Administration from 1750*, vol. I, (London, Stevens and Sons Limited, 1948), p. 92. However, Beattie's figures also suggest that grand juries rejected more indictments in cases of new-born child murder than in other murders throughout the eighteenth century – see Beattie, *Crime and the Courts*, p. 402.

40 It is not always easy to obtain clear information about jury members, but in 1757 a number of the grand jurors hearing the case against Isabella Hailes had apparently previously served as either grand or trial jurors in the case of Dorothy Gatenby in 1754 – see the Gaol Book entries for Newcastle for those years, in ASSI 42/5.

41 On trial procedure and the dynamics of criminal trials, see Beattie, *Crime and the Courts*, pp. 340-78; John H. Langbein, 'The criminal trial before the lawyers', *The University of Chicago Law Review*, 45 (1978), 263-316.

42 Evidence that trial juries heard much the same evidence as that in depositions also comes from the fact that, according to the Northern Circuit indictment files (in which the witnesses appearing in court were listed on the reverse of the indictments), the witnesses giving evidence at trials were the same as those appearing before magistrates and coroners.

43 On the dominant role of the judge, see: Beattie, *Crime and the Courts*, pp. 342-5; Langbein, 'The criminal trial'; Joel Peter Eigen, 'Intentionality and insanity: what the eighteenth-century juror heard', in W. F. Bynum, Roy Porter, and Michael Shepherd (eds.), *The Anatomy of Madness: Volume II*, (London, Tavistock, 1985), pp. 34-49.

44 See Giles Jacob, *New Law Dictionary*, (5th ed., 1744), 'Jury'.

45 P. J. R. King, '"Illiterate Plebians, Easily Misled": Jury composition, experience, and behaviour in Essex, 1735-1815', in J. S. Cockburn and Thomas A. Green (eds.), *Twelve Good Men and True: The Criminal Trial Jury in England, 1200-1800*, (Princeton University Press, 1988), pp. 254-304. See also Douglas Hay, 'The class composition of the palladium of English liberty: trial jurors in the eighteenth century', in Cockburn and Green (eds.), *Twelve Good Men*, pp. 305-57.

46 Examples include: 'The Jury considering the whole matter Acquitted her'; 'the Fact not being proved to the Satisfaction of the Jury, they acquitted her'; and, 'But the Evidence not proving the Fact against the Prisoner, she was acquitted'.

47 Mary Bristow, Old Bailey Sessions Papers, (OBSP), January 1718, pp. 6-7.

48 Ann Masie, OBSP, July 1717, p. 4.

49 See: Elizabeth Shudrick, OBSP No. VIII, October 1743, pp. 276-7; Eleanor Scrogham, OBSP No. VIII, October 1743, pp. 282-4; Grace Usop, James and Magdalen Leger, OBSP No. VIII, October 1745, pp. 245-8.

50 See: William Nelson, *The Law of Evidence*, (London, 1717), p. 4; William Hawkins, *Treatise of the Pleas of the Crown*, (2 vols., London, 1716-1721), vol. II, p. 429.

51 For comments on the development of the hearsay rule in this period, see Langbein, 'The criminal trial', pp. 301-2.

52 Sarah Scott, Surrey Assize Proceedings, July 1741, p. 5.

53 Ann Perry, OBSP, January 1800, p. 82.

54 See Hoffer and Hull, *Murdering Mothers*, p. 68, for a successful plea of benefit-of-linen in 1673. And Edward Hyde East, *A Treatise of the Pleas of the Crown*, (2 vols., London, 1803), vol. I, p. 228, in which he cites a case from 1689 in support of his suggestion that 'evidence is always allowed of the mother's having made provision for the birth, as a circumstance to shew that she did not intend to conceal it'.

55 Ann Seabrook, Surrey Assize Proceedings, August 1756, pp. 17-18.

56 *The Times*, (13 September 1788), p. 3.

57 Ann Morris, OBSP, September 1722, p. 1.

58 Defoe, for example, insisted that women intending to murder their children could easily obtain 'a Scrap or two of Child-Bed Linnen' after the murder had been committed – Daniel Defoe, *The Generous Protector, or a Friendly Proposal to Prevent the Murder and Other Enormous Abuses, By Erecting an Hospital for Foundlings and Bastard-Children*, (London, 1731), pp. 9-10. Anne Bell (1733, ASSI 45/19/3/1G-3) may have attempted to furnish herself with the necessary evidence after the birth.

59 Frances Harrison, 1795, ASSI 45/38/3/51.

60 Sir John Kelyng, *A Report of divers cases in Pleas of the Crown, adjudged and determined in the reign of ... Charles II*, (London, 1708), pp. 32-3.

61 East, *Pleas of the Crown*, vol. I, p. 229.

62 For a discussion of manslaughter in this period, see Beattie, *Crime and the Courts*, pp. 81-96.

63 As Babington indicated, the law implied malice or intent in these cases even though 'none can be presumed to bear malice to a dead child' - *Advice to Grand Jurors*, p. 172. See also the case quoted by Hoffer and Hull, *Murdering Mothers*, p. 76.

64 From Hunnisett's collection of Wiltshire coroners' bills, it would appear that approximately 14 per cent of women accused of new-born child murder between 1752 and 1796 were convicted, and the remainder acquitted. A similar proportion (17 per cent) of defendants on murder charges were also found guilty of murder. However, a further 27 per cent of defendants in adult homicide trials were found guilty of manslaughter, leaving only 56 per cent acquitted - Hunnisett (ed.), *Wiltshire Coroners' Bills*.

65 Mary Morgan, OBSP, March 1724, p. 7.

66 Ann Hullock, OBSP, May 1760, pp. 195-6.

67 Anne Milburne, 1728, ASSI 45/18/5/53, ASSI 45/18/6/88 (list of prisoners); Elizabeth Conney, 1744, ASSI 45/22/4/31-33A, ASSI 41/3, ASSI 41/4.

68 The trial judges, Daines Barrington and James Hayes, recommended Margaret Evans to the King's mercy on the grounds that 'no Proofs of Barbarous or Cruel Treatment were produced'. Although Lord Mansfield suggested that the judges should have stated the nature of the evidence in the case more clearly, Margaret Evans was reprieved and transported. The letters are in the Public Record Office, State Papers Domestic Entry Book SP44/87, pp. 180-5.

69 See Anne Stephens (OBSP, January 1691, p. 2), who was apparently found guilty because 'She had nothing to say for her self'.

70 For example, there are cases in which even a confession of live-birth and manifest evidence of violence were questioned by the court and the woman was acquitted. Similarly, some women were convicted in the absence of obviously inflammatory

evidence. Evidence of live-birth or violence failed to produce a conviction in the cases of Ann Bennison (1788, ASSI 45/36/2/10-12, ASSI 41/8), Sarah Ward (1797, ASSI 45/39/2/121-2, ASSI 41/9) and Elizabeth Packins (OBSP No. IV, April 1771, pp. 200-3). In the case of Mary Inman (OBSP, July 1721, p. 4), evidence similar to that resulting in acquittal in other cases led to a conviction.

71 Beattie, *Crime and the Courts*, pp. 97, 436-9. Beattie points out, however, that men and women were not treated differently by the courts in homicide cases - ibid., p. 97.

72 See, John Brydall, *Lex Spuriorum: Or, the Law Relating to Bastardy*, (London, 1703), p. 2.

73 A similar point has been made by Karen Clarke concerning the high acquittal rate in the nineteenth century – Karen Clarke, 'Infanticide, illegitimacy and the medical profession in nineteenth century England', *Bulletin of the Society for the Social History of Medicine*, 26 (1980), 11-14. Such disinterest in the fate of bastard children may have been encouraged by the influence of Locke's opinion that there were no innate principles in the mind, an opinion later explicitly used by Jeremy Bentham and William Godwin to reduce the significance of the death of a new-born child and to criticise the capital punishment of women accused of murdering such children. See: John Locke, *An Essay Concerning Human Understanding*, ed. John W. Yolton, (London, Everyman's Library [5th ed., 1706], 1976), pp. 1-31; Jeremy Bentham, *Theory of Legislation*, tr. R. Hildreth, (London, Kegan Paul, 1911), pp. 264-5. This work was originally published in French by Etienne Dumont at the turn of the nineteenth century. On Godwin's views on 'infanticide' and abortion, see, Angus McLaren, *Reproductive Rituals: The Perception of Fertility in England from the Sixteenth Century to the Nineteenth Century*, (London, Methuen, 1984), p. 187.

74 See the case in *The Diary of Richard Kay, 1716-1751*, eds. W. Brockbank and F. Kenworthy, (Manchester, Chetham Society, 1968), p. 125, in which Mary Walker's family sent her away from home even after her acquittal.

75 John Morgan, *Essays upon The Law of Evidence*, (3 vols., London, 1789), vol. I, p. 1.

76 For a discussion of this see Langbein, 'The criminal trial', 309-310; J. M. Beattie, 'Scales of justice: defense counsel and the English criminal trial in the eighteenth and nineteenth centuries', *Law and History Review*, 9 (1991), 221-67.

77 Langbein, 'The criminal trial', 311-13.

78 Langbein, 'The criminal trial', 306; Beattie, 'Scales of justice'.

79 According to Langbein ('The criminal trial', 306), the 'formation of the law of evidence from the middle of the eighteenth century is more or less contemporaneous with the onset of lawyerization of the criminal trial. My suggestion, therefore, is that the true historical function of the law of evidence may not have been so much jury control as lawyer control.'

80 Barbara J. Shapiro, *Probability and Certainty in Seventeenth-Century England*, (Princeton, Princeton University Press, 1983).

81 Geoffrey Gilbert, *The Law of Evidence*, (Dublin, 1754), p. 1.

82 Morgan, *The Law of Evidence*, vol. I, p. 2. On the influence of Locke, see also Barbara J. Shapiro, *'Beyond Reasonable Doubt' and 'Probable Cause'*, (Berkeley, University of California Press, 1991), pp. 25-7.

83 Gilbert, *The Law of Evidence*, p. 3.

84 Ibid., p. 112.

85 According to Thomas Peake, whose work owed much to Gilbert, 'the mind, comparing the circumstances of the particular case with the ordinary transactions of mankind, judges from those circumstances as to the probability of the story, and for want of better evidence, draws a conclusion from that before it'. See Thomas Peake, *A Compendium of the Law of Evidence*, (London, 1801), p. 14.

86 The need to assess witnesses in this way was discussed by Locke, *An Essay Concerning Human Understanding*, p. 356. Similar aspects of jurors' evaluation of testimony according to the witnesses' credibility were stressed by: Gilbert, *The Law of Evidence*, pp. 106-12; Morgan, *The Law of Evidence*, vol. I, pp. 7-8.

87 Morgan, *The Law of Evidence*, p. 10. See also Gilbert, *The Law of Evidence*, pp. 112-13.

88 Geoffrey Gilbert, *The Law of Evidence*, enlarged by Capel Lofft, (2 vols., London, 1791), vol. I, p. 309.

89 William Paley, *The Principles of Moral and Political Philosophy*, (2nd ed., London, 1786), pp. 551-2.

90 Reported in *The York Courant*, (28 March 1749).

91 Hale, *Pleas of the Crown*, vol. II, p. 289.

92 According to Morgan (*The Law of Evidence*, vol. I, p. 30), 'all presumptive evidence of felony should be admitted cautiously; for the law holds, that it is better that ten guilty persons escape, than that one innocent suffer'. The belief that it was better for the guilty to escape than for the innocent to suffer was the second maxim that, according to Paley, was contributing to 'injudicious acquittals' – Paley, *Moral and Political Philosophy*, pp. 551-3.

93 On these repeal attempts, see the next chapter.

94 Edward Coke, *The Third Part of the Institutes of the Laws of England*, (London, 1644), pp. 29, 137.

95 *The York Courant*, (28 March 1749).

96 For the emergence of this standard of proof in the late eighteenth and early nineteenth centuries, see J. H. Wigmore, *A Treatise on the Anglo-American System of Evidence in Trials at Common Law*, (3rd ed., Boston, Little, Brown and Company, 1940), vol. 9, para 2497. Also J. B. Thayer, *A Preliminary Treatise on Evidence at the Common Law*, (Boston, Little, Brown and Company, 1898), pp. 551-76.

97 Wigmore, *Treatise*, vol. 9, para 2511; Thayer, *Treatise*, pp. 551-76. See also Shapiro, *'Beyond Reasonable Doubt'*, pp. 1-41.

98 *A Guide to Juries*, p. 81.

99 Gilbert, *The Law of Evidence*, p. 41.

100 William Hunter, 'On the uncertainty of the signs of murder, in the case of bastard children', *Medical Observations and Inquiries*, 6 (1784), 280-1.

101 On the previous experience of trial jurors, especially towards the end of the century, see: King, '"Illiterate Plebians"', 283-90; Langbein, 'The criminal trial', 276.

102 Thomas Percival, *Medical Ethics*, (Manchester, 1803), p. 81.

103 *The Parliamentary History of England*, (1771-4), XVII, col. 452.

104 It may have been the statute's severity on this point that prompted Daines Barrington to suggest that the statute created a 'presumption of guilt, in the room of actual proof against the criminal' - *Observations on the Statutes, Chiefly the More Ancient*, (2nd ed., London, 1766), p. 424.

105 Barrington, *Observations on the Statutes*, p. 424.

106 Blackstone, *Commentaries*, (1765-9), vol. IV, p. 198.

107 Eden, *Principles of Penal Law*, pp. 15-16.

108 For counsel's knowledge of Hunter's work, for example, see Elizabeth Jarvis, OBSP, January 1800, pp. 77-82.

109 For examples of extensive examination and cross-examination of medical witnesses, and the doubts that such questioning raised, see: Elizabeth Packins, OBSP No. IV, April 1771, pp. 200-3; Elizabeth Harris, OBSP No. V, May 1781, pp. 266-9.

110 Hunter, 'On the uncertainty of the signs', p. 286.

111 Hay, 'Property, authority and the criminal law'; Radzinowicz, *A History of English Criminal Law*, vol. I, pp. 83-106. On changing attitudes to capital punishment, see: V. A. C. Gatrell, *The Hanging Tree: Execution and the English People 1770-1868*, (Oxford, Oxford University Press, 1994); Randall McGowen, 'The body and punishment in eighteenth-century England', *Journal of Modern History*, 59 (December 1987), 651-79; Randall McGowen, 'Civilizing punishment: the end of the public execution in England', *Journal of British Studies*, 33 (July 1994), 257-82.

112 Radzinowicz, *A History of English Criminal Law*, vol. I, p. 86.

7

Single women, bastardy and the law: the decline and fall of the 1624 statute

Introduction

In 1743, in a footnote to the report of Elizabeth Shudrick's trial for murdering her new-born child, the editor of the Old Bailey Sessions Papers suggested that such cases 'would not so frequently occur at the Old Bailey, if the law were more generally known, viz. 21 Jac. I. c. 27'.[1] Although a steady stream of cases continued to reach the trial courts throughout the eighteenth century, it would be a mistake to explain the prevalence of such cases in terms of ignorance of the 1624 statute. The provisions of the 1624 statute continued to dominate discussions of new-born child murder both in and out of the courts throughout the century. The statute was referred to in legal texts, in court records, and in newspaper reports, and was discussed by a wide variety of writers interested both in this particular crime and in broader issues relating to penal policy. The statute's influence is also evident in local responses to suspected murders. The statutory emphases on the unmarried mothers of bastards, on concealment, and on intent were echoed both in the selection of suspects and in the testimony of witnesses and suspects before magistrates and coroners.

Although the 1624 statute continued to dominate the legal process, it was increasingly viewed as anomalous. In the light of changing attitudes to the character of accused women, and to the nature of the evidence and the standard of proof required to produce a conviction, extensive discussions of the statutory presumption served only to limit the statute's scope and application in the courts. This process increased the number of trials at common law, and discouraged juries from convicting defendants.

In the 1770s, in response to waning application of the 1624 statute, several members of parliament made four separate, but in some ways related, attempts to repeal it. These attempts were unsuccessful and the statute remained in force until it was repealed in 1803. In this final chapter, I shall examine the circumstances surrounding these frustrated attempts at repeal in the 1770s and explore the factors that influenced eventual repeal at the turn of the nineteenth century. I shall argue that attempts to repeal the statute in the 1770s should be seen in the light of broad debates about the administration of justice, and that the failure of these attempts can be traced to widespread and influential conservative beliefs (typified by the attitudes of the Lords and the judges) that political and social stability would be more readily achieved by the selective use of existing capital statutes than by criminal law reform. I shall also submit that it was, perhaps ironically, the influence of the judiciary and the persistence of conservative beliefs about the maintenance of law and order, rather than the force of arguments for law reform, that inspired successful repeal of the 1624 statute in 1803.

Attempts to repeal the 1624 statute, 1772-6

In November 1770, at the instigation of Sir William Meredith, a committee was appointed from the House of Commons 'to consider of so much of the Criminal Laws as relate to Capital Offences'. In May of the following year, Sir Charles Bunbury reported to the Commons that the committee recommended the repeal of four capital statutes. Before the report could be considered, however, parliament was prorogued. In January 1772, the committee was re-appointed, and in March of that year Sir Charles Bunbury reported the committee's recommendations that eight capital statutes should be repealed: the four statutes previously recommended and an additional four, including the 1624 statute. When the committee's suggestions were debated in the Commons, the House rejected motions to repeal both the 1624 statute and a statute of 1597 according to which the abduction of an heiress against her will had been made a felony without benefit of clergy. A bill to repeal the six remaining statutes was prepared by Sir Charles Bunbury, Sir William Meredith, Henry Herbert, Charles James Fox, Sir George Savile, the serjeant-at-law John Glynn, and Constantine Phipps. The resulting 'Penal Laws Bill' was passed by the Commons on 21 May 1772 but was lost in the Lords, either through the prorogation of parliament or through the opposition of certain members of the House.[2]

On 6 May 1772, only a few days after the Commons had rejected the motion to repeal the 1624 statute as part of wider reforms of the penal law, Thomas Lockhart introduced a new bill aimed exclusively at repealing the 1624 statute and at 'more effectually preventing the Concealment of the Deaths of such Children'. This measure was passed by the Commons, after amendment, on 22 May 1772. It was read for the first time in the Lords on 26 May, but on 1 June the second reading was postponed for a month, during which time parliament was prorogued and the bill was lost.[3]

Eight months later, shortly after the new parliamentary session had opened, Lockhart made a further attempt to repeal the 1624 statute. On 3 February 1773, he was given leave 'to bring in a Bill to repeal the said Act; and to prevent the Concealment of the Deaths of Bastard Children'. Once again, the bill was passed by the Commons but, after delays in the Lords, was lost on prorogation.[4] The fourth attempt to repeal the 1624 statute was introduced in February 1776 by one of the architects of the 'Penal Laws Bill', Sir Charles Bunbury. The bill was passed by the Commons, after amendments, on 5 March 1776. It was read twice and committed by the Lords but the committee stage was repeatedly postponed until the bill was eventually lost when parliament was prorogued in May of that year.[5]

The perseverence of those involved in these attempts to repeal the 1624 statute illustrates the level of attention that this particular crime and the 1624 statute was attracting in this period. However, although this burst of parliamentary activity can be seen partly as a product of specific humanitarian objections to the statute and partly as a consequence of the courts' refusal to utilise the statutory presumption, both the impetus for repeal and the reasons for failure should be viewed in a much wider context.

The initial attempt to include the 1624 statute in the 'Penal Laws Bill' of 1772 was linked to debates about the execution of justice in the eighteenth century. Contemporary perceptions that the broadening scope of capital punishment was failing to control the crime rate or to deter criminals initiated considerable discussion about the most appropriate way in which to administer justice. In the early eighteenth century, tracts such as *Hanging, Not Punishment Enough* and George Ollyffe's *An Essay Humbly Offer'd, for an Act of Parliament to prevent Capital Crimes*, argued that the major aim of punishment was deterrence, and advocated the strict enforcement of capital statutes and the use of aggravated forms of the death penalty, such as breaking on the wheel.[6] This 'doctrine of maximum severity' found support both from the legislature and from writers later in the century, such as the novelist and magistrate Henry Fielding and the lawyer and Methodist minister Martin Madan, who argued that problems with the penal system were to be found not in the nature of the laws but in their application.[7] The severity of the law, they argued, was so frequently mitigated by the decisions of judges and juries and by the use of the royal prerogative of mercy that it was no longer serving as a deterrent. As Madan argued in his *Thoughts on Executive Justice*, published in 1785, 'punishment has been rendered so *uncertain*, or rather the suspension of it so *certain*, as to prevent the operation of the laws'.[8] Madan's solution to the problems apparently associated with this loosening of the law was the full enforcement of all capital statutes.[9]

Writers and members of parliament pushing for reform of the criminal law in the second half of the eighteenth century agreed with writers such as Madan that the main aim of penal law was to deter not punish, and that, as Madan argued, 'to enact a law, and not to enforce the execution of it, is against all reason'.[10] They also conceded that the current uncertainty of punishment undermined the use of the law as deterrent. These reformers, however, refused to accept that capital punishment should be more strictly enforced or aggravated. They argued instead that capital statutes were disregarded by prosecutors, and by judges and juries, simply because they were too severe, that is, because the punishment was in most cases out of proportion to the severity of the crime. As the lawyer and legal writer Sollom Emlyn had asserted in his preface to the second edition of *State Trials*, published in 1730, when death 'is indiscriminately inflicted, it leaves no room to difference the punishments of crimes widely different in their own nature'.[11] The point was reiterated by William Meredith in his initial speech urging the Commons to consider reforming the criminal laws in 1770: 'in a well-regulated state, nothing is more requisite than to proportion the punishment to the crime, and to satisfy the minds of the people that equal justice is administered to every delinquent'.[12] Taking their cue from continental reformers such as Montesquieu and Beccaria and from earlier English works,[13] would-be reformers of the criminal law argued that the solution to the inconsistency of the law was to restrict the number of capital statutes. The consistent application of moderate but certain punishments would then enable the law to function adequately as a deterrent, thereby ensuring the maintenance of social order.

It is apparent that arguments used both for and against repeal of the 1624 statute in the 1770s closely reflected critical elements of this broader debate. In 1772, for example, Edmund Burke, Charles James Fox, Harbord Harbord and Sir William Meredith argued in support of the motion to repeal the 1624 statute 'that nothing could more strongly prove the absurdity and inexpediency of the law, than the impossibility of putting it in execution, under which the judges found themselves; that laws were made to be executed, not dispensed with'.[14] One year later, Lockhart expanded these views in his speech to the Commons:

> I am in hopes, Sir, when this matter becomes seriously considered, the Lords will give their assent; for at present the law is of little use, as the judge, the jury, and auditors, notwithstanding the circumstances are plain, often acquit unfortunate women. Those acquittals, Sir, encourage

women who are unhappily in this predicament; and the law, from its severity, is rendered ineffectual. If any lenity is to be shewn, let it be by the legislature. I hope, Sir, to see the Act made in the reign of James the 1st repealed: it is now indeed of little effect; ... and I would have parliament, however laudable it may be in the judges to dispense with the Act, repeal it, and have a punishment for the future, the certainty of which may deter women from destroying and afterwards concealing the deaths of their bastard children.[15]

Opponents of repeal in 1772 challenged such arguments by insisting that the law was appropriately severe for a destructive crime. Moreover, they contested that judicial leniency in these cases was neither a disadvantage nor a factor inducing uncertainty, but an example of the wisdom of the legal system: they opposed repeal of the statute on the very basis 'that the judges seldom or never put it rigorously in force'.[16] While this argument was later adopted by William Paley in his influential apology of the established system, *The Principles of Moral and Political Philosophy*,[17] it was rejected by would-be reformers who believed that disused statutes undermined the authority of the judicial system. As William Eden argued in the early 1770s:

Obsolete and useless statutes should be repealed; for they debilitate the authority of such as still exist and are necessary. Neglect on this point is well compared by Lord Bacon to the cruelty of Mezentius, who left the living to perish in the arms of the dead.[18]

In addition to employing many of the arguments used to promote reform on a wider scale, would-be repealers of the 1624 statute also introduced a variety of arguments more directly related to the offence in question. They pointed out, for example, that the laws concerning the maintenance of bastard children and the 1624 statute were unjust when taken together, since the former encouraged concealment by rendering the bearing of a bastard shameful and punishable, while the latter then punished that concealment: 'nothing could be more unjust, or inconsistent with the principles of all law, than first to force a woman through modesty to concealment, and then to hang her for that concealment'.[19] Proponents of repeal also adopted the rhetoric of emergent humanitarian constructions of suspects by arguing that defendants were often modest and virtuous, rather than lewd, women and that concealment should not be taken as evidence of murder.[20]

Supporters of repeal in 1772 concluded by suggesting not only that it would be unwise for the English parliament to emulate continental law on the subject (as opponents of repeal had argued that it should) but also that continuance of the 1624 statute was unjust to bastard children since it allowed their deaths to be concealed with impunity:

that the example of Denmark and France, despotic countries, ought to be no model for us; that this observation only proved, that the law of France ought not to be that of England; that the parliament which made this law was not infallible; that, while all due praise was allowed to legitimate children, it was not just to give a squeeze in the neck to bastards; and that humanity and justice pleaded strongly for the alteration contended for.[21]

Although proponents of repeal in 1772 acknowledged humanitarian accounts of suspects as modest virtuous women, they were not suggesting either that the majority of defendants were necessarily innocent of murder (as William Hunter later did) or that women convicted of this crime should remain unpunished. In line with their primary concern with reforming the criminal law and providing courts with appropriately severe deterrents, they were arguing instead for the more certain application of a suitable (that is, lesser) punishment that would effectually discourage women from murdering their illegitmate children. This strategy for law reform was explicitly expressed in Lockhart's bill 'for more effectually preventing the Concealment of the Deaths of such Children', introduced in 1772. Having pointed out that 'it is repugnant to natural Justice that the horrid Crime of Murder should in any Case be presumed without clear and satisfactory Evidence' (echoing the new sensitivity to evidential rules and standards of proof), the bill's preamble insisted that it was nevertheless 'highly expedient and necessary that the Concealment of the Deaths of Bastard Children should be prevented by the Punishment of Persons so offending'. The solution, according to Lockhart, was to transport women convicted of new-born child murder to America rather than hang them.[22] By reducing the severity of the punishment, Lockhart hoped to remove resistance to conviction in these cases and reassert the authority of the courts.

Opposition to the 1624 statute in this period may also have been sustained by doubts about the relative merits of statute and common law. In 1760, Michael Foster, in his discussion of the statute on stabbing, argued that while 'Rules of the Common-Law in Cases of this kind may be considered as the Result of the Wisdom and Experience of many Ages', the statute on stabbing had been made 'upon the Spur of the Times'. He also suggested that prosecution 'with due Vigour and proper Severity' at common law would have rendered the statute unnecessary. 'This Observation', he continued, 'will hold with regard to many of our Penal Statutes made upon special and pressing Occasions, and savouring rankly of the Times.'[23] The belief that such statutes were inferior to common law, that they should be enacted only on a temporary basis, and that they should be repealed once they no longer suited the customs and dispositions of a changing society, may have been in part responsible for the decline of the 1624 statute and the return to common law rules of evidence in the courts.[24] Such beliefs may also have reinforced arguments for the statute's repeal.

Arguments for repeal of the 1624 statute in the 1770s constituted a substantial attack on the construction, the implications, and the application of that statute from a number of directions. However, these arguments were repeatedly deflected by either the Commons or the Lords, and the statute remained in force for another thirty years. The reasons for this are complex. In the Commons in 1772, opponents of reform agreed with reformers that the deaths of bastards should be prevented.[25] They asserted 'that the practice of destroying children of any kind was destructive to population; that it was consequently the part of the legislature to make every possible provision against so dangerous an evil'.[26] They insisted, however, that the 1624 statute was appropriately framed for the purpose since it had been considered more than once by the 'highly and justly esteemed' parliament that had passed it, and had been made at first temporary and only after further debate made perpetual. These circumstances, they argued, 'were at least presumptions in its favour'. They also justified the statute's construction on the basis that 'the same law obtained in Denmark, Sweden, and France', and by emphasising 'that the proof of the crime intended to be provided against by this law was very difficult'. By rendering 'concealment of the birth of a bastard child a capital crime', the statute 'was solely calculated for rendering that proof more easy'. Opponents of repeal concluded by observing that the statute 'had hitherto been attended with advantages, which entirely over-balanced its disadvantages; that the judges seldom or never put it rigorously in force, but used a discreet latitude'.[27]

The initial motion to repeal the 1624 statute in the Commons in 1772 was defeated, and later bills were lost in the Lords, largely because these arguments against repeal were firmly embedded in influential, conservative opinions about crime and the criminal law, and about the growing problems of national and international political stability. These opinions were responsible not only for the failure of reformers to repeal the 1624 statute, but also for the rejection of broader attempts to reform the criminal law in the 1770s and 1780s.

The first factor underlying successful opposition to repeal of the 1624 statute was persistent and widespread support for the doctrine of maximum severity, or at least for the retention, or extension, of capital punishment. In the absence of changes in the administration of criminal justice and the poor law, and in the light of growing fears about the rising incidence of crimes against property, it appeared undesirable to relax the severity of the criminal law. Although most concern was directed against property crimes, the legislature still believed that murder should be punished with loss of life. Indeed, in 1752, 'An Act for better preventing the horrid Crime of Murder' had introduced an aggravated form of the death penalty on the basis that murder had 'of late been more frequently perpetrated than formerly'.[28] Even reformers (except Beccaria and, later, Jeremy Bentham) preferred to retain capital punishment for murder.[29] In this climate, the principle of sentencing women found guilty to death was preferred to Lockhart's suggestion that they be transported.

The suggestion that convicted women should be transported raised further doubts about the wisdom of repeal. Unrest in the American colonies, stemming to a large extent from debts incurred during the war with France and from subsequent attempts to procure some compensation from America in the form of Stamp Duty, was increasingly evident in the late 1760s and 1770s. The situation became critical after the 'Boston Tea Party' in 1773, resulting in the American War of Independence and in the loss of thirteen North American colonies previously under British sovereignty. The implications of these events for the repeal of the 1624 statute were twofold. First, it was increasingly apparent that the colonies would no longer be available for the reception of transported convicts. In the absence of an alternative destination at that time, and amidst a variety of further criticisms of the effects of transportation, motions to increase the number eligible for transportation were unlikely to be approved.[30] Second, events in America contributed to a period of increasing political instability in England. Concern about George III's use of the royal prerogative, the American question, and repeated calls for parliamentary reform, together with a growing number of riots about food prices, turnpikes, popery, low wages, the replacement of manual labour with machines, and a variety of other grievances, combined to instil a feeling of insecurity in the legislature. In these circumstances, parliament resisted attempts to weaken the severity of the criminal law.

It is not clear whether debates about repeal were also influenced by party issues. Some of the men prominently involved in attempts to reform the criminal law were certainly associated with the Rockingham Whigs at some stage in this period. This Whig group, which comprised old corps Whigs such as Lord Rockingham and Sir George Savile and younger men such as Charles James Fox, had been humiliated by their exclusion from Chatham's ministry in 1766, and spent the 1770s in opposition to Lord North's ministry and at odds with other Whig factions. A number of those involved in criminal law reform in the 1770s had associations with this group: Sir William Meredith, who presented the original motion to consider the criminal law relating to capital punishment and who supported the motion to repeal the 1624 statute; Charles James Fox and Edmund

Burke, who both spoke for repeal in 1772; and Sir George Savile, who was part of the committee ordered to bring in the 'Penal Laws Bill' in 1772.[31] On the other side, Jeremiah Dyson, who opposed repeal of the 1624 statute in 1772, had previously voted against Rockingham.[32]

For a number of reasons, it would be a mistake to over-emphasise the importance of party issues or alliance with Rockingham as a factor in determining the outcome of attempts to repeal the 1624 statute. In the first instance, the importance of a party system only developed gradually in the late eighteenth century, largely as a result of the increasing political instability described above. Throughout the 1760s, 1770s and 1780s, neither elections nor parliamentary debates were greatly influenced by party matters: it was accepted that members of parliament would give their votes independent of Crown or party; 'Whigs' and 'Tories' combined in coalition ministries led by statesmen who enjoyed the King's favour; and groups of Whigs frequently opposed each other in the House. While separate groups of politicians could undoubtedly be identified in parliament in addition to the large number of independent members, the concept of party was nevertheless primitive during the years in which repeal of the 1624 statute was attempted.[33]

Moreover, as John Brooke has suggested, the problem of crime and the extent of capital punishment became the concern of a few individuals 'drawn from all quarters of the house'.[34] Constantine Phipps, for example, identified himself with the 'King's friends', and a number of the men involved clearly remained independent of any party interests. Interpretation is also complicated by the fact that even those reformers allied to Rockingham were divided on some issues. For example, while Burke supported repeal of the 1624 statute, he voted against Fox and Harbord on the question of repealing the statute concerning the abduction of heiresses.[35] However, it remains a possibility, open to further investigation, that attempts to repeal a number of capital statutes in the 1770s failed because they had been introduced by men who were to some extent politically isolated not only from the government but also from other Whigs, and who were proposing radical alternatives to the political, social, and penal standards of the day.[36]

Although further research is required to clarify the question of party, it is clear that the House of Lords did exert considerable influence over attempts to repeal both the 1624 statute and other penal laws. While the original motion to repeal the 1624 statute was defeated in the Commons, all three further attempts were lost in the Lords. The 'Penal Laws Bill', eventually passed by the Commons in May 1772, was also lost in the Lords. At first sight, it would appear that these bills were lost simply as a result of prorogation of parliament. On closer inspection, the Lords' influence appears to have been more deliberate than coincidental. When considering bills to repeal the 1624 statute in 1772, 1773, and 1776, the Lords deferred the reading or committal of the bills for one, two, and six months respectively, thereby facilitating their loss through prorogation. Furthermore, when Lockhart introduced his second motion to repeal the statute in the Commons in 1773, he commented that he 'had the honour of being one who was appointed with others last session to bring in a Bill for the more effectually punishing the concealing the death of bastard children; and though it met with a favourable reception here, it was rejected in the other House of Parliament'.[37]

The Lords' opposition to these attempts to repeal the 1624 statute was consistent with their conservative reputation. In 1777, Sir William Meredith, opposing the bill to make arson in dockyards a capital felony, contended that the House of Lords had rejected the 'Penal Laws Bill' in 1772 'for this reason, "It was an innovation, they said, and subversion of law"'.[38] Many years later, in 1819, Sir James Mackintosh also claimed that the Lords had successfully opposed the passage of that bill.[39] The tendency of the House of Lords to oppose 'any relaxation of the severity of criminal law' may have been due in part to the presence in the House of a number of judges who were collectively opposed to reform.[40] The judges supported the principle of maximum severity mitigated only by judicial leniency, an approach that became crystallized in the works of Paley. Judicial influence on attempted reform was increasingly evident during the last decades of the century. Pitt's opinion, expressed in 1787, that any proposed change in punishment ought to be considered by the judges before its adoption, was repeated in the early years of the nineteenth century when it contributed to the failure of Samuel Romilly and others to reform the criminal law.[41] The attitudes of the Lords and the judges were similarly influential in the 1770s and ensured that the 1624 statute, although rarely used, remained in force.

There is, however, a further aspect to persistent opposition to reform in this period. As Douglas Hay has argued, the persistence of a severe penal law which could be extenuated only by the merciful intervention of the king at the suggestion of judges or local elites served to strengthen the authority of the propertied ruling classes: the performance of a regular number of selected executions each year encouraged the populace to fear the law, while the exercise of discretionary powers to pardon offenders fostered deference. Rather than providing grounds for repeal, the non-uniform application of many capital statutes was seen instead as highly expedient, since it represented an important tool in the maintenance of social order. For most of the ruling class, therefore, criminal law reform was simply undesirable.[42]

The failure of reformers to repeal the 1624 statute can be seen in a similar light. Occasional executions and the persistence of the statute on the statute books provided a constant reminder of the potential severity of the law. It may not be coincidental that in cases in which the 1624 statute was referred to in court (according to the trial reports), the defendant was usually found guilty. In 1734, Mercy Hornby was found guilty of murder immediately after the clerk was ordered by the judge to read the statute in court.[43] And at the trial of Mary Curtis at Chelmsford in 1740, the jury found the defendant guilty after the court had noted that 'There is an Act of Parliament that makes it Felony to conceal an Infant after its Birth, if it born living or dead'.[44] It is possible, therefore, that the 1624 statute was employed to encourage, or at least to justify, occasional select convictions intended to create a deterrent. Conversely, restrained application of the statutory presumption and the use of royal pardons resulted in few convictions and even fewer executions, thereby reinforcing the prestige of, and the deference due to, both local and assize officials. In these circumstances, repeal of the 1624 statute was considered unnecessary.

Lord Ellenborough's Act, 1803

In the 1770s, would-be law reformers argued that the causes of both humanity and justice would be better served if the 1624 statute were to be repealed and the death sentence replaced by a lesser punishment in these cases. Repeal was blocked at that time by influential conservative resistance to weakening the criminal law in any direction. At the turn of the nineteenth century, opposition to law reform in general and to arguments for repeal of the 1624 statute in particular was reinforced by a number of factors. Rising levels of bastardy within a rising population contributed to dramatic increases in the poor rates and heightened the antipathy to women who burdened the parish. Opponents of wholesale political and social reform also placed increasing emphasis on the importance of improving individual morality in engineering social change, an emphasis that is evident both in Christopher Hodgson's dismissal of the sympathy towards accused women advocated by William Hunter and in the warnings expressed in printed broadsheets from the period.[45] Concerns about the lawlessness and moral laxity of an expanding population were also intensified by events of the French Revolution, which, while they 'necessitated an immediate confrontation with the issues of reform in Britain',[46] encouraged the adoption only of gradual, conservative methods of achieving that reform.

It is perhaps surprising, therefore, that the 1624 statute was successfully repealed in 1803, during a period of strong opposition to criminal law reform. This aspect of the repeal has generally been ignored by historians who have either explained repeal as the eventual recognition of persistent humanitarian claims that the statute was unjust or have depicted the 1803 statute as the inevitable outcome of a longstanding campaign to repeal the 1624 statute that had begun in the 1770s. Hoffer and Hull, for example, have argued that, in legalising the leniency that juries had been showing during the eighteenth century, the 1803 statute represented a return to conformity between law and humane social opinion.[47] Sauer has also suggested that what he regards as the 'unfairness' of the 1624 statute was 'replaced by a more equitable law' in 1803.[48]

Although humanitarian arguments about the severity of the 1624 statute certainly contributed to the context in which repeal became possible, such historical interpretations of events in 1803 fail to recognise critical elements in the origins, construction, and consequences of the repealing statute.[49] Close analysis of the 1803 statute suggests that repeal was not primarily the fruit of enlightened reforming ideals that had espoused new approaches to suspects and inspired attempts at criminal law reform in the last half of the eighteenth century. On the contrary, repeal appears to have been the product of a conservative legal and political philosophy that had opposed earlier reform.

The bill proposing repeal of the 1624 statute was introduced to the House of Lords on Monday 28 March 1803 by Lord Ellenborough, Lord Chief Justice of the King's Bench.[50] The first section of what he referred to as the 'Maiming and Wounding Bill' rendered a wide variety of offences (including procuring 'the Miscarriage of any Woman, then being quick with Child') capital felonies. The second section concerned repeal of the 1624 statute. In his speech to the House, Ellenborough explained that the reason for including this second clause was 'to relieve the judges from the difficulties they labour under in respect to the trial of women indicted for child-murder in the case of bastards':

> At present the judges were obliged to strain the law for the sake of lenity, and to admit the slightest suggestion that the child was still-born as evidence of the fact. Upon this point, the law, as it now stands, is so severe in a constructive view towards the mother of a bastard child, supposed to have been murdered after its birth, that in case of such child having been found dead, or being made away with, the proof of the mother having previously concealed her pregnancy, is to be taken as sufficient to convict of the murder. A clause was therefore inserted in the present bill, repealing the law as it now stood, and re-enacting a proviso, requiring that evidence should first be duly admitted, that such bastard child was, or was not, born living, previous to the final decision upon any trial.[51]

Although the wording of the initial bill reflected Ellenborough's intent to bring the law in line with the practice adopted by assize courts since the middle of the eighteenth century, it also betrayed the persistent influence of the statute to be repealed. According to Ellenborough's initial drafting of the bill, if any woman endeavoured to conceal the death of a bastard child 'as that it may not come to light whether it was born alive or not, but be concealed, in every such Case the said Mother shall suffer Death as in Case of Murder; except such Mother can make Proof, by One Witness at the least, that the Child (whose Death was by her so intended to be concealed), was born dead, probable Evidence having been first given that such Child was born alive'.[52]

On 27 April, the bill was read a second time and committed to the whole House. Two days later, when the Lords considered the bill, a number of amendments were proposed and incorporated into the second draft. The main amendments were alterations to the first section of the bill and the addition of a new section enacting that procuring the miscarriage of a pregnant woman before 'quickening' (that is, before the child had moved in the womb) was a felony punishable by imprisonment or transportation. Only the final sentence of the section repealing the 1624 statute was amended. According to the amendment, suspects were now to provide proof either 'that the Child ... was born dead, reasonable Evidence having been first given that such Child was born alive, or, that being born alive, the same afterwards died a natural Death'.[53]

On 9 May, the bill was re-committed to the House and further amendments were made. One week later, the bill was read a third time and, after yet further amendment, was passed and sent to the Commons. After the Commons had made minor amendments to the first section, the bill was returned to the Lords and received the royal assent on 24 June 1803.[54]

The text of the statute finally passed by both Houses differed substantially from that of previous drafts printed by the Lords. After repealing both the 1624 statute and an identical Irish statute passed in 1707 because, according to the preamble 'they have been found in sundry Cases, difficult and inconvenient to put in Practice', the 1803 statute enacted:

> that, from and after the said first Day of *July* in the said Year of our Lord One thousand eight hundred and three, the Trials in England and Ireland respectively of Women charged with the Murder of any Issue of their Bodies, Male or Female, which being born alive would by Law be Bastard, shall proceed and be governed by such and the like Rules of Evidence and of Presumption as are by Law used and allowed to take place in respect to other Trials for Murder, and as if the said two several Acts had never been made.

IV. Provided always, and be it enacted, That it shall and may be lawful
for the Jury by whose Verdict any Prisoner charged with such Murder
as aforesaid shall be acquitted, to find, in case it shall so appear in
Evidence that the Prisoner was delivered of Issue of her Body, Male or
Female, which, if born alive, would have been Bastard, and that she
did, by secret Burying, or otherwise, endeavour to conceal the Birth
thereof, and thereupon it shall be lawful for the Court before which
such Prisoner shall have been tried, to adjudge that such Prisoner shall
be committed to the Common Gaol or House of Correction for any
Time not exceeding two Years.[55]

The passage and construction of the 1803 statute provide clues both
about its origins and about the perceptions and intentions of its legislators. In the light of the customary opposition to law reform demonstrated
by the Lords and the judiciary, it is striking that the initial bill was
introduced in the Lords by a judge, Lord Ellenborough, who had succeeded Lord Kenyon as Lord Chief Justice of the King's Bench in 1802.
Ellenborough's views on crime and punishment were strongly influenced
by William Paley, who had dedicated his *Principles of Moral and Political
Philosophy* to Ellenborough's father, Edmund Law, then Bishop of Carlisle. Ellenborough himself frequently corresponded with Paley,[56] and
although his adherence to Paley's views was not uncritical,[57] his speeches
in the Lords (particularly in opposition to Samuel Romilly's efforts to
repeal certain capital statutes in 1810 and 1811)[58] demonstrate his support
for Paley's beliefs that the principal aim of punishment was deterrence
and that the severity of punishment should be founded 'not in the guilt of
the offender, but in the necessity of preventing the repetition of the
offence'.[59] For both Paley and Ellenborough, the most effective means of
preventing crime was to provide punishments of maximum severity in
order to inspire terror, and to allow that severity to be mitigated only at
the discretion of the bench. Both men, therefore, supported the established system and were opposed to reform.

Ellenborough did, however, accept that excessive penalties could
sometimes defeat the purpose of legislation by discouraging conviction.[60]
This factor, allied to his belief in 'expediency, drawn from practical
experience',[61] may have encouraged Ellenborough to consider repealing
what had come to be regarded as an obsolete statute. In this case,
however, it was not the severity of the punishment that Ellenborough
considered counter-productive but the construction of the legal presumption whereby guilt was established. By sanctioning a return to common
law rules of evidence and presumption, Ellenborough hoped to ease the
courts' difficulties in these cases, to discourage the indulgence of judges
and jurymen, and to encourage conviction.

It is possible that Ellenborough was influenced by earlier humanitarian arguments against the statutory presumption of 1624. As A. V. Dicey noted in a series of lectures on law and public opinion originally presented at Harvard Law School in 1898, changes in the law are characteristically the product not only of opinions held at the time, but also of those prevalent twenty or thirty years previously.[62] He also pointed out that laws passed during what he termed 'the period of old toryism or legislative quiescence' (1800-1830) included not only reactionary laws, but also reforms 'due to the increasing development of humanitarianism'.[63]

However, it is apparent that Ellenborough made few concessions to the designs of earlier critics of the 1624 statute. Ellenborough's first draft of the bill retained the wording of the 1624 statute, including its emphasis on concealment, and simply added a qualifying clause condoning the practice followed by most courts from the mid-eighteenth century. Furthermore, in accordance with the doctrine of maximum severity, capital punishment was retained. While the bill therefore brought the law in line with evidential standards developed in the eighteenth century, it failed to countenance any re-evaluation of the character or culpability of accused women. The initial bill, more an amendment, than a repeal, of the 1624 statute, illustrated Ellenborough's preference for expediency over what he later termed the 'visionary plans of speculative improvement'.[64]

The precise origins of the final construction of the 1803 statute remain unclear. Significant differences between the initial bill and the statute can be traced to later debates in the Lords,[65] and, since his personal papers contain a hand-written draft of those sections of the statute relating to new-born child murder and concealment, Ellenborough himself may have been responsible for drafting the amendments.[66] It is clear, however, that the final text of the 1803 statute, like that of the initial bill, failed to recognise humanitarian concerns. Although the 1803 statute certainly repealed the 1624 statute with greater clarity than the initial bill had done, women found guilty of murdering their new-born bastard children were still to be punished capitally.

The last clause of the statute also failed to acknowledge objections to the manner in which suspicions had been generated and guilt established in these cases. The final clause directed that if a single woman was acquitted of murder, but was found to have concealed the birth of her bastard child, she could then be imprisoned for up to two years (even if the child had been still-born). This alternative verdict at first appears to represent a concession to demands for greater leniency in the law. On closer inspection, it reveals the force of persistent prejudices against accused women. As in cases tried under the 1624 statute, indictments needed to specify only that the child was a bastard before the woman could be punished for concealment. By punishing only the mothers of illegitimate children, the statute's final clause ignored humanitarian pleas for a re-assessment of the pressures faced by single women and sustained local preoccupations with the moral and legal significance of concealment.

The persistence of concealment as a criterion of guilt further betrays the legislators' intentions. Although the validity of equating concealment with criminality had been forcefully challenged in the last half of the eighteenth century, the 1803 statute nevertheless continued to judge such behaviour as suspicious and punishable in its own right. The peculiarity of the concealment clause was that it allowed a jury to punish a woman for concealment (which was not in itself a substantive crime) after she had been acquitted of the crime with which she had been charged. Thus, while repeal of the 1624 statute removed what had come to be seen as an anomaly from the statute books, the final clause of the 1803 statute constructed what was soon regarded as another anomaly in its place: that is, the power of the courts to indict a woman for one offence, and yet punish her for another.[67]

The peculiarity and severity of the concealment clause did not pass unnoticed. Even the surgeon Christopher Johnson, who was critical of William Hunter's approach to suspects and who considered that most cases amounted 'to little less than murder', saw no justification for this clause.[68] And in 1819, while testifying to the Select Committee on Criminal Law, William Evans, a barrister and vice-chancellor of the County Palatinate of Lancaster, complained that the clause had increased the chances of a woman being indicted and convicted for the murder of her child on insufficient evidence:

> the late Mr George Hardinge [one of the King's Counsel] actually recommended grand juries to find true bills against persons indicted for murdering their bastard children, upon insufficient evidence of the commission of that crime, in order that the court might have an opportunity of punishing the individuals for the minor offence, if they should be proved to have concealed the birth of the bastard child. In case a woman ought to be punished for concealing the birth of a bastard child who happens to die, that punishment ought not to depend upon collateral circumstances, in consequence of which a jury might be induced to find an indictment for murder.[69]

To some extent, the construction of the 1803 statute was therefore as severe as that of the statute that it replaced. In practice, it also caused the courts as many administrative problems as the terms of the 1624 statute had caused them previously. These problems partly stemmed from the persistent influence of the 1624 statute itself. For example, although the 1803 statute empowered the courts to punish any single woman who endeavoured to conceal the *birth* of her child, references to concealment of *death* continued to appear in the court records. Indeed, the inquisition into the death of Sarah Riley's child in 1806, which concluded that Sarah 'did endeavour privately so to conceal the death of the said female child as that it might not come to light whether it were born alive or not but be concealed', is simply a transcript of the relevant section of the 1624 statute.[70] Assize clerks also appear to have been unsure of precisely how to indict an accused woman for murder and yet bring her under the terms of the concealment clause. In some cases, indictments drawn up against women for murdering new-born bastard children were duplicated with the term bastard removed.[71] In others, the indictment was unnecessarily concluded with the phrase 'against the Form of the Statute'.[72] Such inconsistencies in the records suggest that neither local nor assize officials were thoroughly conversant with the terms of the new statute.

More significantly, there was also confusion as to the nature of the offence with which suspects could be charged. Although the 1803 statute, like that of 1624, did not create a new offence, and although suspects could therefore only be indicted and tried for murder, some women were, according to their committal notes, charged with concealment. In 1804, for example, Sarah Littlewood stood 'charged by the Coroner's Inquest … with secreting the birth of the said male bastard child'.[73] It would appear that some local officials, prosecutors and jurors, perhaps prompted by their own belief in concealment as a mark of criminality, misinterpreted the 1803 statute as having created a new substantive crime of concealment. That this error was prevalent is suggested by the fact that, in 1813, Simon Le Blanc, a Justice of the King's Bench, felt obliged to explain the law in his charge to the grand jury at York:

> concealment of the birth is still a circumstance to be considered, in connexion with the other parts of the case, but it by no means forms a conclusive proof of guilt, and you will not find a true bill, unless from other circumstances, you find probable grounds of guilt; nor can you find a bill for concealing the birth only, in no case, can this of itself form the subject of an indictment, or of a criminal prosecution. I have been induced to make these observations, from the stress which seems to be laid in the order of committal, on the concealment of the birth, as if it was an offence of itself, which might form the ground of a criminal charge.[74]

In spite of reservations about the severity and clarity of its construction, and in spite of the fact that its emphasis on proving live-birth further exposed the uncertainties inherent in medical evidence, the versatility of the 1803 statute appears to have satisfied both parochial hostility towards the bearers of chargeable bastards and dominant legislative opinions about punishment and the prevention of crime. The statute not only enabled rate-paying jurors, witnesses, and prosecutors to inflict some form of punishment on certain women, but also retained the means of making capital examples when necessary. At the first assize session held in York after the 1803 statute was passed, for example, three women were indicted for murdering their bastard children and, in reaching their verdicts, the juries fully utilised the statute's provisions. Hannah Tattersall, a twenty-seven year old single woman, was found not guilty of murder and discharged. Rebecca Beaumont, who had been acquitted of murdering a new-born child in the summer of 1801, was found not guilty of murder, 'but Guilty of concealing the Birth' of her latest bastard child and was sentenced to two years imprisonment in the House of Correction at Wakefield. Martha Chapel, a nineteen year old single woman whose child was found with considerable marks of violence upon it, was tried by the same jury as that hearing the case against Rebecca Beaumont, and, having been found guilty of murder, was executed.[75]

During the next seven years, a further eighteen women appeared in the Northern Circuit courts accused of murdering their new-born children. Seven women were sent to trial by the grand jury (two for the murder of their niece's child), and two women were tried on coroners' inquisitions after the grand jury had rejected indictments against them. The remaining nine women were discharged by the grand jury. Of those women that were tried, six were found not guilty and discharged, two were acquitted of murder but found guilty of concealment, and one woman was found guilty of murder and hanged.[76]

The fact that over fifty per cent of suspects were discharged by the grand jury (as they had been in the decade prior to repeal) suggests that the 1803 statute did not significantly alter the behaviour of that jury, as William Evans and Simon Le Blanc had thought it might. The pattern of trial jury verdicts, however, suggests that trial jurors continued to utilise the options provided by the 1803 statute. Between the statute's passage in 1803 and 1810, a total of three women were found guilty of concealment and sentenced to two years, twelve months and five months imprisonment respectively. According to the gaol calendars, these sentences were served in full.[77]

In addition, within two years of the statute's passage two women had been found guilty and hanged for new-born child murder in the north of England.[78] Both convictions may have been the result of evidence that violence had been inflicted on the child's body, a circumstance acknowledged by contemporary commentators to encourage conviction in crimes of all varieties.[79] Nevertheless, no woman had been convicted of this crime in the Northern Circuit courts for nearly fifty years prior to the conviction of Martha Chapel in 1803, even when marks of violence had been evident. It would appear, therefore, that the 1803 statute not only provided the courts with what was regarded as a fitting alternative punishment to inflict upon accused women, but, having freed judges and jurors from the encumbrance of the 1624 statute, also restored their confidence in finding women guilty of murder.

It is clear that the passage of the 1803 statute resulted in the conviction and punishment of more single women than had previously been possible while the presumption of the 1624 statute remained in force. In eighty-three years prior to 1803 only six women had been punished by the Northern Circuit courts. In the first eight years after the passage of the 1803 statute, two women were found guilty and executed for new-born child murder and a further three were imprisoned for concealment by the same courts. On this evidence, it would be inappropriate to consider the construction of the 1803 statute as more lenient or more humanitarian than the statute that it had repealed. On the contrary, these figures illustrate just how successful Ellenborough was in achieving his stated aim of relieving the courts of the difficulties under which they had previously laboured in the trials of women accused of murdering their new-born children.

Conclusion

The 1803 statute constituted a distinct departure from the legal landscape of the eighteenth century. By repealing the statutory presumption of 1624, Ellenborough ensured that all women accused of murdering their new-born children were once again tried according to common law rules of evidence. At the trials of single women, as well as at those of married women and men, it was once more incumbent upon the prosecution to prove that a dead child had been born alive before it could hope to obtain a conviction for murder.

It would be a mistake, however, to over-emphasise the significance of this reversion to common law or to interpret the 1803 statute as necessarily more humane or more equitable than the statute that it replaced. To a large extent, by requiring proof of live-birth, Ellenborough was doing no more than legitimating a practice adopted by most assize courts over the previous half century. In addition, the 1803 statute made few concessions either to the claims of humanitarian critics of the 1624 statute or to the arguments of criminal law reformers. By retaining capital punishment for women convicted of murder, the statute ignored humanitarian arguments in mitigation of accused women and rejected the claims of would-be reformers that the interests of both humanity and justice would be better served by the application of some lesser form of punishment. Furthermore, by perpetuating the statutory emphasis on concealment and illegitimacy, Ellenborough was endorsing persistent prejudices against unmarried mothers, prejudices that had inspired the regular prosecution of single women for new-born child murder throughout the eighteenth century.

More critically, although Ellenborough had conceded that the 1624 statute was too severe, his self-acknowledged aim in repealing it was not to reduce the harshness of the law but to put a stop to the customary latitude with which the courts had been dealing with suspects. The legislative strategy eventually adopted by Ellenborough and other members of parliament was imperious. By sanctioning a return to common law, the 1803 statute silenced critics of the obsolete and unenforceable statutory presumption of 1624. At the same time, by retaining capital punishment and by providing courts with the option of committing a woman to gaol for concealment, Lord Ellenborough's Act reaffirmed many of the assumptions inherent in the 1624 statute and ensured that male judges and juries retained, or more accurately regained, the power to punish single women who concealed the pregnancies, births and deaths of their illegitimate children.

Notes

1 Elizabeth Shudrick, Old Bailey Sessions Papers (OBSP) No.VIII, October 1743, p. 277.
2 For Meredith's original speech, see *The Parliamentary History of England*, (1765-71), XVI, col. 1124-7. For the bill's subsequent passage, see *The Journals of the House of Commons* (*JHC*), 33, pp. 27, 365, 442, 612, 695, and *The Parliamentary History of England*, (1771-4), XVII, col. 448-53. See also Leon Radzinowicz, *A History of English Criminal Law and its Administration from 1750*, vol. I, (London, Stevens and Sons Limited, 1948), pp. 425-46.
3 A copy of Lockhart's Bill is in the *House of Commons Sessional Papers of the Eighteenth Century*, vol. 22, Bills 1768-72, ed. Sheila Lambert, (1975), pp. 449-50. On the bill's fate, see *JHC*, 33, pp. 732, 743, 777, 784; and *The Journals of the House of Lords*, (*JHL*), 33, pp. 431, 435, 445.
4 Lockhart's speech requesting leave to bring in the bill is in *The Parliamentary History of England*, (1771-4), XVII, col. 699-700. See also *JHC*, 34, p. 106; and *JHL*, 33, pp. 627, 668, 676, 690, 692.
5 *JHC*, 35, pp. 586, 601, 606, 608, 630; *JHL*, 34, pp. 579, 582, 584, 587.
6 *Hanging, Not Punishment Enough*, (1701); George Ollyffe, *An Essay Humbly Offer'd, for an Act of Parliament to prevent Capital Crimes*, (1731).
7 In 1752, an aggravated form of punishment was introduced 'for better preventing the horrid Crime of Murder', by 25 Geo.II c.38. In 1750, Henry Fielding's *An Inquiry into the Causes of the Late Increase of Robbers* advocated, among other measures, the more rigorous enforcement of capital statutes. In 1785, Martin Madan also insisted that the capital law be strictly enforced in his *Thoughts on Executive Justice*, (London, 1785).
8 Madan, *Executive Justice*, p. 34.

9 For a wider discussion of Madan and the doctrine of maximum severity, see Radzinowicz, *A History of English Criminal Law*, vol. I, pp. 231-67, 399-424.

10 Madan, *Executive Justice*, p. 132. According to the would-be repealers of the 1624 statute in 1772, 'laws were made to be executed, not dispensed with' – *The Parliamentary History of England*, (1771-4), XVII, col. 453.

11 Quoted in Radzinowicz, *A History of English Criminal Law*, vol. I, p. 266.

12 *The Parliamentary History of England*, (1765-71), XVI, col. 1124.

13 On the influence of early English and continental reformers, see Radzinowicz, *A History of English Criminal Law*, vol. I, pp. 259-300.

14 *The Parliamentary History of England*, (1771-4), XVII, col. 453.

15 Ibid., col. 699-700.

16 Ibid., col. 452.

17 Paley's work, first published in 1785, supported the construction of the 1624 statute and, according to Radzinowicz, 'became the *credo* of all opponents of the movement for the reform of criminal law' - *A History of English Criminal Law*, vol. I, p. 257.

18 William Eden, *Principles of Penal Law*, (2nd ed., London, 1771), p. 19.

19 *The Parliamentary History of England*, (1771-4), XVII, col. 452-3.

20 Ibid., col. 453.

21 Ibid., col. 452-3.

22 *House of Commons Sessional Papers*, vol. 22, pp. 449-50.

23 Michael Foster, *A Report of Some Proceedings on the Commission of Oyer and Terminer ... to which are added Discourses upon a Few Branches of the Crown Law*, (Oxford, 1762), pp. 299-300.

24 The belief that statutory punishments should be periodically reviewed and readjusted to suit the times can be found in a number of English and Continental writers on the law in this period. On Montesquieu's opinion, for example, see Radzinozwicz, *A History of English Criminal Law*, vol. I, p. 270. On the importance of rendering certain laws temporary, see Eden, *Principles of Penal Law*, p. 305.

25 According to *The Parliamentary History of England*, (1771-4), XVII, col. 451, the opponents of reform were 'Mr. Dyson, Mr. Fuller, and others'.

26 Proposals for more effective prevention of new-born child murder may have reflected views prevalent in the middle of the century that expansion of the nation's population should be actively encouraged. The setting up of the Foundling Hospital and other charitable institutions illustrates the efforts made by certain philanthropists to utilise even illegitimate children for this purpose. Although the birth of bastards certainly met with hostility locally, and although prejudices against bastards persisted, their utility was increasingly recognised in the middle decades of the century. Both proponents and opponents of repeal of the statute therefore sought the protection of bastards not just on humanitarian grounds, but also on utilitarian grounds – that is because they populated the nation and provided men to fight wars.

27 *The Parliamentary History of England*, (1771-4), XVII, col. 451-2.

28 25 Geo.II c.38 enacted that murderers were to be executed the next day but one after the sentence and that their bodies were to be delivered to surgeons at Surgeons Hall to be 'dissected and anatomized'. A judge could also order that the body 'be hung in Chains, in the same Manner as is now practised for the most atrocious Offences'.

29 See Radzinowicz, *A History of English Criminal Law*, vol. I, pp. 284-6 (Beccaria), pp. 303-5 (Eden), p. 315 (Romilly), pp. 389-91, 599 (Bentham).

30 On some of the problems with transportation in this period, see J. M. Beattie, *Crime and the Courts in England 1660-1800*, (Oxford, Clarendon Press, 1986), pp. 538-48.

31 See the individual entries in Sir Lewis Namier and John Brooke, *The History of Parliament: The House of Commons 1754-1790*, (H.M.S.O., 1964). See also Frank O'Gorman, *The Rise of Party in England: The Rockingham Whigs 1760-82*, (London, Allen and Unwin, 1975).

32 See the entry in Namier and Brooke, *The History of Parliament.* Also see John Brooke, *The House of Commons 1754-1790,* (London, Oxford University Press, 1968), p. 176.

33 For a discussion of the rise of party, see: Frank O'Gorman, *The Emergence of the British Two-Party System 1760-1832,* (London, Edward Arnold, 1982); Frank O'Gorman, *The Rise of Party in England.*

34 Brooke, *The House of Commons,* p. 268.

35 *The Parliamentary History of England,* (1771-4), XVII, col. 450-1; Radzinowicz, *A History of English Criminal Law,* vol. I, p. 442. On Phipps, see Radzinowicz, p. 445 fn.

36 In this context, it is interesting that when Minchin was forced to withdraw his motion that leave be given to 'examine into the state of all the Penal Laws now in force' in 1787, he felt it necessary to declare that he had not raised the issue as a party matter. And in the early nineteenth century, Samuel Romilly insisted that his suggestions for penal reform had been thwarted on at least two occasions because the government had viewed his proposals as a party matter. See Radzinowicz, *A History of English Criminal Law,* pp. 447-8 incl. fn., p. 505 fn.

37 *The Parliamentary History of England,* (1771-4), XVII, col. 699.

38 *The Parliamentary History of England,* (1777), XIX, col. 239.

39 *Hansard's Parliamentary Debates,* (1819), XXXIX, col. 781-2.

40 Radzinowicz, *A History of English Criminal Law,* vol. I, pp. 422, 448.

41 Ibid., pp. 448, 497, 507-10.

42 Douglas Hay, 'Property, authority and the criminal law', in Douglas Hay, Peter Linebaugh, John G. Rule, E. P. Thompson, Cal Winslow, *Albion's Fatal Tree: Crime and Society in Eighteenth-Century England,* (London, Allen Lane, 1975), pp. 17-63.

43 Mercy Hornby, OBSP No. IV, April 1734, pp. 108-9.

44 Mary Curtis, Essex Assize Proceedings, 1740, pp. 15-16. Mary was sentenced to death but reprieved by the judge. See also Mary Radford, OBSP, January 1723, p. 6.

45 See C. Hodgson, *A Letter from a Magistrate in the Country, to his Medical Friend at Peterborough,* (Peterborough, 1800). A large number of ballads, trial accounts, and 'lamentations' published in the early nineteenth century warned young single women of the dangers of allowing themselves to be seduced and betrayed by men. On the efforts of writers such as William Paley, Hannah More and Arthur Young to reform lower-class attitudes and improve individual morality, see Maureen McNeil, *Under the Banner of Science: Erasmus Darwin and his Age,* (Manchester, Manchester University Press, 1987), pp. 61-4.

46 McNeil, *Under the Banner of Science,* p. 64.

47 Peter C. Hoffer and N. E. H. Hull, *Murdering Mothers: Infanticide in England and New England 1558-1803,* (New York, New York University Press, 1981), pp. 87, 91.

48 R. Sauer, 'Infanticide and abortion in nineteenth-century Britain', *Population Studies,* 32 (1978), 82. See also: Angus McLaren's opinion that Ellenborough suggested 'relaxing the law on infanticide' – Angus McLaren, *Reproductive Rituals: The Perception of Fertility in England from the Sixteenth Century to the Nineteenth Century,* (London, Methuen, 1984), p. 135; and Lionel Rose's comment that the 1803 statute brought the law 'more into line with modern sentiment' – Lionel Rose, *The Massacre of the Innocents: Infanticide in Britain 1800-1939,* (London, Routledge and Kegan Paul, 1986), p. 70.

49 Previous historical discussions of the 1803 statute have often been cursory and failed to grasp its pertinent features. See: Sauer, 'Infanticide and abortion', 82; Rose, *Massacre of the Innocents,* p. 70; D. Seaborne Davies, 'Child-killing in English law', *Modern Law Review,* 1, (December 1937), 214. Only Angus McLaren and John Keown have discussed some of the issues surrounding the 1803 statute in any depth, but largely from the point of view of the abortion clauses. See: McLaren, *Reproductive Rituals,* pp. 135-8; John Keown, *Abortion, Doctors and the Law: Some Aspects of the Legal Regulation of Abortion in England from 1803 to 1982,* (Cambridge, Cambridge University Press, 1988), pp. 3-25.

50 *JHL,* 44, (1802-4), p. 111. The full title of the bill was 'An Act for the further

Prevention of malicious shooting, stabbing, cutting, wounding, and poisoning, and also the malicious setting Fire to Buildings; and also for repealing a certain Act, made in the First year of the late King James the First, intituled, An Act to prevent the destroying and murthering of Bastard Children, and for substituting other Provisions in lieu of the same'.

51 *The Parliamentary History of England*, (1801-3), XXXVI, col. 1246. Ellenborough's speech was reported in *The Times*, (29 March 1803), p. 2.

52 A copy of the bill is in *House of Lords Sessional Papers 1802-3*, vol. I, ed. F. William Torrington, (New York, Oceana Publications Inc., 1972), pp. 117-19.

53 *JHL*, 44, pp. 151, 156. The amended bill is in *Lords Sessional Papers 1802-3*, vol. I, pp. 149-152.

54 *JHL*, 44, pp. 170, 172, 187, 265, 286; *JHC*, 58, (1802-3), pp. 424-5, 509, 514, 516.

55 The statute was passed as 43 Geo.III c.58.

56 Ellenborough's correspondence with Paley is in the Public Record Office, Kew, PRO 30/12/17/4.

57 In his notes for a speech to the Lords concerning Romilly's proposed repeal of the statute that had made shoplifting a capital offence, Ellenborough criticised Paley's belief that all circumstances could be accounted for in written laws, pointing out instead that there were an 'infinite variety of circumstances by which crime may be aggravated and distinction in punishment founded - which would elude enumeration by positive laws'. Ellenborough's hand-written notes are in PRO 30/12/17/9/243-50. Although differing in some particulars, these notes possibly formed the basis for Ellenborough's speech on the 30 May 1810 (*Hansard's Parliamentary Debates*, (1811), XIX, Appendix, col. lxxxix-xcii), in which he directly opposed Romilly's bill in the Lords.

58 See the speech in PRO 30/12/17/9/243-50; *Hansard's Parliamentary Debates*, (1811), XIX, Appx., col. lxxxix-xcii, cxviii-cxxii; *Hansard's Parliamentary Debates*, (1811), XX, col. 299-300; *The Parliamentary Register*, 3 (1811), 309-10. See also Radzinowicz, *A History of English Criminal Law*, vol. I, pp. 503-17.

59 William Paley, *The Principles of Moral and Political Philosophy*, (2nd ed., London, 1786), p. 527.

60 In the notes for his speech (PRO 30/12/17/9/243-50), Ellenborough admitted 'that if the penalties be so high, that it is in no Case fit to be inflicted, it will counteract its own purpose of Terror in as much as the Criminal will not be deterred by the apprehension of a punishment which never can be inflicted'.

61 See PRO 30/12/17/9/243-50.

62 A. V. Dicey, *Lectures on the Relation between Law and Public Opinion in England during the Nineteenth Century*, (London, Macmillan and Co. Ltd., [2nd ed., 1914] 1962), p. 33.

63 Ibid., Lecture V, esp. p. 106.

64 Ellenborough's opinion of Romilly's attempts to reform the criminal law in 1810 (PRO 30/12/17/9/243-50).

65 Since the Commons made only minor amendments to the first section of the bill, differences between the second printed draft of the bill and the final text can be attributed to the amendments proposed by the Lords during discussions on 9, 10 and 17 May. There are no records of the amendments discussed on these occasions, but the proceedings on those dates are noted in *JHL*, 44, pp. 170, 172, 187.

66 The hand-written draft, which is probably not in Ellenborough's hand, contains minor alterations and has significant passages underlined. The script is in PRO 30/12/17/9/373.

67 Strictly speaking, a woman could not be punished for another 'offence', since concealment was not a substantive crime. Women were, in reality, punished simply for a pattern of behaviour deemed punishable, although not technically criminal.

68 Christopher Johnson, *An Essay on the Signs of Murder in New Born Children*, tr. from the French of Dr. P. A. O. Mahon, (Lancaster, 1813), pp. xviii-xix.

69 *Report from the Select Committee on Criminal Law Relating to Capital Punishments in Felonies:*

House of Commons Order Papers, 1819, 585, (Irish University Press Series, 1968), p. 43.

70 The inquisition is in ASSI 44/121iii.

71 See the indictments against Martha Chapel, 1803, in ASSI 44/118i, and Ann Airton, 1807, in ASSI 44/122ii.

72 In 1804, Hannah Errington's indictment (in ASSI 44/119i) was concluded 'against the Form of the Statute in such Case made and provided'. In the same year, this phrase was deleted from Sarah Littlewood's indictment - ASSI 44/119iii.

73 From the Gaol Calendar for the summer assize session at York, in ASSI 44/119iii.

74 This charge was printed in *The York Herald*, (13 March 1813), and was quoted in full by Johnson, *An Essay on the Signs of Murder*, p. xviii, fn.

75 Hannah Tattersall, 1803, ASSI 45/42, ASSI 44/118i-ii, ASSI 41/10; Rebecca Beaumont, 1803, ASSI 44/118i-ii, ASSI 41/10, ASSI 42/11; Martha Chapel, 1803, ASSI 44/118i-ii, ASSI 41/10, ASSI 42/11. Details of Rebecca Beaumont's previous indictment in 1801 are in ASSI 45/41, ASSI 44/116i, ASSI 41/10.

76 These figures are taken from the unindexed Northern Circuit records between 1804 and 1810.

77 The women found guilty of concealment were Rebecca Beaumont (see above, note 75), who was sentenced to two years imprisonment, Hannah Young (1806, ASSI 45/43, ASSI 44/121ii, ASSI 44/122ii, ASSI 41/10, ASSI 42/11), who was imprisoned for twelve months, and Mary Lockham (1810, ASSI 45/45, ASSI 41/11, ASSI 42/11), who was imprisoned for five months.

78 In addition to Martha Chapel, Ann Haywood was also found guilty of murder and executed in 1805 - for details, see ASSI 45/42, ASSI 44/120iii, ASSI 41/10, ASSI 42/11.

79 A number of witnesses giving evidence to the Select Committee on Criminal Law in 1819 testified that the reluctance with which juries convicted defendants of capital crimes was less marked in cases where violence had been used. There was generally no reluctance to convict for murder, for example, if there was sufficient evidence of violence. Thomas Shelton, however, pointed out that the only form of murder in which juries were reluctant to convict was in cases of the murder of bastard children (*Report from the Select Committee*, p. 22).

BIBLIOGRAPHY

Archive sources – Public Record Office, London
Northern Circuit Assize Records

ASSI 41/2-11 Minute Books, 1719-1817
ASSI 42/4-12 Gaol Books, 1718-1810
ASSI 43/7-9 Account, cash and note books, 1730-1840
ASSI 44/46-125 Indictments, inquisitions, recognizances, and gaol calendars, 1730-1810
ASSI 45/18-45 Depositions, 1720-1810
ASSI 47/1-21 Miscellaneous papers

Other Assize Circuit Records

ASSI 2/21 Oxford Circuit Crown Book
ASSI 66/1 Chester coroners' inquisitions, 1798-9.
CHES 24/171/5-6 Chester gaol files

Miscellaneous Papers

SP 44/87 State Papers, Domestic – Entry Book
PRO 30/12 Ellenborough Papers

Printed trial reports
Guildhall Library, London

Old Bailey Sessions Papers, 1714-1800

British Library

Surrey Assize Proceedings – Lent 1739-Summer 1741
Summer 1751
Summer 1756
Lent 1759
Essex Assize Proceedings, 1740

York City Reference Library

The Trials at Large of the Felons in the Castle of York, 1775-8

Printed statutes

23 H. VIII c. 1, 1531, 'An Act concerning convicts in Petit Treason, Murder, &c. '.

1 & 2 Ph. & M. c. 13, 1554, 'An Act touching Bailment of Persons'.

2 & 3 Ph. & M. c. 10, 1555, 'An Act to take Examination of Prisoners suspected of any Manslaughter or Felony'.

5 Eliz. c. 4, 1562, 'An Act containing divers Orders for Artificers, Labourers, Servants of Husbandry and Apprentices'.

18 Eliz. c. 3, 1576.

39 Eliz. c. 3, 1597, 'An Act for the Reliefe of the Poore'.

43 Eliz. c. 2, 1601, 'An Act for the Relief of the Poor'.

1 Jac. I c. 8, 1604, 'An Act to take away the Benefit of Clergy for some kind of Manslaughter'.

7 Jac. I c. 4, 1610, 'An Act for the due Execution of divers Laws and Statutes heretofore made against Rogues, Vagabonds and sturdy Beggars, and other lewd and idle Persons'.

21 Jac. I c. 6, 1623, 'An Act concerning Women convicted of small Felonies'.

21 Jac. I c. 27, 1624, 'An Act to prevent the Destroying and Murthering of Bastard Children'.

13 & 14 Car. II c. 12, 1662, 'An Act for the better Relief of the Poor of this Kingdom'.

Scottish Acts 1690 c. 50, 'Act anent Murthering of Children'.

3 Will. & Mar. c. 9, 1691, 'An Act to take away Clergy from some Offenders, and to bring others to Punishment'.

7 Will. III c. 3, 1696, 'An Act for regulating of Trials in Cases of Treason and Misprision of Treason'.

8 & 9 Will. III c. 26, 1697, 'An Act for the better preventing the counterfeiting the current Coin of this Kingdom'.

1 Ann. c. 9, 1702, 'An Act for punishing of Accessories to Felonies, and Receivers of stolen Goods, and to prevent the wilful burning and destroying of Ships'.

6 Ann. c. 4, Irish Statutes, 1707, 'An act to prevent the destroying and murthering of bastard children'.

6 Geo. II c. 31, 1733, 'An Act for the Relief of Parishes and other Places from such Charges as may arise from Bastard Children born within the same'.

25 Geo. II c. 29, 1752, 'An Act for giving a proper Reward to Coroners for the due Execution of their Office; and for the Amoval of Coroners upon a lawful Conviction for certain Misdemeanours'.

25 Geo. II c. 36, 1752, 'An Act for the better preventing Thefts and Robberies, and for regulating Places of Publick Entertainment, and punishing Persons keeping disorderly Houses'.

25 Geo. II c. 37, 1752, 'An Act for better preventing the horrid Crime of Murder'.

27 Geo. II c. 3, 1754, 'An Act for the better securing to Constables and others the Expences of conveying Offenders to Gaol; and for allowing the Charges of poor Persons bound to give Evidence against Felons'.

18 Geo. III c. 19, 1778, 'An Act for the Payment of Costs to Parties, on Complaints determined before Justices of the Peace out of Sessions; for the Payment of the Charges of Constables in certain Cases; and for the more effectual Payment of Charges to Witnesses and Prosecutors of any Larceny, or other Felony'.

43 Geo. III c. 58, 1803, 'An Act for the further Prevention of malicious shooting, and attempting to discharge loaded Fire-Arms, stabbing, cutting, wounding, poisoning, and the malicious using of Means to procure the Miscarriage of Women; and also the malicious setting Fire to Buildings; and also for repealing a certain Act, made in England in the twenty-first Year of the late King James the First, intituled, An Act to prevent the destroying and murthering of Bastard Children; and also an Act made in Ireland in the sixth Year of the Reign of the late Queen Anne, also intituled, An Act to prevent the destroying and murthering of Bastard Children; and for making other Provisions in lieu thereof'.

6 & 7 Will. IV c. 89, 1836, 'An Act for the Attendance and Remuneration of Medical Witnesses at Coroners' Inquests'.

12 & 13 Geo. 5 c. 18, 1922, 'An Act to provide that a woman who wilfully causes the death of her newly-born child may, under certain conditions, be convicted of infanticide'.

1 & 2 Geo. 6 c. 36, 1938, 'An Act to repeal and re-enact with modifications the provisions of the Infanticide Act, 1922'.

Other contemporary sources

Albertus the Second: or the Curious Justice, (n. d.).

Alexander, William, *The History of Women*, (2 vols. in one, London, 1779).

'The Apprehending and Taking of Phoebe Cluer, On Suspicion of the Murder of her Bastard Child', (n. d.).

Aristotle's Compleat Master-Piece, (11th ed., London, 1725).

Babington, Zachary, *Advice to Grand Jurors in Cases of Blood*, (London, 1677).

Barrington, Daines, *Observations on the Statutes, Chiefly the More Ancient*, (2nd ed., London, 1766).

Bartholinus Anatomy; Made from the Precepts of his Father, (London, 1668).

Battie, William, *A Treatise on Madness*, (London, 1758).

Bentham, Jeremy, *Theory of Legislation*, tr. R. Hildreth, (Kegan Paul, London, 1911).

Blackstone, William, *Commentaries on the Laws of England*, (4 vols., Oxford, 1765-9).

Blackstone, William, *Commentaries on the Laws of England*, (4 vols., Dublin, 1770).

Bond, J., *A Complete Guide for Justices of Peace*, (1685).

Broughton, Thomas, *Serious Advice and Warning to Servants*, (4th ed., London, 1763).

Browne's General Law List, (London, 1799).

Brydall, John, *Lex Spuriorum: Or, the Law Relating to Bastardy*, (London, 1703).

Burn, Richard, *The Justice of the Peace, and Parish Officer*, (3rd ed., London, 1756).

Burn, Richard, and Burn, John, *The Justice of the Peace and Parish Officer*, (17th ed., 4 vols., London, 1793).

Cheselden, William, *The Anatomy of the Humane Body*, (London, 1713).

Cheselden, William, *The Anatomy of the Humane Body*, (2nd ed., London, 1722).

Cheselden, William, *The Anatomy of the Human Body*, (3rd ed., London, 1726).

Coke, Edward, *The Third Part of the Institutes of the Laws of England*, (London, 1644).

The Cumberland Pacquet, 1774-1783.

Curry, James, *Popular Observations on Apparent Death from Drowning, Suffocation, &c. with an Account of the Means to be Employed For Recovery*, (Northampton, 1792).

Dalton, Michael, *The Countrey Justice*, (1619).

Defoe, Daniel, *The Generous Protector, or a Friendly Proposal to Prevent Murder and Other Enormous Abuses, By Erecting an Hospital for Foundlings and Bastard-Children*, (London, 1731).

Deposition Book of Richard Wyatt, J. P. 1767-1776, ed. Elizabeth Silverthorne, (Surrey Record Society, XXX, 1978).

The Diary of a Country Parson: The Reverend James Woodforde 1759-1802, ed. John Beresford, (5 vols., Oxford, 1924-31).

The Diary of Richard Kay, 1716-51, eds. W. Brockbank and F. Kenworthy, (Manchester, Chetham Society, 1968).

The Diary of Thomas Turner 1754-1765, ed. David Varsey, (Oxford, Oxford University Press, 1984).

Dionis, Pierre, *A General Treatise of Midwifery*, (London, 1719).

Downright, Sir Daniel (pseudonym), *The Bastard Child, or a Feast for the Church-wardens*, (London, 1768).

Duncan, Andrew, *Heads of Lectures on the Institutions of Medicine*, (5th ed., Edinburgh, 1801).

East, Edward Hyde, *A Treatise of the Pleas of the Crown*, (2 vols., London, 1803).

Eden, William, *Principles of Penal Law*, (2nd ed., London, 1771).

Farr, Samuel, *Elements of Medical Jurisprudence*, (London, 1788).

Fielding, Henry, *An Inquiry into the Causes of the Late Increase of Robbers*, (1750).

Fitzherbert, Sir Anthony, and Crompton, Richard, *L'Office et Aucthoritie de Justices de Peace*, (2nd ed., 1584).

Foster, Michael, *A Report of Some Proceedings on the Commission of Oyer and Terminer ... to which are added Discourses upon a Few Branches of the Crown Law*, (Oxford, 1762).

Friend, J., *Emmenologia*, tr. Thomas Dale, (London, 1729).

'A Full and True Account of a barbarous and bloody Murder Committed by Nelly Salvy, a Cook-Maid, who Liv'd in a Gentlemans House the upper end o Caple-Street, on the body of her own young Child just Born, the 25th of this Instant January 1725', (Dublin, 1725).

'A full and True Account of a most horrid and barbarous Murder committed Yesterday, April 24th in St James's House, by Eliz. Smith, upon the Body of her own Male Child', (London, 1711).

Galen, *De Usu Partium*, tr. Margaret Tallmadge May, (2 vols., New York, 1968).

The Genuine Sentiments of an English Country Gentleman, upon the Present Plan of the Foundling Hospital, (London, 1759).

The Gentleman's Magazine.

Gilbert, Geoffrey, *The Law of Evidence*, (Dublin, 1754).

Gilbert, Geoffrey, *The Law Of Evidence*, enlarged by Capel Lofft, (2 vols., London, 1791).

'God's Judgment against False Witnesses. To which is added. An Account of the Execution of Mary Shrewsbury, for the Murder of her Bastard Child', (n. d.).

Gouge, William, *Of Domesticall Duties*, (London, 1622).

The Guardian.

A Guide to Juries: Setting Forth their Antiquity, Power, and Duty, From the Common Law and Statutes, by a Person of Quality, (London, 1699).

Hale, Matthew, *Pleas of the Crown: A Methodical Summary*, (1678).

Hale, Matthew, *History of the Pleas of the Crown*, ed. Sollom Emlyn, (2 vols., London, 1736).

Hamilton, Alexander, *Elements of the Practice of Midwifery*, (London, 1775).

Hanging, Not Punishment Enough, (1701).

Hansard's Parliamentary Debates.

[Hanway, Jonas], *A Candid Historical Account of the Hospital For the Reception of Exposed and Deserted Young Children; Representing The Present Plan of it as Productive of Many Evils, and Not Adapted to the Genius and Happiness of this Nation*, (London, 1759).

Harvey, William, *Lectures on the Whole of Anatomy*, tr. C. D. O'Malley, F. N. L. Poynter, K. F. Russell, (Berkeley, University of California Press, 1961).

Harvey, William, *Anatomical Exercitations, Concerning the Generation of Living Creatures*, (London, 1653).

Haslam, John, *Observations on Insanity*, (London, 1798).

Hawkins, William, *Treatise of the Pleas of the Crown*, (2 vols., London, 1716-21).

Hawkins, William, *A Treatise of the Pleas of the Crown*, ed. Thomas Leach, (Dublin, 1788).

[Haywood, Elizabeth], *A Present for a Servant-Maid: Or, The Sure Means of gaining Love and Esteem*, (London, 1743).

Heywood, Oliver, *The Rev. Oliver Heywood, B.A. 1630-1702; His Autobiography, Diaries, Anecdote and Event Books*, ed. J. Horsfall Turner, (4 vols., Brighouse, 1881-5).

Highmore, Anthony, *Pietas Londinensis: the History, Design, and Present State of the Various Public Charities in and near London*, (London, 1814).

Hodgson, C., *A Letter from a Magistrate in the Country, to his Medical Friend at Peterborough*, (Peterborough, 1800).

House of Commons Sessional Papers of the Eighteenth Century, vol. 22, Bills 1768-72, ed. Sheila Lambert, (1975).

House of Lords Sessional Papers 1802-3, ed. F. William Torrington, vol. I, (New York, Oceana Publications Inc., 1972).

Hunter, William, 'On the uncertainty of the signs of murder, in the case of bastard children', *Medical Observations and Inquiries*, 6 (1784), 266-90.

Jackson, Rowland, *A Physical Dissertation on Drowning*, (London, 1746).

Jacob, Giles, *New Law Dictionary*, (5th ed., 1744).

James I, *The Political Works of James I*, (Harvard University Press, [1616] 1918).

Johnson, Christopher, *An Essay on the Signs of Murder in New Born Children*, translated from the French of Dr. P. A. O. Mahon, (Lancaster, 1813).

Johnson, Samuel, *A Dictionary of the English Language*, (London, 1755; 1756; 1778; 1785; 1799).

The Journals of the House of Commons.

The Journals of the House of Lords.

Kelyng, Sir John, *A Report of divers cases in Pleas of the Crown, adjudged and determined in the reign of ... Charles II*, (London, 1708).

Laconics: or, New Maxims of State and Conversation, (1701).

'The Lamentation of Mary Butcher, Now confined in WORCESTER-CITY-GAOL, On Suspicion of murdering her Male Bastard Child, in April last', (n. d.).

'The Last Dying Speech and Confession of Matthew Barker, who was Executed this September 11, 1784, on the Castle-Hill, Norwich'.

'The Last Speech and Dying Words of Ellinor Sils, who is to be Burn't alive this present Wednesday being the 19th, of this Instant May 1725, For Murdering her own Child', (Ireland, 1725).

The Leedes Intelligencer, 1754-75.

The Leeds Mercury, 1775-77.

The Letters of Erasmus Darwin, ed. Desmond King-Hele, (Cambridge, Cambridge University Press, 1981)

Locke, John, *An Essay Concerning Human Understanding*, ed. John W. Yolton, (London, Everyman's Library [5th ed., 1706], 1976).

Madan, Martin, *Thoughts on Executive Justice*, (London, 1785).

Mandeville, Bernard, *A Modest Defence of Public Stews: or, an Essay upon Whoring, As it is Now Practis'd in these Kingdoms*, (Augustan Reprint Society, No. 162, [1724] 1973).

Mandeville, Bernard, *The Fable of the Bees: or, Private Vices, Publick Benefits*, (2 vols., Oxford, [6th ed., 1732] 1924).

Mayo, Richard, *A Present for Servants*, (London, 1693).

Middlesex County Records, ed. J. C. Jeaffreson, (6 vols., The Middlesex County Records Society, 1886-1892).

Morgagni, Giovanni Battista, *The Seats and Causes of Diseases*, tr. Benjamin Alexander, (3 vols., London, 1769).

Morgagni, Giovanni Battista, 'The Third Medicolegal Response of Giovanni Battista Morgagni: On whether an infant can be born alive and perfect seven months after conception?', English tr. in *Archives of the Forensic Sciences*, 1 (1972), 384-7.

Morgan, John, *Essays upon the Law of Evidence*, (3 vols., London, 1789).

Nelson, William, *The Law of Evidence*, (London, 1717).

Nelson, William, *The Law of Evidence*, (3rd ed., London, 1739).

The Northampton Mercury, 1731-68.

A Northern Circuit: Described, in a Letter to a Friend: A Poetical Essay, (London, 1751).

Ollyffe, G., *An Essay Humbly Offer'd for an Act of Parliament to prevent Capital Crimes, and the Loss of many Lives, etc.*, (1731).

Paley, William, *The Principles of Moral and Political Philosophy*, (2nd ed., London, 1786).

The Parliamentary History of England.

The Parliamentary Register.

Parr, Bartholomew, *The London Medical Dictionary,* (3 vols., London, 1809).

Peake, Thomas, *A Compendium of the Law of Evidence,* (London, 1801).

Pechey, J., *The Compleat Midwife's Practice Enlarged,* (5th ed., 1698).

Percival, Thomas, *Medical Ethics,* (Manchester, 1803).

Portal, M., 'Memoire dans lequel on demontre l'action du Poumon sur l'Aorte, pendant le temps de la Respiration; et ou l'on prove que dans l'Enfant qui vient de naitre, le Poumon droit respire avant le gauche', (1769), reviewed in *Medical and Philosophical Commentaries,* vol. I, part IV (London, 1773), 409-12.

A Rebuke to the Sin of Uncleanness, (London, 1704).

A Remedy for Uncleanness. Or, Certain Queries propounded to his Highness the Lord Protector, (London, 1658).

Report from the Select Committee on Criminal Law Relating to Capital Punishments in Felonies: House of Commons Order Papers, 1819, 585, (Irish University Press Series, 1968).

'A short View of the remarkable Differences in the State of the Defence made use of at the Coroner's Inquest from that which was afterwards brought and made use of at the Old Bailey', (n. d.).

Smellie, William, *A Treatise on the Theory and Practice of Midwifery,* (London, 1752).

Smellie, William, *A Treatise on the Theory and Practice of Midwifery,* (2 vols., 1762-4).

Smellie, William, *A Treatise on the Theory and Practice of Midwifery,* (a new and corrected edition, n. d.).

Somers, John Lord, *The Security of Englishmen's Lives: or the Trust, Power and Duty of Grand Juries of England,* (London, 1766).

The Times, 1785-1803.

Tong, W., *An Account of the Life and Death of Mr. Matthew Henry,* (London, 1716).

Townsend, John, *A Dissertation on the Poor Laws,* (London, 1786).

'A Trophy of Christ's Victory; Or, The great Mercy of God in Christ, Examplified, in the speedy and seasonable Repentance of Elizabeth Blackie, who was Executed for Child Murder, at Jedbergh, 27th of May, 1718', (Dumfries, 1719).

Umfreville, Edward, *Lex Coronatoria: Or, The Office and Duty of Coroners,* (London, 1761).

W., T., *The Office of the Clerk of Assize: Containing The Form and Method of the Proceedings at the Assizes, and General Gaol-delivery, as also on the Crown and Nisi Prius Side,* (London, 1676).

[Walsh, William], *A Dialogue Concerning Women, Being a Defence of the Sex,* (London, 1691).

Willughby, Percivall, *Observations in Midwifery,* ed. H. Blenkinsop, (Yorkshire, S. R. Publishers Ltd, [1863] 1972).

Wood, Thomas, *An Institute of the Laws of England,* (5th ed., London, 1734).

The York Courant, 1729-74.

Secondary Sources

Ackerknecht, Erwin H., 'Legal medicine in transition (16th–18th centuries)', *Ciba Symposia*, 11 (1950), 1224-8.

Adair, Richard, *Courtship, Illegitimacy and Marriage in Early Modern England*, (Manchester, Manchester University Press, 1996).

Allen, Carleton Kemp, *Legal Duties and other Essays in Jurisprudence*, (Oxford, Clarendon Press, 1931).

Andrew, Donna T., 'London charity in the eighteenth century', (PhD thesis, University of Toronto, 1977).

Andrew, Donna T., *Philanthropy and Police: London Charity in the Eighteenth Century*, (Princeton, Princeton University Press, 1989).

Andrew, Donna, 'Two medical charities in eighteenth-century London: The Lock Hospital and the Lying-In Charity for Married Women', in Jonathan Barry and Colin Jones (eds.), *Medicine and Charity Before the Welfare State*, (London, Routledge, 1991), pp. 82-97.

Arnot, Margaret L., 'Infant death, child care and the state: the baby-farming scandal and the first infant life protection legislation of 1872', *Continuity and Change*, 9:2 (1994), 271-311.

Atkinson, Stanley B., 'Life, birth, and live-birth', *Law Quarterly Review*, LXVIII (1904), 134-59.

Bailey, Victor, 'Bibliographical essay: crime, criminal justice and authority in England', *Bulletin of the Society for the Study of Labour History*, 40 (1980), 36-46.

Baker, A. Barrington, 'Artificial respiration, the history of an idea', *Medical History*, 15 (1971), 336-51.

Baker, J. H., 'Criminal courts and procedure at common law 1550-1800', in J. S. Cockburn (ed.), *Crime in England 1550-1800*, (London, Methuen, 1977), pp. 15-48.

Baker, J. H., 'Male and married spinsters', *The American Journal of Legal History*, 21 (1977), 255-9.

Baker, J. H. (ed.), *Legal Records and the Historian*, (London, Royal Historical Society, 1978).

Bayne-Powell, Rosamond, *The English Child in the Eighteenth Century*, (London, John Murray, 1939).

Beattie, J. M., 'Towards a study of crime in 18th century England: a note on indictments', in Paul Fritz and David Williams (eds.), *The Triumph of Culture: 18th Century Perspectives*, (Toronto, A. M. Hakkert Ltd., 1972), pp. 299-314.

Beattie, J. M., 'The criminality of women in eighteenth-century England', *Journal of Social History*, VIII (1975), 80-116.

Beattie, J. M., *Crime and the Courts in England 1660-1800*, (Oxford, Clarendon Press, 1986).

Beattie, J. M., 'Scales of justice: defense counsel and the English criminal trial in the eighteenth and nineteenth centuries', *Law and History Review*, 9 (1991), 221-67.

Berg, Maxine, *The Age of Manufactures: Industry, Innovation and Work in Britain 1700-1820*, (London, Fontana, 1985).

Brant, Clare, and Purkiss, Diane (eds.), *Women, Texts and Histories 1575-1760*, (London, Routledge, 1992).

Brittain, R. P., 'The hydrostatic and similar tests of live birth: a historical review', *Medico-Legal Journal*, 31 (1963), 189-94.

Brock, Helen, 'The many facets of Dr William Hunter (1718-83)', *History of Science*, xxxii (1994), 387-408.

Brooke, John, *The House of Commons 1754-1790*, (London, Oxford University Press, 1968).

Brownlow, John, *The History and Objects of the Foundling Hospital*, (4th ed., London, 1881).

Bynum, W. F., and Porter, R. (eds.), *William Hunter and the Eighteenth-century Medical World*, (Cambridge, Cambridge University Press, 1985).

Clark, Alice, *Working Life of Women in the Seventeenth Century*, (London, Routledge, [1919] 1992).

Clark, Michael, and Crawford, Catherine (eds.), *Legal Medicine in History*, (Cambridge, Cambridge University Press, 1994).

Clarke, Karen, 'Infanticide, illegitimacy and the medical profession in nineteenth century England', *Bulletin of the Society for the Social History of Medicine*, 26 (1980), 11-14.

Cockburn, J. S., 'The Northern Assize Circuit', *Northern History*, 3 (1968), 118-30.

Cockburn, J. S., *A History of English Assizes, 1558-1714*, (Cambridge University Press, 1972).

Cockburn, J. S., 'Early-modern assize records as historical evidence', *Journal of the Society of Archivists*, 5 (1975), 215-31.

Cockburn, J. S., 'The nature and incidence of crime in England 1559-1625: a preliminary survey', in J. S. Cockburn (ed.), *Crime in England 1550-1800*, (London, Methuen, 1977), pp. 49-71.

Cockburn, J. S. (ed.), *Crime in England 1550-1800*, (London, Methuen, 1977).

Cockburn, J. S., 'Trial by the book? Fact and theory in the criminal process, 1558-1625', in J. H. Baker (ed.), *Legal Records and the Historian*, (London, Royal Historical Society, 1978), pp. 60-79.

Cockburn, J. S., and Green, Thomas A. (eds.), *Twelve Good Men and True: The Criminal Trial Jury in England, 1200-1800*, (Princeton, Princeton University Press, 1988).

Cockburn, J. S., 'Patterns of violence in English society: homicide in Kent 1560-1985', *Past and Present*, 130 (1991), 70-106.

Crawford, C., 'The emergence of English forensic medicine: medical evidence in common-law courts, 1730-1830', (D. Phil. thesis, University of Oxford, 1987).

Crawford, Catherine, 'A scientific profession: medical reform and forensic medicine in British periodicals of the early nineteenth century', in Roger French and Andrew Wear (eds.), *British Medicine in an Age of Reform*, (London, Routledge, 1991), pp. 203-30.

Crawford, Catherine, 'Legalizing medicine: early modern legal systems and the growth of medico-legal knowledge', in Michael Clark and Catherine Crawford (eds.), *Legal Medicine in History*, (Cambridge, Cambridge University Press, 1994), pp. 89-116.

Crawford, Patricia, 'Attitudes to menstruation in seventeenth-century England', *Past and Present*, 91 (1981), 47-73.

Damme, Catherine, 'Infanticide: the worth of an infant under law', *Medical History*, XXII (1978), 1-24.

Davies, D. Seaborne, 'Child-killing in English law', *Modern Law Review*, 1 (December 1937), 203-23.

Davis, Natalie Zemon, *Fiction in the Archives: Pardon Tales and their Tellers in Sixteenth-century France*, (Cambridge, Polity Press, 1987).

Day, Shelley, 'Puerperal insanity: the historical sociology of a disease', (PhD thesis, Cambridge, 1985).

Dicey, A. V., *Lectures on the Relation between Law and Public Opinion in England during the Nineteenth Century*, (2nd ed., London, Macmillan and Co. Ltd., [1914] 1962).

Ditton, Jason, *Controlology: Beyond the New Criminology*, (London, Macmillan, 1979).

Donnison, Jean, *Midwives and Medical Men: A History of Inter-Professional Rivalries and Women's Rights*, (London, Heinemann, 1977).

Duden, Barbara, *The Woman Beneath the Skin*, (Massachusetts, Harvard University Press, 1991).

Eccles, Audrey, *Obstetrics and Gynaecology in Tudor and Stuart England*, (London, Croom Helm, 1982).

Edwards, Valerie C., 'The case of the married spinster: an alternative explanation', *The American Journal of Legal History*, 21 (1977), 260-5.

Eigen, Joel Peter, 'Intentionality and insanity: what the eighteenth-century juror heard', in W. F. Bynum, Roy Porter and Michael Shepherd (eds.), *The Anatomy of Madness*, vol. II, (London, Tavistock, 1985), pp. 34-51.

Eigen, Joel Peter, *Witnessing Insanity: Madness and Mad-Doctors in the English Court*, (New Haven, Yale University Press, 1995).

Emsley, Clive, *Policing and its Context 1750-1870*, (London, Macmillan, 1983).

Emsley, Clive, *Crime and Society in England, 1750-1900*, (London, Longman, 1987).

England Jr., R. W., 'Investigating homicides in Northern England, 1800-1824', *Criminal Justice History*, VI (1985), 105-23.

Erickson, Robert A., *Mother Midnight: Birth, Sex, and Fate in Eighteenth Century Fiction*, (New York, AMS Press, 1986).

Faller, Lincoln B., *Turned to Account: The Forms and Functions of Criminal Biography in Late Seventeenth- and Early Eighteenth-century England*, (Cambridge, Cambridge University Press, 1987).

Forbes, T. R., *The Midwife and the Witch*, (New Haven, Yale University Press, 1966).

Forbes, T. R., 'Crowner's Quest', *Transactions of the American Philosophical Society*, 68 (1978), 1-48.

Forbes, Thomas Rogers, *Surgeons at the Bailey*, (New Haven, Yale University Press, 1985).

Foss, Edward, *The Judges of England; with Sketches of their Lives*, vol. VIII, (London, 1864).

French, Roger, and Wear, Andrew (eds.), *British Medicine in an Age of Reform*, (London, Routledge, 1991).

Fritz, Paul, and Williams, David (eds.), *The Triumph of Culture: 18th Century Perspectives*, (Toronto, A. M. Hakkert Ltd., 1972).

Gatrell, V. A. C., *The Hanging Tree: Execution and the English People 1770-1868*, (Oxford, Oxford University Press, 1994).

Gattrell, V. A. C., Lenman, Bruce, and Parker, Geoffrey, (eds.), *Crime and the Law: The Social History of Crime in Western Europe since 1500*, (London, Europa Publications Limited, 1980).

Geyer-Kordesch, Johanna, 'Infanticide and medico-legal ethics in eighteenth century Prussia', in Andrew Wear, Johanna Geyer-Kordesch and Roger French (eds.), *Doctors and Ethics: The Earlier Historical Setting of Professional Ethics*, (Amsterdam, Rodopi, 1993), pp. 181-202.

Gillis, John R., 'Servants, sexual relations, and the risks of illegitimacy in London, 1801-1900', *Feminist Studies*, 5 (1979), 142-73.

Gillis, John R., *For Better, For Worse: British Marriages, 1600 to the Present*, (Oxford, Oxford University Press, 1985).

Green, Thomas A., 'A retrospective on the criminal trial jury, 1200-1800', in J. S. Cockburn and Thomas A. Green (eds.), *Twelve Good Men and True: The Criminal Trial Jury in England, 1200-1800*, (Princeton, Princeton University Press, 1988).

Greenwald, Gary I., and Greenwald, Maria White, 'Medicolegal progress in inquests of felonious deaths: Westminster, 1761-1866', *The Journal of Legal Medicine*, 2 (1981), 193-264.

Greenwald, Maria White, and Greenwald, Gary I., 'Coroners' inquests: a source of vital statistics: Westminster, 1761-1866', *The Journal of Legal Medicine*, 4 (1983), 51-86.

Hair, P. E. H., 'Bridal pregnancy in rural England in earlier centuries', *Population Studies*, 20 (1966), 233-43.

Hair, P. E. H., 'Bridal pregnancy in earlier rural England further examined', *Population Studies*, 24 (1970), 59-70.

Hand, Learned, 'Historical and practical considerations regarding expert testimony', *Harvard Law Review*, 15 (1901), 40-58.

Harley, David, 'Ignorant Midwives - a persistent stereotype', *Bulletin of the Society for the Social History of Medicine*, 28 (1981), 6-9.

Harley, David, 'Historians as demonologists: the myth of the midwife-witch', *Social History of Medicine*, 3 (1990), 1-26.

Harley, David, 'Rape, bastardy, and infanticide: the midwife as investigating agent in pre-industrial England', (1990), unpublished paper.

Hausfater, Glenn, and Hrdy, Sarah Blaffer, *Infanticide: Comparative and Evolutionary Perspectives*, (New York, Aldine Publishing Company, 1984).

Havard, J. D. J., *The Detection of Secret Homicide*, (London, Macmillan and Co. Ltd., 1960).

Hay, Douglas, 'Property, authority and the criminal law', in Douglas Hay, Peter Linebaugh, John G. Rule, E. P. Thompson, Cal Winslow, *Albion's Fatal Tree: Crime and Society in Eighteenth-Century England*, (London, Allen Lane, 1975), pp. 17-63.

Hay, Douglas, 'War, dearth and theft in the eighteenth century: the record of the English courts', *Past and Present*, 95 (1982), 117-60.

Hay, Douglas, 'The class composition of the palladium of English liberty: trial jurors in the eighteenth century', in J. S. Cockburn and Thomas A. Green (eds.), *Twelve Good Men and True: The Criminal Trial Jury in England, 1200-1800*, (Princeton, Princeton University Press, 1988), pp. 305-57.

Hecht, J. Jean, *The Domestic Servant in Eighteenth-Century England*, (London, Routledge and Kegan Paul, 1980).

Hill, Bridget, *Eighteenth-Century Women: An Anthology*, (London, Allen and Unwin, 1987).

Hill, Bridget, *Women, Work, and Sexual Politics in Eighteenth-Century England*, (Oxford, Basil Blackwell, 1989).

Hoffer, Peter C., and Hull, N. E. H., *Murdering Mothers: Infanticide in England and New England 1558-1803*, (New York, New York University Press, 1981).

Houlbrooke, Ralph A., *The English Family 1450-1700*, (London, Longman, 1984).

Hunnisett, R. F., 'Pleas of the Crown and the Coroner', *Bulletin of the Institute of Historical Research*, XXXII (1959), 117-37.

Hunnisett, R. F., (ed.), *Wiltshire Coroners' Bills 1752-1796*, (Wiltshire Record Society, 1981).

Hunt, Lynn (ed.), *The New Cultural History*, (Berkeley, University of California Press, 1989).

Innes, Joanna, and Styles, John, 'The crime wave: recent writing on crime and criminal justice in eighteenth-century England', in Adrian Wilson (ed.), *Rethinking Social History*, (Manchester, Manchester University Press, 1994).

Jackson, Mark, 'New-born child murder: a study of suspicion, evidence, and proof in eighteenth-century England', (PhD thesis, University of Leeds, 1992).

Jackson, Mark, 'Suspicious infant deaths: the statute of 1624 and medical evidence at coroners' inquests', in Michael Clark and Catherine Crawford (eds.), *Legal Medicine in History*, (Cambridge, Cambridge University Press, 1994), pp. 64-86.

Jackson, Mark, 'Developing medical expertise: medical practitioners and the suspected murders of new-born children', in Roy Porter (ed.), *Medicine in the Enlightenment*, (Amsterdam, Rodopi, 1995), pp. 145-65.

Jackson, Mark, 'Childbirth's mental toll', *The Times*, (13 June 1995), p. 14.

Jackson, Mark, '"Something more than Blood": conflicting accounts of pregnancy loss in eighteenth-century England', in Rosanne Cecil (ed.), *The Anthropology of Pregnancy Loss*, (Berg, 1996).

Jones, Vivien (ed.), *Women in the Eighteenth Century: Constructions of Femininity*, (London, Routledge, 1990).

Jordanova, L. J., 'Natural facts; a historical perspective on science and sexuality', in Carol P. MacCormack and Marilyn Strathern (eds.), *Nature, Culture and Gender*, (Cambridge, Cambridge University Press, 1980), pp. 42-69.

Jordanova, L. J., 'The history of the family', in Cambridge Women's Studies Group, *Women in Society*, (London, Virago, 1981), pp. 41-54.

Jordanova, L. J., 'Gender, generation and science: William Hunter's obstetrical atlas', in W. F. Bynum and R. Porter (eds.), *William Hunter and the Eighteenth-century Medical World*, (Cambridge, Cambridge University Press, 1985), pp. 385-412.

Jordanova, Ludmilla, *Sexual Visions: Images of Gender in Science and Medicine between the Eighteenth and Twentieth Centuries*, (Harvester Wheatsheaf, 1989).

Keeble, N. H. (ed.), *The Cultural Identity of Seventeenth-Century Woman*, (London, Routledge, 1994).

Kellum, Barbara A., 'Infanticide in England in the later middle ages', *History of Childhood Quarterly*, 1 (1974), 367-88.

Kent, Joan R., 'Attitudes of Members of the House of Commons to the regulation of "Personal Conduct" in late Elizabethan and early Stuart England', *Bulletin of the Institute of Historical Research*, XLVI (1973), 41-71.

Keown, I. J., '"Miscarriage": a medico-legal analysis', *The Criminal Law Review*, (October 1984), 604-14.

Keown, John, *Abortion, Doctors and the Law: Some Aspects of the Lgal Regulation of Abortion in England from 1803 to 1982*, (Cambridge, Cambridge University Press, 1988).

Kermode, Jenny, and Walker, Garthine (eds.), *Women, Crime and the Courts in Early Modern England*, (London, UCL Press, 1994).

King, Peter, 'Decision-makers and decision-making in the English criminal law, 1750-1800', *The Historical Journal*, 27 (1984), 25-58.

King, P. J. R., '"Illiterate Plebians, Easily Misled": Jury composition, experience, and behaviour in Essex, 1735-1815', in J. S. Cockburn and Thomas A. Green (eds.), *Twelve Good Men and True: The Criminal Trial Jury in England, 1200-1800*, (Princeton, Princeton University Press, 1988), pp. 305-57.

Knafla, Louis A. (ed.), *Crime and Criminal Justice in Europe and Canada*, (Ontario, Wilfred Laurier University Press, 1981).

Kussmaul, Ann, *Servants in Husbandry in Early Modern England*, (Cambridge, Cambridge University Press, 1981).

LaFleur, William, *Liquid Life: Abortion and Buddhism in Japan*, (Princeton, 1992).

Langbein, John H., 'The origins of public prosecution at common law', *The American Journal of Legal History*, XVII (1973), 313-35.

Langbein, John H., 'The criminal trial before the lawyers', *The University of Chicago Law Review*, 45 (1978), 236-316.

Langer, William, 'Infanticide: a historical survey', *History of Childhood Quarterly*, 1 (1974), 353-66.

Laqueur, Thomas, 'Bodies, details, and the humanitarian narrative', in Lynn Hunt (ed.), *The New Cultural History*, (Berkeley, University of California Press, 1989), pp. 176-204.

Larner, Christina, *Enemies of God: The Witch-hunt in Scotland*, (London, Chatto and Windus, 1981).

Laslett, Peter, *Family Life and Illicit Love in Earlier Generations*, (Cambridge, Cambridge University Press, 1977).

Laslett, Peter, 'Introduction: comparing illegitimacy over time and between cultures', in Peter Laslett, Karla Oosterveen and Richard M. Smith (eds.), *Bastardy and its Comparative History*, (London, Edward Arnold, 1980), pp. 1-65.

Laslett, Peter, and Oosterveen, Karla, 'Long-term trends in bastardy in England', *Population Studies*, 27 (1973), 255-86.

Laslett, Peter, Oosterveen, Karla, and Smith, Richard M., (eds.), *Bastardy and its Comparative History*, (London, Edward Arnold, 1980).

Lee, James, Campbell, Cameron, and Tan, Guofu, 'Infanticide and family planning in late imperial China: the price and population history of rural Liaoning, 1774-1873', in Thomas G. Rawski and Lillian M. Li (eds.), *Chinese History in Economic Perspective*, (Berkeley, 1992), pp. 145-76.

McClure, Ruth K., *Coram's Children: The London Foundling Hospital in the Eighteenth Century*, (New Haven, Yale University Press, 1981).

MacDonald, Michael, 'The secularisation of suicide in England 1660-1800', *Past and Present*, 111 (1986), 50-97.

Macfarlane, Alan, 'Illegitimacy and illegitimates in English history', in Peter Laslett, Karla Oosterveen and Richard M. Smith (eds.), *Bastardy and its Comparative History*, (London, Edward Arnold, 1980), pp. 71-85.

Macfarlane, Alan, *Marriage and Love in England: Modes of Reproduction 1300-1840*, (Oxford, Blackwell, 1986).

McGowen, Randall, 'The body and punishment in eighteenth-century England', *Journal of Modern History*, 59 (December 1987), 651-79.

McGowen, Randall, 'Civilizing punishment: the end of the public execution in England', *Journal of British Studies*, 33 (July 1994), 257-82.

McHugh, Mary Patricia, 'The influence of the coroner's inquisition on the development of the common law and the medico legal system', (PhD thesis, London, 1976).

McLaren, Angus, *Reproductive Rituals: The Perception of Fertility in England from the Sixteenth Century to the Nineteenth Century*, (London, Methuen, 1984).

McLynn, Frank, *Crime and Punishment in Eighteenth-century England*, (London, Routledge, 1989).

Macnair, M. R. T., 'The early development of the privilege against self-incrimination', *Oxford Journal of Legal Studies*, 10 (1990), 66-84.

McNeil, Maureen, *Under the Banner of Science: Erasmus Darwin and his Age*, (Manchester, Manchester University Press, 1987).

Malcolmson, R. W., 'Infanticide in the eighteenth century', in J. S. Cockburn (ed.), *Crime in England 1550-1800*, (London, Methuen, 1977), pp. 187-209.

Michel, Robert H., 'English attitudes towards women, 1640-1700', *Canadian Journal of History*, 13 (1978), 35-60.

Montag, Beverley A., and Montag, Thomas W., 'Infanticide: a historical perspective', *Minnesota Medicine*, (May 1979), 368-72.

Namier, Sir Lewis, and Brooke, John, *The History of Parliament: The House of Commons 1754-1790*, (H.M.S.O., 1964).

Nemec, Jaroslav, *International Bibliography of the History of Legal Medicine*, (US Department of Health, Education, and Welfare, 1973).

Nichols, R. H., and Wray, F. A., *The History of the Foundling Hospital*, (London, Oxford University Press, 1935).

Ober, William B., 'Infanticide in eighteenth-century England: William Hunter's contribution to the forensic problem', *Pathology Annual*, 21 (1986), 311-19.

O'Donovan, Katherine, 'The medicalisation of infanticide', *The Criminal Law Review*, (May 1984), 259-64.

O'Gorman, Frank, *The Rise of Party in England: The Rockingham Whigs 1760-82*, (London, Allen and Unwin, 1975).

O'Gorman, Frank, *The Emergence of the British Two-Party System 1760-1832*, London, Edward Arnold, 1982).

Oldham, James C., 'On pleading the belly: a history of the Jury of Matrons', *Criminal Justice History*, VI (1985), 1-64.

Pelling, Margaret, 'Child health as a social value in early modern England', *Social History of Medicine*, 1 (1988), 135-64.

Piers, Maria W., *Infanticide: Past and Present*, (New York, W. W. Norton and Company, 1978).

Pike, Luke Owen, *A History of Crime in England Illustrating the Changes of the Laws in the Progress of Civilisation*, (Patterson Smith, 1968).

Pinchbeck, Ivy, and Hewitt, Margaret, *Children in English Society*, (2 vols., London, Routledge and Kegan Paul, 1969-73).

Porter, Roy, *English Society in the Eighteenth Century*, (London, Penguin Books, 1986).

Prior, Mary (ed.), *Women in English Society 1500-1800*, (London, Routledge, 1991).

Quaife, G. R., *Wanton Wenches and Wayward Wives: Peasants and Illicit Sex in Early Seventeenth Century England*, (London, Croom Helm, 1979).

Radzinowicz, Leon, *A History of English Criminal Law and its Administration from 1750*, vol. 1, (London, Stevens and Sons Limited, 1948).

Rose, Lionel, *The Massacre of the Innocents: Infanticide in Britain 1800-1939*, (London, Routledge and Kegan Paul, 1986).

Rosen, George, 'A slaughter of innocents: aspects of child health in the eighteenth-century city', *Studies in Eighteenth-Century Culture*, 5 (1976), 293-316.

Rowlands, Alison, '"Inhuman and unnatural": Infanticidal women in sixteenth- and seventeenth-century Germany', paper presented to an international conference entitled 'Gender and Crime in Britain and Europe Early Modern and Modern' held at Roehampton Institute, London, 2-4 April 1995.

Sauer, R., 'Infanticide and abortion in nineteenth-century Britain', *Population Studies*, 32 (1978), 81-93.

Shapiro, Barbara J., *Probability and Certainty in Seventeenth-Century England*, (Princeton, Princeton University Press, 1983).

Shapiro, Barbara J., *'Beyond Reasonable Doubt' and 'Probable Cause'*, (Berkeley, University of California Press, 1991).

Sharpe, J. A., *Crime in Seventeenth-century England: A County Study*, (Cambridge, Cambridge University Press, 1983).

Sharpe, J. A., *Crime in Early Modern England 1550-1750*, (London, Longman, 1984).

Sharpe, J. A., 'The history of violence in England: some observations', *Past and Present*, 108 (1985), 206-15.

Sharpe, Jim, 'Women, witchcraft and the legal process', in Jenny Kermode and Garthine Walker (eds.), *Women, Crime and the Courts in Early Modern England*, (London, UCL Press, 1994), pp. 106-24.

Short, R., 'Female criminality 1780-1830', (M. Litt thesis, Oxford, 1989).

Shorter, Edward, 'Illegitimacy, sexual revolution, and social change in modern Europe', *Journal of Interdisciplinary History*, 2 (1971), 237-72.

Shorter, Edward, *The Making of the Modern Family*, (London, Collins, 1976).

Shorter, Edward, 'The management of normal deliveries and the generation of William Hunter', in W. F. Bynum and R. Porter (eds.), *William Hunter and the Eighteenth-century Medical World*, (Cambridge, Cambridge University Press, 1985), pp. 371-83.

Smith, Roger, *Trial by Medicine: Insanity and Responsibility in Victorian Trials*, (Edinburgh, Edinburgh University Press, 1981).

Speck, W. A., 'The harlot's progress in eighteenth-century England', *British Journal for Eighteenth-Century Studies*, 3 (1980), 127-39.

Staves, Susan, 'British seduced maidens', *Eighteenth-Century Studies*, 14 (1980/1), 109-34.

Stenton, Doris Mary, *The English Woman in History*, (London, Allen and Unwin, 1957).

Stone, Lawrence, 'A Rejoinder', *Past and Present*, 108 (1985), 216-24.

Stone, Lawrence, *The Family, Sex and Marriage in England 1500-1800*, (London, Penguin Books, 1990).

Stone, Lawrence, *Broken Lives: Separation and Divorce in England 1660-1857*, (Oxford, Oxford University Press, 1993).

Taylor, James Stephen, 'Philanthropy and Empire: Jonas Hanway and the infant poor of London', *Eighteenth-Century Studies*, 12 (1979), 285-305.

Thayer, J. B., *A Preliminary Treatise on Evidence at the Common Law*, (Boston, Little, Brown and Company, 1898).

Thomas, Keith, 'The double standard', *Journal of the History of Ideas*, 20 (1959), 195-216.

Tilly, Louise A., and Scott, Joan W., *Women, Work, and Family*, (London, Routledge, 1989).

Tobias, J. J., *Crime and Police in England 1700-1900*, (Dublin, Gill and Macmillan, 1979).

Trexler, Richard C., 'Infanticide in Florence: new sources and first results', *History of Childhood Quarterly*, 1 (1973), 98-116.

Walker, N., *Crime and Insanity in England: Vol. 1 The Historical Perspective*, (Edinburgh, Edinburgh University Press, 1968).

Watson, Alan A., *Forensic Medicine: A Handbook for Professionals*, (Aldershot, Gower, 1989).

Werner, Oscar Helmuth, *The Unmarried Mother in German Literature*, (New York, AMS Press Inc., [1917] 1966).

Wessling, Mary Nagel, 'Infanticide trials and forensic medicine: Württembergs 1757-93', in Michael Clark and Catherine Crawford (eds.), *Legal Medicine in History*, (Cambridge, Cambridge University Press, 1994), pp. 117-44.

Wiener, Carol Z., 'Is a Spinster an unmarried woman?', *The American Journal of Legal History*, 20 (1976), 27-31.

Wigmore, J. H., *A Treatise on the Anglo-American System of Evidence in Trials at Common Law*, (3rd ed., vol. 9, Boston, Little, Brown and Company, 1940).

Williams, Katherine, S., *Textbook on Criminology*, (London, Blackstone Press Limited, 1991).

Wilson, Adrian, 'William Hunter and the varieties of man-midwifery', in W. F. Bynum and R. Porter (eds.), *William Hunter and the Eighteenth-century Medical World*, (Cambridge, Cambridge University Press, 1985), pp. 343-69.

Wilson, Adrian, 'Illegitimacy and its implications in mid-eighteenth-century London: the evidence of the Foundling Hospital', *Continuity and Change*, 4 (1989), 103-64.

Wilson, Adrian (ed.), *Rethinking Social History*, (Manchester, Manchester University Press, 1994).

Wilson, Adrian, *The Making of Man-midwifery: Childbirth in England, 1660-1770*, (London, UCL Press, 1995).

Wrightson, Keith, 'Infanticide in earlier seventeenth-century England', *Local Population Studies*, 15 (1975), 10-22.

Wrightson, Keith, 'Two concepts of order: justices, constables and jurymen in seventeenth-century England', in J. Brewer and J. Styles (eds.), *An Ungovernable People: The English and their Law in the Seventeenth and Eighteenth Centuries*, (London, Hutchinson, 1980), pp. 21-46.

Wrightson, Keith, 'Infanticide in European history', *Criminal Justice History*, 3 (1982), 1-20.

Wrightson, Keith, *English Society 1580-1680*, (London, Routledge, 1993).

INDEX

abortion, 75, 76; *see also* miscarriage
accessories to murder, *see* accomplices
accomplices, 43, 63, 80 n. 33, 143
acquittal rates, 3-4, 11, 133-4, 140-5
   passim
  contemporary explanations of, 3-4
Acts of Parliament, *see* statutes
administration of justice, 16, 23, 148,
   160-8 *passim*
Alexander, William, 47
America
  transportation to, 163, 165
  unrest in colonies, 165
Appleby, assizes at, 21
assizes, 2, 3, 17-22 *passim*, 23 n. 3, 36,
   49; *see also* court records;
   trial reports

Babington, Zachary, 33, 137, 139
bail, 17, 27 n. 69
baptism of abandoned child, 46
Barrington, Daines, 35, 100, 150
Bartholin, 94
bastard-bearers
  hostility towards, 30-2, 115-16,
   122, 168, 174, 177
  and suspicions of murder, 42, 77
  see also single women; spinsters;
   suspects; widows
bastards, 23 n. 1
  financial burden of, 15, 30-1
  maintenance of, 30-1, 35, 46
  status of, 35, 45-6, 145
  as victims, 3, 29, 36, 39, 55 n. 59
  see also nullius filius
bastardy
  chargeable, 37-45
  and the generation of suspicion,
   29-51, 77
  laws relating to, 30-1, 37, 45-6
  rates, 13, 37, 77, 168

see also nullius filius
Beale, Caroline, vii
Beattie, J. M., 5, 6, 8, 9, 146
  on indictments, 19
  on role of medical evidence, 98, 103
Beccaria, Cesare, 161, 165
benefit of clergy, 33-4, 144
benefit-of-linen, 34, 142-3
Bentham, Jeremy, 165
'beyond a reasonable doubt', 53 n. 16,
   148-9; *see also* proof
birth, *see* child-birth
Blackstone, William, 135, 137, 138, 139,
   150
blood
  as evidence of recent delivery, 66-7,
   75, 77
  as source of nutrition to embryo, 76
  see also menstruation
'bloody code', 152
bodies
  discovery of, 84
  examination of, 84-104 *passim*
  as focus of local inquiries, 84
  as source of evidence, 15, 71-2, 84,
   87-8, 93
  viewed at the inquest, 84, 89
Bond, John, 127
broadsheets, 7, 76, 112-13, 117, 120, 168
Brooke, John, 166
Brydall, John, 43
Bunbury, Sir Charles, 159, 160
burden of proof, 53 n. 16, 148-9; *see*
   also proof
Burke, Edmund, 161, 165-6
Burn, Richard, 40, 126

capital punishment
  extension of, 134, 160, 164
  reluctance to employ, 144, 161
Carlisle, assizes at, 21

certainty needed for conviction, 146-9; *see also* burden of proof; probability; proof

character evidence in court, 118-19, 144

chastity, 47-8, 113-14, 117

Cheselden, William, 94, 95

Chester, assizes at, 2-3

child-birth
  accidental or sudden nature of, 75, 76, 77, 120
  conflicting interpretations of, 74-7
  premature, 74, 75, 90-3
  signs of, 60, 72-4
  value in court, 74
  without assistance, 69

churchwardens, 37, 41, 60, 140

clergy, *see* benefit of clergy

clergymen, 7

Cockburn, J. S., 19

Coke, Edward, 148

committal to gaol, 17, 78

common law, 20, 23, 99
  return to, 71, 87, 93, 100, 150-1, 163-4, 171, 176-7
  rules of evidence, 31-2

concealment, 11, 31, 39
  of birth and 1803 statute, 171-4, 175
  of death and 1624 statute, 32-5, 142-4
  evidential weight of, 116-17, 124, 149-50
  of pregnancy, 49-50, 61-3
  see also intent

conception, false, 76

confessions, weight in court, 142

constables, 42, 60, 68, 69, 140

conviction, certainty needed for, 146-9; *see also* burden of proof; probability; proof

conviction rates, 3, 9, 13, 23, 46, 103, 133-4, 152 n. 2, 175-6
  in the seventeenth century, 36, 54 n. 41

convictions (specific cases), 2-3, 101, 111, 121, 143, 144, 168, 175

Coram, Thomas, 114

coroners, 7, 17, 20, 44, 60, 77, 84

experience of, 89, 105 n. 22
  increasing importance of, 88-9
  influence on inquest verdicts, 136
  payment of, 88
  status of, 85-6

counsel for defence, 101, 145-6, 148, 149

counsel for prosecution, 142, 145

court records, 7-10
  Northern Circuit, 16-23, 37-45 *passim*

courts, *see* assizes; grand juries; inquest juries; inquests; trial juries; trials

crime
  'dark figure' of, 12
  historical approaches to, 4, 8-14

criminal law reform, 4, 13, 164-8, 176-7

criminal statistics, 8, 9-12, 13-14

criminal trials, *see* trials

Crompton, Richard, 35

Cumberland, 2, 20, 21

Danish law, influence of, 35, 164

Darwin, Erasmus, 95, 102

death, concealment of and 1624 statute, 32-5, 142-4

defence, absence of, 144

defendants, *see* suspects

Defoe, Daniel, 45, 92, 111

delivery, *see* child-birth

depositions, 17, 22, 23, 75
  as historical evidence, 19-20
  survival of, 21

deterrent
  conviction and punishment as, 168, 171
  penal law as, 160-1
  prosecution as, 45-7
  trials as, 46-7, 145

Dicey, A. V., 172

Dionis, Pierre, 73

discharge by proclamation, 18, 137

discretion, of magistrates and judges, 50, 152, 171

dissection, *see* examination of bodies

'doctrine of maximum severity', 160, 164-5, 167

double standard of sexual morality, 30
Durham, County Palatinate, 21
Dyson, Jeremiah, 166

Eden, William, 127, 139, 150, 162
Edwards, Valerie C., 44
Ellenborough, Lord Chief Justice
    (Edward Law), 14, 169-77
    passim
Emlyn, Sollom, 138, 139, 161
Evans, William, 173
evidence, 15, 16
    circumstantial, 31-2, 90, 146-8
    common law rules of, 31-2
    laws of, 134, 145-51
    see also medical evidence
examination of bodies, post-mortem,
    72, 84-104 *passim*
examination of suspects, physical, 60-
    78 *passim*
    internal ('touching'), 61
    refusal to be examined, 70
    for signs of delivery, 69-74
    for signs of pregnancy, 64-5

families
    role of women in, 29, 47
    shame and grief of, 48
Farr, Samuel, 61, 90, 95
fathers
    as accomplices, 80 n.33, 143
    and bastardy laws, 30
    identification of, 50, 118
    on inquest jury, 135
    as suspects, 3, 29, 117, 118
    see also men
Fielding, Henry, 160
filiation of bastard children, 31, 41, 64,
    65, 77, 117
Foster, Michael, 163
Foundling Hospital, 46, 114
Fox, Charles James, 159, 161, 165, 166
French Revolution, 168

Galen, 93
gaol books, 18, 21
gaol calendars, 17, 18, 21, 39
gender

and exploration of bodies, 88
    history, 5, 14, 16, 20
    and the legal process, 12
Germany, studies of 'infanticide' in, 17
Gilbert, Sir Geoffrey, 146, 149
Glynn, John, 159
grand juries, 17, 18, 22, 137-40, 174
    composition, 137
    rules governing, 137-40
    verdicts, 133-4, 139-40, 175
A Guide to Juries, 138, 139, 149
guilt, assumptions of, 4, 11, 12, 14, 111

Hale, Sir Matthew, 40, 85, 86, 92-3,
    137, 138, 146, 148
Hamilton, Alexander, 95
Hanging, Not Punishment Enough, 160
Harbord, Harbord, 161, 166
Hardwicke's Marriage Act (1753), 29, 44
Harvey, William, 93
Havard, J. D. J., 87
Hawkins, William, 126
Hawles, Sir John, 139
Hay, Douglas, 134, 167
hearsay rule, 142
Henry, Matthew, 111
Herbert, Henry, 159
'history from below', 8, 9
Hodgson, Reverend Christopher, 125-
    7, 168
Hoffer, Peter C., 5-13 *passim*, 35, 36,
    128, 169
hostility towards suspects, locally, 3,
    14, 30-2, 115-16, 124,
    136, 174, 177
House of Commons, 159-70 *passim*
House of Correction, 30, 31, 175
House of Lords, 159-72 *passim*
    opposition to law reform, 166-7,
    171
Hull, N. E. H., 5-13 *passim*, 35, 36, 128,
    169
Hunter, William, 97, 124, 149, 151,
    168, 173
    on suspects' character, 115-23
humanitarian accounts of suspects,
    113-23, 162-3
    and attempts to repeal the 1624

statute, 4, 13-14, 162-3, 169, 171-3
  opposition to, 123-7, 151
humanitarian narrative, 119-23
hydrostatic lung test, *see* lung test

illegitimacy, *see* bastardy
illegitimate children, *see* bastards; *nullius filius*
indictments, 10, 17, 36, 39, 174
  drafting of, 18-19
  survival of, 21
  use by historians, 8, 9, 14
infanticide, 4-7 *passim*, 13, 16
Innes, Joanna, 8, 9, 13
inquest juries, 38, 39-40, 133-4, 135-6
inquests, 17, 46, 74, 84-104 *passim*
  as major form of pre-trial inquiry, 88-9, 135
  verdicts, 99, 133-4, 135-6
  see also coroners
inquisitions, 17, 19, 21, 38
insanity defence, 5, 40, 120-3
  influence in court, 121-2
  opposition to, 126-7
intent
  to conceal, 34, 142-4
  to murder, 35, 127, 142-4

Jackson, Rowland, 96
Jacob, Giles, 33
James I, 35
Johnson, Christopher, 102, 125, 173
Johnson, Samuel, 6
Jordanova, Ludmilla, 88
judges
  discretion of, 152, 171
  opposition to criminal law reform, 167, 171
  role in court, 140, 147, 149, 151
juries, *see* grand juries; inquest juries; and trial juries
Jury of Matrons, 70
justice, administration of, 16, 23, 148, 160-8 *passim*
justices of the peace, 7, 17, 20, 30, 31, 44, 50, 69, 77, 85, 137
  changing role of, 88-9

Kelyng, Sir John, Lord Chief Justice, 116, 143
Kent, Joan R., 35
Kermode, Jenny, 16
'kite case', 35

labour
  as cause of incapacity, 120-1
  signs of, 60, 65-6, 68
    conflicting interpretations of, 74-7
Lancaster, County Palatinate, 2, 21, 173
Langbein, John, 146
Laqueur, Thomas, 119-23 *passim*
Larner, Christina, 12
law, *see* common law; statute law
Law, Edmund, 171
Law, Edward, *see* Ellenborough, Lord Chief Justice
laws of evidence, 134, 145-51
lawyers, 7, 99, 101, 142, 145-6, 148, 149
Le Blanc, Simon, 174
legal medicine
  development of, 85-90
  neglect of in England, 86
  see also inquests; medical evidence
leniency of the courts, 4, 13-14, 98-9, 124, 169
live-birth, 7, 15, 31, 84, 87, 141
  medical and legal definitions of, 99
  signs of, 93; *see also* lung test
local hostility towards suspects, 3, 14, 30-2, 115-16, 124, 136, 174, 177
Locke, John, 146
Lockhart, Thomas, 159-60, 161, 163, 167
Lofft, Capel, 100, 147
Lord Ellenborough's Act (1803), *see under* statutes
lung test, 93-100
  acceptance by courts, 94, 100
  doubts about, 95-100

Mackintosh, Sir James, 167
McLynn, Frank, 12
Madan, Martin, 160-1
Magdalen Hospital, 114

magistrates, *see* justices of the peace
Malcolmson, R. W., 5, 8, 11
Manchester Conversation Society, 118
Mandeville, Bernard, 62, 113-16
man-midwifery, rise of, 71
manslaughter, 34, 125, 143-4
marriage, 29, 43-5, 47, 117
    as defence against the 1624 statute,
        43, 44, 141
    promise of, 49, 117
married women, as suspects, 3, 29, 35,
    43-5, 47
maturity and viability of dead child,
    evidence of, 32, 90-3, 103
medical evidence/testimony, 15, 20,
    72, 84-104 *passim*
    impact in court, 74, 103-4
    increasing forensic interest in, 86-
        90, 151
    uncertainties in, 103-4
    see also child-birth; labour; live-
        birth; lung test; maturity;
        medical practitioners;
        pregnancy; still-birth;
        violence
medical practitioners, 7, 15, 20, 22,
    65, 69, 84, 87-8, 120
    forensic experience of, 89
    role in examining suspects, 70-4,
        77, 88
    see also medical evidence
men
    responsibility of, 116-18
    as suspects, 3, 29, 117, 118
menstruation, 64, 67
    conflation with miscarriage, 75-7
Meredith, Sir William, 159, 161, 165,
    167
midwives, 20, 22, 65, 69, 74, 91, 122
    experience and status of, 70-1
    as witnesses, 70-2
milk in breasts as proof of delivery,
    72-4
minute books, 18, 39
    survival of, 21
miscarriage, 74, 75, 76, 77
    procurement of, 169, 170
    see also abortion

modesty of suspects, 113-15, 124, 162
    as character evidence, 118-19
    as a virtue (not a vice), 115-17
    see also shame
Morgagni, Giovanni Battista, 6, 95
Morgan, John, 146
Morpeth, assizes at, 21

navel string, 102, 121
neighbours
    hostility towards suspects, 3, 14,
        30-2, 115-16, 124, 136,
        174, 177
    involvement in investigations, 60-
        78 *passim*
Nelson, William, 138, 139
New England, 5, 13
Newcastle-upon-Tyne, assizes at, 21,
newspapers, 2, 21, 22, 38, 110, 111-12
non compos mentis, 121, 126; *see also*
    insanity defence
Northern Circuit, 20-1
    court records, 16-23, 37-45 *passim*
Northumberland, 20, 21
nullius filius, 145

oath, 17
Old Bailey, conviction rates at, 152 n.2
Old Bailey Sessions Papers, 22
Ollyffe, George, 160
overseers of the poor, 31, 37, 41, 60,
    64, 65, 68, 69, 140

Paley, William, 124, 147, 162, 167, 171
parish officers, *see* overseers of the
    poor; churchwardens
parliamentary debates, 22, 23
    and repeal of the 1624 statute, 158-
        77 *passim*
Parr, Bartholomew, 61-2, 97
party, *see* political parties
Penal Laws Bill (1772), 160, 166, 167
Percival, Thomas, 116-17, 124
Piers, Maria W., 6
Phipps, Constantine, 159, 166
Plouquet's test, 100, 108-9 n. 89
political parties, and criminal law
    reform, 165-6

poor rates, 31, 37, 41, 45, 46, 77, 168
poor relief, 31, 35, 37, 41
positivist social science, influence of,
      8-13
pregnancy
   concealment of, 49-50, 61-3
   denials of, 61, 64, 65
   physical examination during, 64-5
   signs of, 60, 61-5
pre-marital sexual relationships, 47-9
premature birth
   claims of, 74, 75
   evidence of, 90-3
      impact in court, 91-3
presumption of innocence, 53 n.16,
      148-9, 150
pre-trial examinations, 19
probability
   and grand juries, 138-9
   and trial jury verdicts, 146-9
proof
   'beyond a reasonable doubt', 53 n.
      16, 148-9
   'by experts', 100
   standards of, 134, 145-51
prosecution
   as a deterrent, 45-7
   as a process, 47-51
prosecution rates, 3-4, 9, 13-14, 26 n.
      61, 28 n. 90, 46
prostitutes, 114
puerperal insanity, 120, 128; *see also*
      insanity defence
punishment, attempts to avoid, 31, 35
puritanism, 5, 35
putrefaction, 95-6

Quarter Sessions, 49
'quickening', 170

Radzinowicz, Leon, 8
recognizances, 17, 19, 21
reform of the criminal law, 4, 13, 164-
      8, 176-7
'reform perspective', 8-9, 13-14
repeal of 1624 statute, *see under*
      statutes
reprieves, 144

resuscitation attempts, 96
Rigge, Fletcher, 39, 150
Rockingham, Lord, 165
Rockingham Whigs, 165-6
Romilly, Samuel, 167, 171
rules of evidence, common law, 31-2

Sauer, R., 169
Savile, Sir George, 159, 165, 166
search warrant, 69, 77
seduction, 48-9, 76, 117-19, 123
self-incrimination, 19, 27 n.81
servants, 48-9, 62
   dismissal of, 49
sexual relationships, pre-marital, 47-9
shame, as motive for concealment and
      murder, 4, 31, 35, 48, 111,
      113-14, 116, 117, 124-5; *see
      also* modesty
Shapiro, Barbara, 146
Sharpe, J. A., 5, 8, 9, 12, 13
sin, 48, 111
single women, as suspects, 3, 29-51
      passim, 84; *see also* bastard-
      bearers; spinsters; suspects
Smellie, William, 62, 73, 96
Somers, John, Lord, 138-9
sources, 16-22
spinsters, 29, 42, 44; *see also* single
      women
standards of proof, 134, 145-51
statute law, 20, 23, 163-4
statute of 1624, *see* under statutes
statutes
   1 & 2 Ph. & M. c. 13 (1554), 135
   18 Eliz. c. 3 (1576), 30, 31
   1 Jac. I c. 8 (1604), 33-4
   7 Jac. I c. 4 (1610), 30, 31
   21 Jac.I c. 27 (1624), 4, 7, 13, 16, 18,
      29, 37, 43, 45, 51, 71, 78
   construction of, 32-6
   declining support for, 93, 150-1,
      158-9
   dominance of, 37-9
   exemptions from, 34, 141-5, 149-
      50, 151
   impact on legal medicine, 87
   repeal (1803), 168-77

repeal attempts (1772-6), 148, 159-60
Scottish Acts, c. 50 (1690), 34
7 Will. III c. 3 (1696), 145
8 & 9 Will. III c. 26 (1697), 124
6 Ann. c. 4, Irish statutes (1707), 165
6 Geo. II c. 31 (1733), 37, 65
25 Geo. II c.29 (1752), 88
25 Geo. II c.37 (1752), 165
43 Geo. III c. 58 (1803), 13, 168-77
12 & 13 Geo. 5 c. 18 (1922), 6-7
1 & 2 Geo. 6 c.36 (1938), 6-7
Staves, Susan, 48
still-birth, 15, 34, 68-9, 74, 75, 84, 87, 99
    evidence of, 90-3
        influence in court, 91-3
    verdicts of, 46, 97, 99
Styles, John, 8, 9, 13
suicide, 122, 126
Surrey Assize Proceedings, 22
suspects
    character and conduct of, 110-28 *passim*
    married women as, 3, 29, 35, 43-5, 47
    men as, 3, 29, 117, 118
    mental state of, 120-3
    as modest virtuous women, 113-23
    selection of, 42-5
    single women as, 3, 29-51 *passim*, 84
    as victims of male deceit, 76, 118, 123, 128
    as wicked murderers, 111-13
suspicions of murder, 3, 15
    factors generating, 29-51 *passim*, 60-78 *passim*, 84
    potency of, 78
    suspects' responses to, 74-6
Sussex Assize Proceedings, 22

Thompson, E. P., 8
transportation, 163, 165
trial juries, 18, 22, 140-5
    composition, 140
    verdicts, 133-4, 140-5
trial reports, printed, 8, 9, 10, 22

trials
    as deterrent, 46-7, 145
    as theatre, 16
Turner, Thomas, 37

umbilical cord, *see* navel string
Umfreville, Edward, 33, 85, 86, 111, 135
unmarried women, as suspects, *see* bastard-bearers; single women; spinsters; widows

verdicts, 133-4
    grand jury, 137-40, 175
    inquest jury, 88, 99, 135-6
    trial jury, 140-5, 175-7
    see also acquittal rates; conviction rates
viability and maturity of dead child, evidence of, 32, 90-3, 103
violence, evidence of, 32, 85-6, 92, 100-2
    influence on verdicts, 101
    problems with, 101-2

Walker, Garthine, 16
warrant to search, 69, 77
Wessling, Mary Nagle, 5
Westmorland, 2, 20, 21
widows, 29, 42-3, 47, 66; *see also* suspects
Wiener, Carol Z., 44
Willughby, Percival, 69, 90
witchcraft trials, 46
witnesses, 11, 17
    credibility of, 145-7
    'expert', 100
    interpretation of signs by, 76-7
    medical witnesses, *see* medical evidence; medical practitioners
Woodforde, Reverend James, 49
women
    history of, 5, 14, 16, 20
    as investigators and witnesses, 12, 60, 65, 68, 69
    married, as suspects, 3, 29, 35, 43-5, 47

treatment of by courts, 144
  see also bastard-bearers; single
    women; spinsters; suspects
Wyatt, Richard, J.P., 50

York, assizes at, 21, 22
Yorkshire, 20-1